D0513382

Different Aspects

Michael Ball OBE is a singer, actor, presenter and now author. He's been a star of musical theatre for over three decades, winning the Laurence Olivier Award for Best Actor in a Musical twice, he's also won two BRIT Awards and been nominated for a Grammy. Michael regularly sells out both his solo tours and his Ball & Boe shows with Alfie Boe and has multiple platinum albums. He published his first novel, *The Empire* to great acclaim in 2021. *Different Aspects* is his first non-fiction book.

A Memoir
MICHAEL
BALL
Different Aspects

BLINK
bringing you closer

First published in the UK by Blink Publishing
An imprint of The Zaffre Publishing Group
A Bonnier Books UK company
4th Floor, Victoria House,
Bloomsbury Square,
London, WC1B 4DA

Owned by Bonnier Books
Sveavägen 56, Stockholm, Sweden

Hardback – 9781785120060
Trade Paperback – 9781785120077
Ebook – 9781785120091
Audio Digital Download – 9781785120107

A CIP catalogue of this book is available from the British Library.

Designed by Envy Design Ltd
Printed and bound by Clays Ltd, Elcograf S.p.A.

3 5 7 9 10 8 6 4 2

Blink Publishing is an imprint of Bonnier Books UK
www.bonnierbooks.co.uk

For all the family, friends and fans who have been such an integral part of my life and supported and encouraged me on every step.

For all the Twirlies and Turns it has been my pleasure to have shared a stage with.

Contents

Introduction

13 May 2023, 7.29pm

We were ready.

Well, I say that. Not quite ready. You have to take into account that this was the opening night of previews, so although it was our first time performing *Aspects of Love* to a paying audience, the show wasn't locked. We'd use those days of previews to fine-tune it, make it ready for press night.

So, 'sort of ready'.

Or, as ready as we'd ever be. Considering.

At the warm-up, before the theatre opened and the audience assembled, I'd made a little speech. I'd reminded the company how good they were and how much we loved the show. If everybody loved it as much as we did, we couldn't lose; we had a sure-fire hit on our hands.

The safety curtain came down, and we retreated to our

various backstage hidey-holes as the audience took their seats. Out front was my partner, Cathy, texting me to say she was in place, wishing me luck. Most of the cast had family and friends present. Later on, I saw Jamie Bogyo's dad wearing a badge that said 'Jamie's Dad'. It was that kind of atmosphere: a big old bundle of raw nerves, anticipation and goodwill.

And if the rest of the company was jangling, then what did that make me? This, after all, was my baby. Thirty-four years ago, I'd headed the cast of *Aspects* in the West End, and now I was returning to the show that had made my name. Nervous? You might say that.

Show time. And down in my dressing room, I awaited my entrance call, feeling and indeed feeding off those legendary first-night nerves but having every faith in the brilliant cast and company, in the production as a whole, and in the material.

My faith was repaid. It went well. Really bloody well. As the show ended we were treated to a standing ovation, the praises of a beaming Lord of the Realm (spoiler: it was Andrew Lloyd Webber), and a producer who was as pleased as punch. We all had pizza in the bar out by the stalls, and then we went home, knowing that our run had begun, and that this – the Lyric Theatre in London's glittering West End – was to be our home for the next six months.

Except, of course, it didn't work out like that.

And if you don't know what I'm talking about when I say it didn't work out like that, then keep reading – we have a great twist ending in store. And if you do, then keep reading anyway, because although you already know the twist, this is about the journey not the destination. A biography, not just of me, thank God, but of a musical – a tale of how *Aspects of Love*, a weird and very wonderful show, has changed my life, not once, but twice. A story that includes as many downs as it does ups, because at the end of the day, that's showbiz.

Ready?

Sort of?

Ready as you'll ever be?

PART ONE

Rules and the Game

Chapter 1

Around October or November of 2021, I instigated a game that I'd play with various friends, acquaintances, delivery drivers etc.

I'd say to them, 'Guess what I'm going to do next? As in, my next project . . .'

What made this such a bloody great game was the way it put people on the spot. I'd watch them be worried about saying the wrong thing but intrigued nonetheless.

'Nobody else has got this,' I'd say, raising the stakes.

'Is it an album of Joy Division songs?'

'No. No, it's not. Look, I tell you what. I'll give you a clue. It's a show.'

'Of course a show. Um . . . *Oklahoma!*?'

'No.'

'*My Fair Lady*?'

'No.'

'*Carousel*?'

'No.'

'Oh, I know. You're going back to *Les Mis* – only this time as Valjean?'

'No.'

Enthusiasm is waning. They're wondering what to make for dinner. Is that lasagne safe to reheat? 'I'm going to need a clue,' they say. 'Is it a British musical?'

'Yes.'

'Is it by Andrew Lloyd Webber?'

'Yes.'

Confidence returning. 'And it's played in the West End?'

'It has.'

'Oh God, I know. *Evita.* And you're playing Evita.'

'No.'

'Joseph.'

'No.'

And then the penny drops. They roll their eyes as though to say, *How could I have been so stupid*? 'Of course,' they sigh. 'You're going back into *The Phantom of the Opera*, playing the Phantom.'

'No.'

'What then?'

'Well . . . ,' I'd say.

We will of course be talking about *Aspects of Love* in great detail, but for now here's a quick bluffer's guide to be getting on with, just so that we're all on the same page. An Andrew Lloyd Webber musical that he'd tinkered with since the fag end of the 1970s and written towards the close of the 1980s, *Aspects* was based on a 1955 novella by David Garnett, a bisexual writer known to his pals as 'Bunny' thanks to his penchant for wearing a cloak made of rabbit skin.

Garnett was a member of the Bloomsbury Group, a band of writers and thinkers including Virginia Woolf and E M Forster, who had what you might call a liberated approach to relationships and sexuality – so much so that Dorothy Parker once remarked that 'they lived in squares, painted in circles and loved in triangles'.

It was this 'love triangle' sensibility that Garnett brought to his novella. God knows what 'novella' means, but it's a very short book, and its story begins with star-struck teen Alex (called Alexis in the book) falling in love with older actress Rose.

Being devilishly handsome and charming, Alex has no problem persuading Rose to accompany him to a villa owned (but not occupied) by his rich and worldly uncle, George, where they break in, consummate the relationship and play dress-up with various outfits hanging round.

The next thing you know, George turns up, and on seeing Rose, promptly falls in love with her, a feeling that is reciprocated. Alex is miffed, things at the villa end messily, and all three go their separate ways.

Cut to two years later, when Alex, now a soldier of 19, discovers that Rose has taken up with George. Old feelings between him and Rose are reignited, and from here, the web weaved becomes even more tangled as bedsheets are ruffled and at one stage a gun is pulled and Rose is injured. Among the many aspects of love explored is same-sex attraction, as Rose forms a bond with George's former mistress, Giulietta, while things take a troubling (and from our perspective vastly more problematic) turn when it becomes clear, 12 years later, that Rose and George have had a daughter, Jenny, who develops a pash for Alex. Love triangle be damned. Garnett was telling the story of a love pentagon. Heptagon, if you want to include Rose's manager, Marcel, and her new lover, Hugo, which we don't.

Andrew's score for *Aspects* is elegant and genteel, quite a departure from the bombastic and operatic leanings of his previous work, while the lyrics by Don Black and Charles Hart tease out the nuance of the narrative.

And it is indeed nuanced. Those anticipating what they assumed to be the usual 1980s Lloyd Webber fare were as disappointed as those who had expected a wide-eyed Rodgers and Hammerstein celebration of the strength and power of love. Not a bit of it. This was about the fickleness and frailty of love – love not as a healing force, but as a destructive one. It was, in a word, downbeat.

And then there was me. As in, me: Michael Ball, your narrator. *Aspects of Love* gave me a number two hit single with 'Love Changes Everything'; it introduced me to my life partner, Cathy, and took me to Broadway; it boosted me from being known mainly in West End circles to virtually a household name, and it marked if not the beginning then very much the flowering of relationships with Andrew, Don, Charles and the director, Trevor Nunn. *Aspects of Love* may be considered a minor Lloyd Webber, but for me it was about as big, both personally and professionally, as a big thing can be.

In terms of a revival, there was a snag. Except you can't really call it a snag because in fact it was the entire basis of the brainwave, and it took the idea from being a decent wheeze to something that blew my mind, not to mention the reason that not a soul managed to win my little game. It was this: back in 1989, when *Aspects of Love* first premiered at the Prince of Wales

Theatre in London's glittering West End, I was a mere pup of 27 and played the devilishly handsome and charming Alex.

Over 30 years later, however, aged – cough – 60, I am no longer young enough to convincingly play a man of Alex's tender years.

'No, no, Michael,' I hear you cry. 'With the right lighting and a bit of make-up . . .'

You're too kind. You really are. But no. I will not be playing Alex, and that's final.

Chapter 2

The idea came to me like snow falling off a shed roof – a tiny bit, then a bigger wodge and then *flump*, the whole lot on your head – and it happened as a result of several things. One of them was me turning 60. Another one was *Hairspray*.

Hairspray was a project that was, and is, very close to my heart. For a start, I'd actively pursued the role of Edna Turnblad to the extent that I dragged my carcass along to a casting session and auditioned, something I hadn't done since *Les Mis* about twenty years earlier. At that time – in 2007, this was – I didn't need to audition for shows, because after almost two decades of being the British musical star who's not Elaine Paige, I happened to be in that fortunate position of having people call me (or to be precise calling my agent, who called me).

But nobody had called me about playing Edna Turnblad in *Hairspray*, and having seen Harvey Fierstein's brilliant portrayal on Broadway, I *really* wanted that part, so along I went, and I've got to say, it was probably my best audition ever. Maybe it was because I wanted it so much or probably more because I'd based my portrayal of Edna on my maternal grandmother, Agnes, otherwise known as Lil, who'd been my greatest supporter in the early days, always encouraging me to get up and do a turn. Suffice to say, if you've seen my Edna in *Hairspray*, you've seen Lil. 'It was like watching Gran up there,' said Mum, when she saw it, which was praise indeed.

I won my first Olivier Award for *Hairspray* (Best Actor) and the show itself broke records with 11 nominations that year. The whole thing was such a gargantuan success that it wasn't until four years and a huge tour later that I finally hung up my Edna wig.

Drum roll. *Or so I thought.*

Fast-forward to 2020 and I found myself dusting off the wig for a London revival. Delayed by the pandemic, it eventually opened in September 2021 at which point Covid restrictions meant we could only have 1,000 people in a 3,000-seater, all of whom had to be in their respective households, with a metre between them and the next bubble.

Was their enjoyment hampered by these restrictions? Was it buffalo! They didn't care. Having been cooped up at home eating Pringles for the best part of two years, the reception was practically religious. They whooped it up. Went absolutely nuts. From a performer's point of view, it was an incredible thing to witness.

Audiences went even more nuts when the production opened up and we were allowed full houses. *Hairspray* was perfect for an audience starved of live entertainment. Again, the reaction each night was positively rapturous.

On stage, things were verging on chaotic. This was during

the time when you had to isolate if you so much as made eye contact with someone who had a sore throat. With our principals falling foul of the rules, we had to rehearse 12 actors that none of us had ever met who could take our places at a moment's notice. The dirty dozen were banished to a room in the eyrie until such time as someone in the main cast dropped out, at which point they were parachuted in to perform.

And when I say that it could take place at a moment's notice, I'm really not kidding. It happened in the interval a few times: you'd have characters played by a different actor in the second half – an actor none of us had even met. Corny Collins goes off at the half. When he comes back on again, he's a different guy.

There were supposed to be special routes around the backstage areas to prevent performers coming into close proximity, but then most of us were doing scenes together anyway, and if you were in a scene with someone who'd tested positive you were supposed to go into isolation. We were doing our best to practise due diligence (more than our job's worth etc.) but doing so in the full knowledge that half the cast were getting in via public transport, so it was probably all in vain anyway.

Still. Even with all that going on, nothing could take the shine off what was a fabulous production so appreciatively received each night, the only trouble being that it had to finish.

And with any show that finishes without another ready to come down the pipe, you find yourself sitting at your kitchen table, wondering what comes next. Every turn on earth will tell you the same. You worry, *Will I ever work again?* This is why I've diversified so much. It's because I'm paranoid I won't get work.

So I was sitting there cogitating, thinking *What show next?* and I couldn't think of one, and at some point I must have left the kitchen table and flown to Majorca, because it was there that I found myself watching the Bond film *Moonraker*, starring Roger Moore as Bond. It's not my favourite Bond movie – that honour goes to *The Spy Who Loved Me* – but it happened to be on, and if there's one thing guaranteed to arrest my progress through a living room, it's a Bond movie.

Have I mentioned that Roger was due to play George in *Aspects of Love*? No, I haven't. And I realise that it's a terrible tease saying that he 'was due to play' George. 'So why didn't he eventually play the part?' you're asking. 'Tell us, Michael.'

Bear with. We'll get to it. For now, that's all you need to know: back in 1989, Roger Moore was due to be in *Aspects*.

Watching him in *Moonraker*, ('How do you kill five hours in Rio if you don't samba?') got me thinking about the circumstances under which he and I first met, and our respective ages at that time. I was thinking about *Aspects* and how important it was to me. How it had supercharged my career and introduced me to Cathy. How I knew from *Les Mis* how fascinating it was to go back to a show and chart its evolution, especially if you do what I'd done in that instance, which was to start off playing Marius and go back as Javert. How in 1989, when we started rehearsals for the first *Aspects*, Roger would have been knocking on the door of 60, which was my age. And that was it. The final bit of snow. *Flump*. I'll do *Aspects*, and I'll step into shoes once filled by Roger Moore and play George.

Chapter 3

I slapped the cast album on, the first time I'd done so in decades. I mean, I've heard 'Love Changes Everything', maybe once or twice since, but not the entire *Aspects*. What a great show it was. What an underrated show. Listening to it reawakened all these feelings in me. I found myself appreciating it anew.

I didn't tell anyone for a couple of days. I sat on it like a hen sits on an egg, just keeping it warm for a while. Perhaps I'd wake up one wet morning and decide that it was a daft idea after all. Like what was I thinking?

But I didn't. Next thing you know, I was doing what I always do before I run with an idea, which is speak to Cathy. Her response is always the most important one, always has been, always will be. 'I think I've got my next show, and you've got to guess what it is,' I told her. 'Here's the premise: "Michael Ball in . . ." What will make people go, "Oh my God, that's a no-brainer," but no one will think of it?'

'Well, what?' she sighed, 20 guesses later.

'*Aspects of Love*,' I told her.

And instantly she got the same buzz. 'Get on the phone,' she said. 'Get on the phone now.'

The first thing to do when you have an idea that Cathy likes is to take her advice and pick up the phone, which in this case was to speak to my agents, Alastair and Helen at Curtis Brown.

'Michael, this is really exciting. And the reason it's exciting is because it's yours,' they told me.

'Mine?' Well, perhaps that was overstating it. The question remained, though, as to who would produce. After all, the original had fallen under the auspices of the Really Useful Group, a company set up by Andrew Lloyd Webber in 1977 to produce and manage his musicals. He took the name from *Thomas the Tank Engine*, where they call the trains 'really useful engines'. The RUG includes Really Useful Films – which takes care of film versions of Andrew's productions (the biggest one to date being the Joel Schumacher production of *The Phantom of the Opera*) – Really Useful Records and LW Theatres, which owns six West End theatres: the Adelphi Theatre, the Cambridge Theatre (home to *Matilda*), the Gillian Lynne Theatre, His Majesty's Theatre (home to *Phantom*), the London Palladium and Theatre Royal, Drury Lane.

So if I was to do *Aspects of Love*, an Andrew Lloyd Webber musical, there was every chance that it would be produced by Really Useful at an LW theatre. On the other hand, I knew that Andrew was incredibly busy with *Bad Cinderella* in the West End and also preparing for a transfer to Broadway, while at the same time I was wondering if the fates were telling me that now was the time to bring a new team to the project – a fresh perspective.

Either way, I would soon find out whether Andrew wanted to keep a tight rein on it, because at some point in the near future, I was going to have to speak to him and ask for his input. At the very least, we would need the rights.

In the meantime, it was Alastair at Curtis Brown who suggested I speak to Nica Burns, who with Max Weitzenhoffer is one half of the Nimax group. As well as being producers, Nimax own six West End theatres – the Palace, the Lyric, the Apollo, the Garrick, the Vaudeville and the Duchess – and I liked the idea of working with her for a bunch of reasons, not least among them being that we get on like a house on fire; that she's a good producer, and that if Nica's on board then she comes with a theatre, the theatre is free, and she can make it work for the schedule.

Off I went, planning to speak to Nica, and little knowing when I left the house that morning that I was about to have the most exciting and productive day ever.

*

I got to the Nimax offices on Maiden Lane at about 11am, where I sat down with Nica and Laurence Miller, the Nimax commercial director and her producing partner.

I did the game. Of course I did the game. The usual answers. *Oklahoma!*, *The Rocky Horror Picture Show* . . . you name it.

Until I told them, and they went, 'Oh, of course, it's a no-brainer,' and the questions started coming: When do you want to do it? How long do you want to do it for? Where do you want it going next? What do you plan to do with it?

Which were all the questions I wanted asking. Music to my ears. I told them I planned to do a limited run; initially, three or four months, while also being aware that in order for it to make money, it might need to be for a longer period of time. All producers like to see a return on their investment so my top tip is not to say anything that might endanger, cap or otherwise limit that return.

'As for where, I'd like to be on Shaftesbury Avenue,' thinking that the Lyric, Apollo and Palace – three Nimax theatres – are all on Shaftesbury Avenue. 'I'd like Jonathan Kent to direct, and . . . now this is a tricky one. I'm not saying this out of ego, but sort of am, I'm going to sing "Love Changes Everything".'

By which I meant that in the 1989 original, Alex, played by me, had sung it; in the 2023 revival, George (played by me) was going to sing it.

'People will be expecting me to do it,' I explained. 'So we need to find a way that he does.'

There was plenty of head nodding going on. Lots of broad agreement. 'Okay,' said Nica, 'But we have to ask Andrew if . . .'

I held up a finger (one of my own), 'I tell you what,' I said, 'if you're okay to wait for a bit, I'm meeting Andrew any minute now.'

I was, in fact, lunching with Andrew at Rules, which as well as being London's oldest restaurant, famed for its pies and oysters, is virtually opposite the Nimax offices. In order to get my answer, all I had to do was cross the road, eat pie, admire one of the most beautiful and unique interiors in the capital (seriously, it's incredible) and persuade the world's most famous living composer to give his blessing to a new *Aspects*. Easy.

Chapter 4

And you know what? It *was* pretty easy.

Because although Andrew can certainly have his moments, he's a really easy-going guy. He's approachable, quick to laughter, fond of reminiscing, and in his old age way more amenable and flexible than he was in his more fiery youth.

At the time – that was the tail end of 2021 – he was going through some issues with *Cinderella* in the West End, so we talked about that; we talked about the Covid situation that had buggered the theatres so royally, and then he asked me what I was doing next, to which I said, 'Well, I've got an idea.'

I didn't play the game. Of course I didn't play the game. Instead I said, 'Well, I was sitting down thinking about what show to do, when Roger Moore came on the telly – and then I got the idea.'

I know Andrew. I can read him really well. The physical change that I saw in him as he instantly related to and began engaging with the idea said way more than words.

'Well, this is absolutely . . . yes, of course, of course, I see this absolutely.' His brain was straight into gear. 'Since we did it originally, it's been through a few incarnations. It's changed,' he said.

I was nodding.

'Who shall we get to produce it?' he said.

He wasn't suggesting that Really Useful produce it. That was handy.

'Well,' I said, 'what about Nica? Because then we can get one of her . . .'

'Absolutely,' he agreed enthusiastically, 'Shall we go and see her? I mean, she's only across the road.'

'No,' I said quickly. 'No, you're all right. I'll call her later maybe.'

'Who do you see directing it?' he asked.

I told him about Jonathan Kent. 'You've never worked with him, but he did the brilliant *Sweeney* that I did; he did *Gypsy*. He's this kind of show's director and he'll come at it with really fresh and interesting ideas.'

Andrew was nodding, agreeing to a meeting between him and Jonathan. The cogs were still whirring. He was thinking ahead to Don Black and Charles Hart, our lyric writers. 'We'll sit down with them to work out if and what needs to be changed. Then of course there's the Jenny issue . . .'

Yes, the Jenny issue. In Garnett's book, Jenny is 13. For the 1989 version of *Aspects*, we aged her so that the birthday she celebrates during the narrative takes her to 15.

Since 1989, the conversation around consent and sexual power dynamics has become louder, more complex and a good deal more sensitive. In short, people now wince where once they might not have done. Alex doesn't groom Jenny; she has her own agency. But even so, 15 is very young for her to be discarding her water wings and playing in the deep end of the pool. We were going to have to think about that. Nica had raised it; Andrew had raised it. If two of Theatreland's biggest brains were throwing up red flags then whether I liked it or not (and my own opinion was not yet formed) we were going to have to think about it.

Anyhow, we placed the Jenny issue to one side for the time being and went on to discuss 'Love Changes Everything', which Andrew agreed I should sing. Another box ticked. As for the placing of the song?

Andrew's received pronunciation lends many of his statements a categorical air. '"Love Changes Everything" should never have started the show,' he told me, emphatically. But of course it's easy to say that *now*, with the benefit of hindsight. Back in 1989, the issue of where to put 'Love Changes Everything' had been a truly vexing question, with a number of factors in play: firstly, the song had been a huge hit well in advance of the show opening (number two in the charts, kept off the top spot by Jason Donovan, something I may have mentioned before), and this meant that Andrew couldn't take the song from Alex and give it to another character because there was a public expectation that I would sing it; secondly, it's a song of wisdom and experience, and thus should be sung by a character who has amassed a bit of both (i.e. not the present-day Alex); thirdly, it couldn't come at the end of the show, because we already had what we call 'the 11 o'clock number' – in other words, a big climactic song towards the end of Act II – and that was 'Anything But Lonely' sung by

Ann Crumb as Rose. 'Anything But Lonely' was a stand-alone number, whereas 'Love Changes Everything' featured as a recurring motif throughout.

Now, if you have a prominent song complete with big ending, it needs to earn its place. You want it early in the show in order to establish its importance; the character singing it has to make it theirs. It really should go up front.

So that was the hand as it was dealt: the song needed to be sung by me as Alex and it had to go at the beginning. It was our director, Trevor Nunn, who had the idea of making it a flash-forward, so that the show would begin with an older, love-weary Alex reflecting on his recent experience before the audience then discovers how he acquired it.

Which, back in 1989, is what we did.

In the 2023 version, however, two things were for sure: one, I was going to play George. Two, George was going to sing 'Love Changes Everything'. Why? Well, partly because there would be a certain expectation; the audience want to see me sing 'Love Changes Everything'. Hell, *I* want me to sing 'Love Changes Everything'. It's my signature song. But also because it really does make a hell of a lot more sense to the story having George sing it.

In the course of writing this book, and in the period between that Rules lunch and rehearsals beginning, I arranged to meet with Andrew, who very graciously agreed to be interviewed, despite the fact that he had recently suffered a terrible personal loss, the death of his son, Nicholas. On a personal note, I was terribly, terribly saddened by this. I knew Nick as a young man of around ten years old when we first did *Aspects*, and I watched him grow into a charming, funny, generous and talented man who, having written the music for *The Little Prince* at The National Theatre, and *Fat Friends The Musical*, among others, had tasted success and would surely have gone on to even greater things. A sad loss.

During our interview, Andrew and I returned to the subject of 'Love Changes Everything'. Our 1989 staging had taken the song 'out of the body of the show', said Andrew. But giving it to George 'makes that song part of the fabric of the show in a way that it wasn't before'. He said something else that was very telling. '"Love Changes Everything" is George's creed. It goes along with [another *Aspects* song sung by George] "A Memory of a Happy Moment"; that's what this week will always be. It makes complete and total sense.'

Anyway, back to our lunch at Rules, where such decisions still lay in the future. At that moment, I was just pleased that my idea to produce a new version of *Aspects* had been given the seal of approval. I was ticking boxes left, right and centre. Literally everything I thought of, he pre-empted.

'Are we on?' I said, as our meeting drew to a close.

'Absolutely,' he said.

'Excellent. I'll try and talk to Nica later,' I told him.

'Well, I'll call her,' he said, and thinking, *I'd better reach her first*, I let him leave and hurried back across the road, knocked on the door, and went up and talked Nica through the conversation.

'Are we on?' I asked her.

'We're on,' she said. And that was it. Incredibly, we had managed to get the whole production green-lit in two hours. Unreal. (By the way, Andrew, if he's reading this, will be learning about this particular chain of events for the first time.)

'What theatre do you want?' she asked me.

'I don't want it in a big theatre. I want this to be closer to how it was originally conceived, which was as a chamber piece – a show that's less about the spectacle and more about the music and characters.'

At first she earmarked the Apollo, which is smaller and has its challenges, but sometime later she called to say she was putting it in the Lyric. As we both knew, that would mean disappointing someone else hoping to have the Lyric, but that's Nica's department, that's what she does. All I know is that every show has a breakpoint, and as long as you hit that and you're paying rent then they can't end your lease. However, if the show falls below breakpoint, the landlords can give you notice. At that time the Lyric had *Get Up, Stand Up!*, which while a great show, had closed, and in came *2:22 A Ghost Story*, which would run until May, when it would transfer with a new cast to the Apollo, and we'd move into the Lyric.

And that was perfect with me. It's just under 1,000 seats and not a wide theatre, but it has huge wing space with room for all the designs we'd be having, as well as space for the orchestra who would sit behind and above the performers.

That night, having done the easiest deal in history, I returned home and sat with Cathy who wanted to know how things had gone. 'Well, be careful what you wish for,' I said. 'It's happening.'

Perhaps 'easy' isn't quite right. But it had been smooth. Me, Cathy, Nica, Andrew – we all wanted a new *Aspects* to happen. The question now was whether the world at large wanted it, too.

PART TWO

Deplored of the Dance

Chapter 5

I can't tell the story of *Aspects of Love* without telling at least a little of my own, chiefly because it's a sequence of events so closely associated with the show's creator, Andrew Lloyd Webber, and a trip to see *Jesus Christ Superstar* when I was a child. It wasn't my first theatre experience but it was perhaps the most significant.

First? That would be when I was in a panto at three and a half. A production of *Babes in the Wood* with the local am-dram that I did because my dad was in it. Dad was the big theatre fan of the family. He wanted to be an actor, but his parents didn't encourage it so he followed my grandad into the motor industry. Mind you, he managed to exorcise his performing instinct by inventing a sort of 'industrial theatre' for launching a project – most notably with the then-new Mini, which he presented to the world's press in suitably striking fashion. With a budget of £500, which was slightly more than a Mini cost at the time, he had a huge top hat constructed and then, in front of the assembled press and dressed as a magician, tapped the hat with his wand. Out of the top hat drove a Mini, inside which were my mum, my brother, Kevin – a babe in arms – and two grown men. The idea, as they then decanted various bits of luggage, including golf clubs, was to show that the Mini, despite its size, could operate as a family car.

Dad also loved after-dinner speaking and, like I say, amateur dramatics, hence my small part in *Babes*. Well, I say small part, but I built it up by going to the front and pretending to play the trumpet. Scene-stealer, even then.

Throughout my childhood, I would put on plays and skits with my gran, Lil, (that was my maternal grandmother, Agnes Lil, the one who was the inspiration for Edna) pulling clothes out of our dressing-up box and slipping gratefully into a fantasy world. I wasn't interested in football or other sports; I was into superheroes, never happier than when I was wearing a cloak made out of a towel, running around the garden being Superman.

Dad left the Austin Motor Company and went to work for a multinational who had a Ford franchise in Cape Town. So, we lived in South Africa for three years, up until I was about 10, and at school there I discovered a talent for singing in a sort of cod-opera funny voice that proved popular with teachers and classmates. I put into practice a valuable lesson that I had learned during those days playing dress-up with Gran. I learned when to come in, but more importantly when to get out. I didn't overstay my welcome. I didn't milk it.

Living in South Africa, we didn't have a telly (nobody did; TV didn't reach South Africa until 1976, four years after we left) so we had to make do with either the cinema, the theatre or by listening to records at home. And we did a lot of all three. At a very young age I was listening to *Round the Horne*, a radio comedy show packed with double entendre and therefore like a foreign language to my young ears. On the whole, getting old is awful – the osteopath bills alone – but on the plus side, you do get to play George in *Aspects*, and with each passing year you understand more of the jokes in *Round the Horne*. Which is just as well, because all this time later, I still love to listen to it.

We were at the theatre whenever we could. Close to where we lived in Cape Town was the Nico Malan Theatre, where we used to watch a hypnotist called The Great Romark; we saw Cilla Black in concert there, supported by Lionel Blair. On one occasion, watching The King's Singers, I was introduced to the joy of corpsing when my gran, startled by a particular note made by the King's Singers' countertenor, spilled her bottle of pop and exclaimed, 'Jesus Christ alive!' This caused the entire Ball family on the front row to erupt into barely contained hilarity, which in turn caused the King's Singers themselves to begin corpsing. Here, then, is one of the many things I love about corpsing: it's infectious. You can literally watch other performers catch a corpse – and no amount of PPE will stop its relentless march. If you're a fellow fan, I can promise you plenty of corpses to come in these pages, including My Favourite-Ever Corpse.

We had a piano in our rented South African home. Mum hadn't played since she was a kid but she got back into it and we'd have singing around the piano: show tunes and the 'Great American Songbook'. Our landlord had a collection of records: movie scores and Broadway musicals. Listening to those, my musical appreciation moved on a stage. The combination of characterisations, story and music fascinated me. I loved emotional songs. I loved dramatic songs. I loved songs that told stories. Musicals and I were a match made in heaven.

From then on, it was Disney at the cinema, musicals at the theatre or on the record player. From an early age, I could recite the whole of *The Sound of Music*. Not long after that I added *Mary Poppins* and *Chitty Chitty Bang Bang* to my repertoire. I loved *Star*, with Julie Andrews, about the life of Gertrude Lawrence. That idea of telling a story with music was a language I understood.

The next epiphany was seeing *Jesus Christ Superstar*, which was my first taste of large-scale major theatre, my first visit to London's West End – sorry, London's *glittering* West End – and my first live experience of an Andrew Lloyd Webber musical. This was in 1974, I was 12, and we had returned from South Africa by then – my brother and I went to boarding school at Plymouth College, the rest of the family to Farnham. In those days, just visiting London was an enormous thrill. I mean, London. The capital. Prior to that the only time I'd made the trip was for an FA Cup final. My dad had got tickets somehow, and so we decided to make a day of it, and all was going well until we had lunch somewhere opposite the Houses of Parliament, where I ate some bad chicken. As a result, I spent the cup final throwing up in the Wembley car park with my mum rubbing my back as we listened to the roar of the crowd from inside the stadium – two of whom were my brother, Kevin, and my dad. I'm pretty sure that every childhood contains at least one memorable vomit story, and that one's mine.

Returning for *Superstar* was a very different kettle of fish. Who cares about football? Well, okay, lots of people. Just not me. But seeing the lights of the West End? Now, that was another thing entirely. Riding in a black cab for the first time, wearing my best bib and tucker (purple corduroy suit, kipper tie, really sharp) was something else.

At that time you could drive around Cambridge Circus before coming on to Shaftesbury Avenue. There it was: the edifice that is the Palace Theatre. A jewel in the crown of the Avenue, one of the greatest frontages of any theatre anywhere in the world, with no buildings either side to distract you from its almost overwhelming beauty.

This was at a time when The Palace wasn't even looking its best. Needing to give it a lick of paint, the owners had bought a job lot of railway paint, meaning its original marble and gilt had been rendered in a typically 1970s shade of gaudy purple. From today's perspective, an aesthetic and cultural crime. At the time? To my eyes? Big psychedelic wow. The perfect location for *Jesus Christ Superstar*. The fact that there were protesters outside – the show being a controversial religious hot potato in its day – was just the icing on the cake.

Although The Palace is four storeys tall, it's not that wide, but to me it seemed massive. I loved the pre-show buzz: getting an ice cream and a programme, joining the mass of people taking their seats, craning to see the stage. *What's going to happen there?* Then the lights going down. The music starting up and . . .

I was practically levitating. I already knew the soundtrack back to front and loved the fusion sound of it, but experiencing it live was an entirely different matter. I mean, the sound wasn't just better or bigger than anything I'd ever seen before – with apologies to Cilla and the King's Singers, but it's true – it was just *huge*. It was a sound that picked me up and carried me away. I was floating. Absolutely sent.

Detailed memories of the night are few. I recall that a different actor played Herod, a black actor who played it quite unlike the performance I knew from the soundtrack, doing it like Muhammad Ali. Watching him in action taught me how an actor can take a role, put a spin on it and make it their own. I don't think that had ever occurred to me before.

Other than that, what I remember about that night is the feeling. I was just taken. Lost. Abducted. Maybe because the music was modern and edgy. Or because the story is told entirely through song, like an opera. Maybe it was just the whole *live* experience. Or perhaps it was the light and spectacle, the realisation of the power of musical. How they can move, transport and change you. How they can make you think things you didn't before. Whatever. All I can say is that I had a reaction. It was literally transformative.

Having said all that, it still didn't occur to me to make a career out of it. I wasn't exactly passing a hand across my forehead and declaring, 'Darling, I've had my calling. I want to be on stage.'

Okay, correction: I *wanted* to be on stage. Difference being, I never thought that I could, that I was capable of it. I didn't dare imagine that life would ever be so good to me that I could make a legitimate career out of it.

Chapter 6

Although I didn't imagine life as a performer, it didn't stop me dreaming. In my head, or to myself, I would perform. Emulating the musicals was my home-made version of singing lessons. Musicals taught me how to hold a note, how to add lyrical inflexion and find my own way of phrasing. Through musicals I worked out the effective emotional beats. I'd listen, be moved and think, *Now, how can I make* me *do that?* I'd be my own judge as to whether or not it was working.

As an aside, I've had a total of three singing lessons throughout my life. They sent me for a couple when I was doing *Pirates of Penzance* in 1985, and then, doing *Phantom* in 1987, I was seen by the legendary Ian Adam, who could boast Michael Crawford and Sarah Brightman among his clients. (It was hearing Michael singing at Ian's studio that prompted Sarah to recommend him for the *Phantom* role.) Ian said to me, 'You know what you're doing,' and that was that.

So anyway, whenever the opportunity presented itself, I'd get up and do a turn for real. It's difficult to believe, I know, but although I was never going to be captain of sports at school, I was really quite funny back then. I'd do impersonations culled from the previous night's episode of *Steptoe & Son*. 'You dirty old man,' and all of that.

After *Superstar* in 1971 came *Evita* in 1978. I remember being at school when 'Don't Cry for Me Argentina' got to number one. Everyone was turning their nose up at it, going, 'It's not as good as Queen,' or Status Quo or whatever, and I'm going, 'Er, no, this is amazing, this is brilliant,' and then being blown away by the album. Like that guy in the advert who used to creep down and drink R Whites Lemonade at night, I was getting my musicals fix any way I could. The difference being that it wasn't a secret and nor was I trying to give it up. Quite the reverse. I was gorging on it. Glugging it down. *Oklahoma!* on TV on a Sunday afternoon? I was there. *My Fair Lady*? *Carousel*? Reserve me a spot on the sofa.

At 14, my dad took me to see Donald Sinden as *King Lear* at Stratford. Fans of synchronicity will be pleased to know that this was a production directed by Trevor Nunn during his triumphant reign as artistic director of the RSC. My dad and I returned that season to see Donald and Judi Dench do *Much Ado About Nothing*, directed by John Barton, and although that was wonderful, it was *Lear* that had the greatest effect on me, not least because at school the upper sixth were doing a production of it, and as I'd been to see the play, I got a part as The Fool, even though I was a lowly fourth year.

That was brilliant for me, and that love of Shakespeare and theatre is why later, at drama school, I studied acting rather than musical theatre. This is why I will always regard myself as an actor first, singer second.

Around this same time, my godparents' daughter, Jackie, got into the original cast of *Annie*, with Stratford Johns from *Z Cars* playing Daddy Warbucks. I think it's fair to say that there's some kind of musical theatre gene embedded deep in the Ball family's DNA. We all went to see Jackie at the Victoria Palace Theatre in London and were invited backstage, which was brilliant. That glorious chaos at the end of the show, people running around in their scanties, costumes flying everywhere, wigs coming off, bald caps on their heads. I knew nothing of the world of dressers and chaperones; I didn't know about the stage crew. I just saw fabulous creatures and thought, *This is my tribe.* This is where I want to be. I want to be part of this.

Leaving school (I returned 35 years later to open their drama room, The Michael Ball Studio), I went on to Farnham Sixth Form College, where some lads in a band asked me to join. It was a time when The Police were a huge group, so we called ourselves Prime Suspect. When it came to choosing what songs to cover, I was going, 'Do you think we could try "The Way We Were"?'

They'd go, 'What the fuck are you talking about?'

I said, 'Well, it's a great song. Think about it.'

I believe there was a clash of musical styles.

'What about "Evergreen", again by Streisand? Cracking song.'

That didn't last too long. I got asked to leave the band, which was probably just as well. By then I'd also joined Surrey Youth Theatre, which was run by a wonderful woman called Kay Dudeney, now sadly passed. At that stage, I knew that my passion wasn't musical or theatrical, it was a symbiosis of the two. I'll tell you exactly what it was: it was being in another world, being someone else. That thing of taking on a character, or a song, and inhabiting it.

*

I was in two productions with The Surrey Youth Theatre. The first was Dylan Thomas's 'play for voices' *Under Milk Wood*, which I loved because it was Welsh, and I could do the accent, you see?

The girl playing Polly Garter was meant to come on and sing about loving Tom, Dick and Harry, and how Little Willy Wee was the man for her. Except that she came on and dried, couldn't remember the words. So there she was, scrubbing the floors, going, 'I love all the boys and all the boys love me, they love me, I love them, I love all the boys.' Genius. My lifelong love of stage fuck-ups was born. File that one alongside corpsing.

I wasn't in the following year's production – they liked to revolve the casts – but I was in the one after that: *The Boyfriend*, which was my first proper, proper musical. Funnily enough, I was given my best-ever note on *The Boyfriend*, and it came from my dad. There was a scene towards the end, a fancy-dress party in which I was dressed as Henry VIII. I was sitting at the back, not part of the action, not doing anything. Later, my dad said to me, 'When you're on stage, even if you're not doing anything, you still have to be the person that you're pretending to be.'

'What do you mean?' I said.

He said, 'Well, I saw you looking around and checking everyone out, utterly as yourself.'

He was right. I was using the opportunity to study my surroundings. Best note ever: stay in character.

It was also the moment that I understood just how brilliant it can be, putting on a musical. The excitement of watching all that hard work come together. By this time I was at Guildford Tech because I'd failed my A levels, and I'd been wondering what I was going to do with my life – still not thinking that performing could be any kind of career – when Kay said to me, 'What about going to drama school? I think you've got something.'

And if someone tells you that you've 'got something' then firstly, you hope they mean something nice, not something catching for which you're going to need ointment; secondly, you listen. Especially if that person is Kay Dudeney.

Why she said it, I can't remember. However, I do recall that it was around the same time that my dad asked me about my plans for the future. He was driving, me in the passenger seat – the traditional configuration for important father-son talks since time immemorial – when he posed the question, 'What the hell are you going to do with your life?'

I looked out of the window, saw a For Sale sign and said, 'I want to be an estate agent.'

I mean, really, it could have been anything. I could have looked outside, seen a traffic cone and gone, 'I want to be a traffic cone.' But bugger me, a week later, he'd organised an interview with a local estate agents.

Perhaps I mentioned it to Kay. Maybe that's when she pulled the drama-school rabbit out of the hat. This all happened in the summer, so I'd missed out on applying for auditions to all the drama schools. 'I have a way of getting in touch with Guildford

School of Acting,' she told me. 'It's local, very reputable. If I can get you an audition there, would you be interested?'

I bit her hand off. I still didn't know what I wanted to be, but I knew that I loved the world of theatre. I loved the community of it. I *loved* being part of a company. And I didn't want be an estate agent.

Chapter 7

Somebody asked me recently if Andrew Lloyd Webber was my Beatles. The answer was no. My Beatles were Abba and the Bee Gees. But Andrew was very much there. He was A Thing. His own thing.

Since *Superstar* his star had been on the rise. There was *Evita*, which was huge, and then *Tell Me on a Sunday*, which, being a one-woman show, was on a much smaller scale but still a massive success. Both were accompanied by chart hits and albums that I listened to on repeat.

Cats was next for Andrew, and it happened at around the same time that I began life at Guildford School of Acting (GSA) in 1981. We were rapt by those extraordinary stories of how Judi Dench had torn her Achilles tendon, meaning that Elaine had to parachute in and take over the role. We listened to the cast album and turned up the volume whenever 'Memory' came on the radio.

And then going to actually see the show. Wow. By then I

thought Andrew was a genius. A composer who could turn his hand to anything and do it with equal skill. He wrote rock songs but on the other hand could craft a ballad like no other; he'd do interesting, cool things with tempo; he could do fun, but he could also do high emotion. His songs were sticky. They were earworms.

Plus, he was flying the flag for the UK. Almost single-handedly Andrew was the standard-bearer for a new dawn of British musicals. Shows like *The Boyfriend* or *Salad Days* were lovely and funny and all that, but maybe a bit . . . slight and / or safe by comparison. Andrew was innovative, boundary pushing. He was embracing big themes.

Did the wheels fall off around the time of *Starlight Express*? Maybe a little. And even then only temporarily. *Starlight* was accused of being a bit gimmicky and cashing in on current trends. It certainly wasn't as strong as *Cats*, although it's still fabulous. But then *The Phantom of the Opera* came along, and that blew everything out of the water.

By the time of *Phantom*, I was in *Les Misérables*, playing Marius. We'd just done 11 weeks at the Barbican and got terrible reviews but were still going to transfer to the West End – a brave but ultimately astute move on behalf of Cameron Mackintosh, who was producing.

Around the same time, Andrew had bought the Palace Theatre, thinking it was going to host *Phantom*, but *Phantom* wasn't ready so Cameron had asked him to put *Les Mis* in there.

Certainly, said Andrew, no doubt thinking it would be a short-term thing. And so *Phantom* ended up in Her Majesty's Theatre, where it still plays, and *Les Mis* transferred to the Palace, where it eventually ran for 19 years.

It was there in the Palace Theatre during my *Les Mis* stint that I met, or perhaps that should be 'encountered', Andrew for the very first time. At that point, he and Sarah Brightman had a flat at the top, and one night we were hanging round for curtain calls when this old cage lift that we weren't allowed to use during the performance, in case someone got stuck, clattered down. There getting out was Andrew in his best bib and tucker, and Sarah, who looked amazing, both on their way out to the *Phantom* opening-night party.

We in the *Les Mis* cast were looking at each other, thinking, *That's Andrew Lloyd blimmin' Webber.*

'How did it go?' we said to him, referring to the opening of *Phantom*.

'Oh, very, very well. Very, very well,' he said, probably wishing that we weren't all hanging around gawping at him. And that was it.

Anyway. Stop. Rewind. And back to my education, where thanks to Kay, I was offered a place at the Guildford School of Acting. The first year was a foundation year, while the next two you spent studying either acting or musical theatre. As I've already said, I chose acting.

Why? For two reasons: one lofty, the other not so much. Lofty one: I loved acting and was in love with Shakespeare. Less lofty: I didn't want to dance. Although I loved singing and would do it at the merest hint of a hat dropping, I was a dance refusenik. Every morning at Guildford, regardless of your course, you had to do an hour of prancing around that they called 'ability'. Well, I'm neither a dancer nor an early bird, so I invented a heart condition to get out of the sessions. Never did another. My special ability? Getting out of 'ability'.

And the biggest irony regarding all that dance avoidance is that the GSA is now part of the University of Surrey, who as well as awarding me an honorary doctorate, named their dance studio The Ball Room after me.

Overall, I liked it at the GSA. I enjoyed learning about life and friendship; I enjoyed being around my fellow students, *my* people; I liked being taught how to do what we do: the voice classes, the singing, the acting.

So was I a goody two shoes? A teacher's pet? Not quite, because having moved out of home for the first time, I was embracing freedom wholeheartedly; the candle was well and truly burned at both ends. Put it this way, I dropped a lot of weight during my time at GSA. Years later, Gaby Roslin, another former pupil, interviewed me for her podcast and told me that she and all the girls in her year fancied me. That was why. I was on the G-Plan Diet, with G standing for 'going out an awful lot'.

My lifestyle didn't always endear me to the tutors. I remember one of them saying to me, 'Do you know what, Ball? You're probably never going to work until you're 40, and then you might get the odd character role.'

Yes, well. Whatever. It was a version of that thing I've been told all my life, that I 'get away with doing the bare minimum', and if I actually bothered to focus, work hard and take things seriously, I might amount to something. It's not true now, and it wasn't true then, and anyway, I didn't totally neglect the work at college. Yes, that particular end of the candle might have flickered at times, but it never fully went out.

For graduation we staged a showcase, the idea being that everybody in the year could do a turn and hopefully shine.

Parents, agents, casting directors and producers came along to watch this big show, in which I performed a 1950s number wearing a shiny red drape coat and brothel creepers, with all the girls around me in *Grease*-style clothes. It was the penultimate song before we went into the big 'whole company number' finish – for which, again, I was fortunate to be front and centre – and it absolutely stole the show.

By then, I'd already landed my first job, which was with Rob Mitchell, who'd been the music department head and who must have seen something in me, for having landed a job as musical director at the Theatre Llewellyn in Aberystwyth, he invited me to try out for their summer season: *Godspell.*

Was that my first audition? Actually it wasn't. That had come earlier when I tried out for a part in *There's a Girl in My Soup* starring Gerald Harper aka Adam Adamant from *Adam Adamant Lives!* How I got that audition is lost in the mists of time, but it might have had something to do with my dad, who'd become friends with Ernest Maxin, a producer of *The Morecambe & Wise Show* at the BBC.

The audition was for the part of a beatnik drummer.

'What should I wear?' I asked my dad.

My dad, bless him, being old school, said firmly, 'It's an interview. If you're going to an interview, you must look smart.'

Taking his advice and attending the interview dressed more like a Mormon than a beatnik drummer meant I didn't get the part. On the upside, I did get to meet Adam Adamant and was suitably star-struck (not hard; I get star-struck easily; still do) while also being invited to eat lunch at the BBC canteen, the whole time thinking, *This is just about the most exciting thing in the world. The BBC canteen.*

But anyway. I got the *Godspell* part with Rob Mitchell, which was a dream job because it meant I'd have an Equity card – a provisional one, at least – and an agent, the holy grail. On top of which, it was a fantastic company.

As a result, I had the best summer ever. I mean, really. For me there hasn't been an ensemble experience as good as that until, well, the rehearsals for *Aspects* in 2023. You know it's good when you spend the whole time laughing like drains. It was the case during *Aspects* and it was the case back then.

Not only that, but I was paid – really, somebody actually *paid* me to do the thing I love (rather than pay me not to, which is always a possibility). It was only £95 a week, Equity minimum, but who cared about that? Fresh out of college, I was already up and running. I was seeing from the other side the power that a musical could wield over its audience.

Godspell opens with this amazing horn sound. There are big gates on the stage and from behind the gates I'd sing a cappella, '*Preeeepare yee, the way of the Lord,*' and then the gates would swing open and I'd come down centre stage, back-lit, bit of dry ice, '*Preeeepare yee . . .*' before it goes uptempo. '*Preeeepare yee the way of the Lord*'. Absolutely spellbinding.

I was suddenly in the place that those stars of *Superstar* had been in when I was in the audience. We even had fans. Girls from the local school would wait outside. Will anything ever match being asked for my first autograph? I doubt it somehow.

Chapter 8

Next thing you know, Rob Mitchell had moved to a rep theatre down in Basingstoke, The Horseshoe, which was doing Neil Simon's *Sweet Charity*. I auditioned and was accepted into the repertory company, which is where you have a permanent company who put on shows in two-week cycles, performing one in the evening and rehearsing a new one during the day. I ended up doing *Sweet Charity*, followed by *Lark Rise* and then, for Christmas, *The Adventures of Mr Toad*.

Our production of *Sweet Charity* was done on a budget. I was playing famous Italian movie star Vittorio Vidal. We didn't have enough people to play all the girls for the big number 'Big Spender', so four of the boys – though not me, I was playing a dirty old man wandering around in the background – had to dress up as women. This wasn't woke times. It wasn't done ironically, tongue-in-cheek or for any other post-modern reason. It was just that we didn't have enough female performers and couldn't afford more. 'Big Spender', indeed.

These minor budget issues aside, life at The Horseshoe was

great. Even so, you've still got an eye on what comes next. You're always looking to move up in the world. At that time, we all read *The Stage*, keen to know about any upcoming auditions, and in there was news of *Pirates of Penzance* at the Manchester Opera House. Paul Nicholas, Bonnie Langford, Victor Spinetti and Dilys Laye were already confirmed. For other parts they were having open auditions for Equity members.

Well, I was an Equity member (provisionally) with a copy of *The Stage* in his hand and what's more, a spring in his step, so off I went to join 600 other hopefuls.

What you're looking for in an open audition is a recall. So you do your singing, your movement and a line audition, bugger off and then keep your fingers crossed.

You get recalled. Then you're looking for another recall. And another. Until, like me, you're on your third or fourth, thinking, *I might get into the show*. I got five for *Pirates*, the first four of which were in London.

Word filtered through that it was down to me and one other guy for the lead role of Frederick. The producer and director visited The Horseshoe to audition me, and the guys at The Horseshoe were so excited. They couldn't have been more delighted. They set aside a little room for me to meet with the *Pirates* people, who put me through my paces.

And I got it. Got the part. They even waived the rule about needing a full Equity card in order to work. Provisional or not, I was in.

*

Now, this was huge. This production would reopen the opera house in Manchester, and its two leads were huge names.

Even so, and as star-struck as I was, I had the presence of mind to ask for a special 'introducing' credit on the poster, which they gave me.

Good thing too, because the reviews were glowing. Far be it from me to blow my own trumpet (that's not true, I'm quite happy to blow my own trumpet), but no less an organ than the *Manchester Evening News* said, 'Newcomer Michael Ball gives Mr Nicholas a run for his cutlass in the beefcake stakes. With a cheeky sense of fun, commanding stage presence and sweet and strong tenor voice, he's a discovery of some importance. It is his first major role but won't be his last.'

The *Manchester Evening News* was by no means a solitary voice. All the reviews said the same. They praised Paul and Bonnie, Victor and Dilys, great work from seasoned troupers kind of thing, while for me it was all 'a star is born'.

Talk about a big-head. I was still on not-great wages, £200 a week, if memory serves, but again, so what? Less than a year out of drama school, playing the lead in *Pirates* at the Manchester Opera House, there for a total of seven months. It felt as though I'd arrived.

The sad thing was that my gran, Lil, had died a matter of days before we opened, which was absolutely heartbreaking. She'd been to see pretty much everything up until then. And it was funny, because she'd often say to me, 'Oh, Mike, I'm so proud of you, but if you ever got into *Coronation Street*, I can't tell you what that would mean.'

Well, as it turned out, the opera house was opposite Granada Studios so there was quite a lot of mixing, and I was able to audition for *Corrie*. The outcome was that there were two episode of *Corrie* done on OB – outside broadcast – and I played a tennis player. Again it's a great sadness that Lil was not around to see it.

It must have been around that time that my dad said to me, 'It's so wonderful, what's happening to you. Imagine if you had got into the RSC? I couldn't be more proud.'

That's family for you. Still, you can hardly blame them. He and I had such a history with the RSC, just as Lil was a lifelong *Corrie* fan.

Well, wouldn't you know it, but the RSC began holding auditions for *Les Misérables* while I was in Manchester, and Barry Burnett, who was Bonnie's agent, had asked the producer, Cameron Mackintosh, to come and have a look at Bonnie, with a view to her possibly being in *Les Mis*. At the same time, Barry had mentioned my name as a promising up-and-comer, currently getting good reviews in Manchester.

So up came Cameron. I had no real idea who he was back then, even though I knew all about Andrew Lloyd Webber. I was far more interested in the fact that it was an RSC production with Trevor Nunn directing.

The first audition was with Cameron as well as the executive producer Nick Allott and the writers Alain Boublil and Claude-Michel Schönberg.

I was looking perfect for the part with my bouffy *Pirates* hair (look, it was the 1980s, and you should have seen Paul Nicholas) and I sang a sort of nonsense version of 'Empty Chairs', which went well enough that I got a call back, this time to the New London Theatre on the set of *Cats*, where I met Trevor Nunn.

Things were getting surreal now. Trevor Nunn. *Cats*. There I sang a few songs I'd been asked to prepare, after which I was asked if I'd be prepared to take on a 'non-singing role', to which I replied, 'Oh, gosh, I thought this was a through-sung musical, and I'm rubbish at stage management, so I'm probably no good to you.'

He was just testing me out, it seemed, and the next day the call came through: they offered me Marius.

And if you're puzzling over that story, then that's because I haven't explained 'through-sung musical'. *Les Misérables* is through-sung, which means that it's not a book musical. A book musical is like *Oklahoma!* or *Grease*. As in, acting, acting, acting, underscore, sing the song. But a through-sung musical is where the characters sing all the way through, and any dialogue, such as it is, is sung in the form of recitative. You know another musical that's through-sung? *Aspects of Love*.

Anyhow, *Pirates* was coming to an end, so they let me go. There were a couple of people in the cast they wouldn't release, who had to commute, but as for me, I waved a very fond farewell to the *Pirates* of Manchester and joined four others living in a one-room place in Finsbury Park until I could find somewhere else to live. That ended up being a house in Hampstead that I shared with Patti LuPone who was playing Fantine in *Les Mis*. I stayed there until she got fed up of me, at which point I moved to a terrible flat hemmed in by building works in Crouch End.

On *Pirates* I'd learned showbiz, but *Les Mis* was all about the pitfalls and politics of actually creating a show. It wasn't fully written when I came on board, and so at Trevor's instigation we had a lot of trust exercises – he loves all that – as well as spending time working on character and all the stagecraft that went along with it.

In short, *Les Misérables* was a new thing altogether, a complete step up, even from *Pirates*, and I think that this is where I really started to learn my craft.

Chapter 9

If, with the introduction of Trevor into my life, it feels as though the *Aspects* stars were beginning to align, well, in actual fact I discovered recently that the seeds had been sown even earlier than that. It was during my interview with Andrew in his London flat – previous occupant: Tom Cruise – that he told me how *Aspects* had landed in his life just after *Evita*, when Tim Rice had handed him Garnett's novella.

'It came via a friend of Tim's,' he told me. 'He had an idea about the book being a movie, so he asked Tim and me whether we'd like to do a few incidental songs for it. Tim and I went on a little trip away, which was quite interesting and not entirely a success, because we spent our time playing pinball and never really got around to the work. Anyway, in the end Tim didn't really fancy it, and I sort of forgot about it, and then *Phantom* happened. It was only later that I came back to it.'

The book, he said, had been considered shocking in its time, 1955. 'People like Noël Coward found the character of Rose really immoral.'

'Okay, but what about the character of Jenny?' I wanted to know, thinking about those 'problematic' issues raised previously.

'No, no, Alex is not grooming her at all,' declared Andrew. 'To Alex, Jenny is the one thing that he absolutely has to resist, and does. To be honest, the character of Jenny doesn't frighten me, because one knows a lot of young girls *do* get crushes on older men, but as far as *Aspects* is concerned, Alex doesn't go there, or even consider going there.

'One of the other things that appealed to me, and possibly resonated with me more than Tim at the time, was that I had this wonderful Aunt Viola who was the naughtiest woman who ever lived in history. "Too many cocks spoil the breath" was the tamest of Auntie's pronouncements. Anyway, she went and lived in the South of France, just over the border, and when I was a little boy, longing to get away from my parents and my home in South Kensington as quickly as I possibly could, I used to go and stay there. And the thing was that every holiday there I saw exactly the same people, except they were all married to different people, but the same people. So there was a great deal of swapping that went on, which to me, aged 14, was really quite interesting and exciting. And these were all the characters in Garnett's book.'

History tells us, of course, that Tim's involvement with *Aspects* came to an end there and then, whereas for Andrew it was moved to the back burner for a period of time that encompassed *Cats*, *Starlight Express* and then *Phantom*.

Meanwhile, I was having the time of my bloomin' life on *Les Misérables*. We opened in October 1985 at the Barbican Centre, which was the base for the RSC. In December, we transferred to the Palace Theatre, and I was there for a short while, still enjoying it, until I started to get ill. They sent me for blood tests and I was diagnosed with glandular fever which, so the doctor said, would put me out of action for two weeks.

I took the fortnight off. In retrospect it wasn't nearly enough, and I went back feeling well below par. One night early on in my return, I took the stage and had my first panic attack.

It's not good to have a panic attack during a West End performance. Not good at all.

As for what happened next, well, it was a very, very dark time and not one I intend to go into here. Suffice to say that the biggest joy of my life, performing, had become the biggest terror. I went into a spiral of doubt, self-hatred and despair. It was as though something inside me had snapped and, unable to get well, I felt I had no choice but to leave the show.

It was the first time I had ever been so afflicted, having previously felt fairly immune from these issues, and it hit me extremely hard. For a long time, I sat in my flat and mouldered, gripped by an awful, terrible state of mind, a total prisoner of it, the solitude and surrounding building work only serving to make things worse. For a while I wondered if that was it. Was I finished as a performer? Would I be unwell for the rest of my life? It was as though I was frozen. Made a captive of the dark thoughts.

What helped to bring me out of it was an opportunity to perform on Miss England. I literally got a call from my agent who said they'd requested me. God knows how that came about, but the way it worked was that they'd stage the beauty contest and then, as the votes were being counted, a turn would come on and sing. My bit was due to be broadcast at 11pm, right after the news, and Miss England was not much of a big deal – literally tens of people watched it. Even so, it was live television. Live.

Thoughts of panic attacks presented themselves, marching through my head during sleepless nights. From somewhere I found the strength, and I told myself, *If I can get on, get through this, not die, and do it all on live television, it'll never be harder. Nothing will ever be more challenging than that.*

So I agreed to do it. Wearing a terrible shiny suit (again with the suits!) and a green bow tie, I sang what was a pretty average ballad.

I was terrified during the performance. Literally rigid with fear. I couldn't even feel my arms.

But I got through it.

'Okay,' I said to myself, 'It'll never get worse than that. I can find a way to blag this.'

After that, I got a spot on *3-2-1*, the game show starring Dusty Bin, which the more ancient among you will remember well. I bet you're even doing the 3-2-1 thing with your fingers right now.

Again I was nervous, but again I got through it. And the thing was that I'd do these bits of telly, watch myself back and see that the nerves didn't show. On stage I felt like a jelly, but to everyone watching I just looked like a turn doing my job.

Armed with that knowledge my confidence began to return, and I reasoned that as long as I could go on stage and actually do my stuff, then perhaps I might be able to recover the joy of performing at some later stage. The question remaining was whether anybody in Theatreland would give me another chance.

Chapter 10

They did. Cameron rang to say that *Phantom* was coming to the end of its first year. Michael Crawford, who played the Phantom, Sarah Brightman, who played Christine, and Steve Barton, who played Raoul, were all leaving to do the show on Broadway. Cameron wanted to know if I'd like the part of Raoul.

Maybe I *ummed*. Perhaps I also *ahhed*.

'Look, it's time for you to shit or get off the pot,' Cameron said, or words to that effect. 'You need a job and you're perfect for this role. I'll tell you exactly why it's great for you right now: it's because it's a good part but not the central role. All eyes will be on whoever takes over from Michael, not who's taking over from Steve Barton, so the pressure won't be on you. What do you think? Do you want to come in and meet Andrew?'

What an offer. Points in its favour were, firstly, as Cameron said, the eyes of the world would be on whoever took the

Phantom role – Dave Willetts, as it turned out; secondly, as I was going into an established company it would be a nice gentle reintroduction to that world; thirdly, I thought that *Phantom* would be a good one for me. *Les Misérables* is a really hard, emotional show, whereas *Phantom* is just love. I mean, it's all dramatic and over the top and massive, but it's lovely, right up my street; fourthly, and most importantly, it was a second chance, simple as that. A way back. In Cameron, I was lucky to have someone fighting my corner, and no way was I going to stare that gift horse in the mouth.

I can only thank Cameron for that, and often do, because he's remained a great friend and supporter. I remember once I was doing the worst production of *Kismet* but knowing Cameron I was sure he'd love it.

'Come and see this,' I told him. 'You love a really bad show. You'll never see anything worse. What's more, there's a young guy in it who I think you'll be interested to see.'

He and I went for what you might call a robust pre-*Kismet* lunch. Well, I say that. I was performing that night and didn't touch a drop. Cameron, on the other hand, was suitably refreshed. 'Darling,' he slurred, after the show. 'You were absolutely right, it is conceivably the worst thing that I've ever been to, but that boy's very good; we're going to have words.'

'That boy' was Alfie Boe, who ended up playing Jean Valjean.

I remember doing the *Les Misérables* 25th Anniversary show. It was the matinee and something had gone wrong – it wasn't showing on all the screens in the huge, sold-out O2 arena – and Cameron, bless him, was screaming and shouting, absolutely incensed, driving everyone mad. I grabbed his hand. I said, 'You come with me now,' pulled him out into the auditorium and stood halfway back at the side, just as Alfie was starting to sing 'Bring Him Home'.

'Just stop,' I said to Cameron. 'Just listen and look. There are 30,000 people here and they're all focused on Alfie singing. You've created this, you've done this. Smell the fucking roses.'

'Darling,' he said. 'You're absolutely right.'

And there aren't many performers who can boast that kind of closeness with Cameron. I really cherish that. I love knowing that if ever the chips were down, he'd be there for me. 'I'd say, "Giz a job," and he'd say, "Well, what do you want to do, darling? You can do Thénardier but I'm not paying you much," which is typical Cameron. I remember when we transferred *Les Mis* from the Barbican to the West End, he told me I'd have to take a £5 a week pay cut. I'd been on an RSC weekly rate of £250, but Cameron wanted me on £245 a week. I subsequently found out this was because he gave Frances Ruffelle a £5 rise to £255 a week so I was financing Frances. Makes you wonder how he became a billionaire, doesn't it? *The show's the star.* That's his mantra.

As for his relationship with Andrew, Charles Hart describes it as 'love-hate'. I'm not sure I'd go that far, but there's definitely a healthy (and I would say friendly) competition between them, with each wanting to be the best and most successful in their field and nowhere was that better exemplified than in their ongoing *Phantom* v *Les Mis* contest. Put it this way, if the bomb ever drops, there'll be two shows left standing, it'll be those two, and standing outside their respective theatres will be Cameron and Andrew, bullhorns in their hands.

Anyway, I guess that my relationship with Cameron really flowered the moment he offered me *Phantom* with his 'shit or get off the pot' speech, and I said to him, 'Yes, Cameron. Of course yes.'

I remember going into the audition room at the top of Her Majesty's, this beautiful rehearsal space with its large, curved window, ballet bars and mirrors all around – the absolute epitome of a rehearsal room – and who should be sitting at a grand piano on the corner? Andrew Lloyd Webber. Just him, me and Mike Reed, the musical director, in the room.

This was my first *proper* meeting with Andrew, who was as gracious as you might hope. 'Lovely to meet you,' he said, 'well done,' before turning his attention to the music, saying, 'Are you familiar with "All I Ask of You"?' which I knew from Cliff Richard and Sarah Brightman's chart hit.

'Yes,' I said. 'I don't read music, but give me the lyrics, we'll have a go.'

If he was surprised by that, he didn't say, and we got into it. Now, as the song ends it's meant to go into harmony, with a high note for the girl and what was supposed to be me underneath it. Muggins here goes for the high note, the soprano, and I remember seeing Andrew wince, but very kindly say, 'I think it'll work in the show.'

Having been offered the part and worrying somewhat about a recurrence of the panic attacks, I spoke to my doctor, who introduced me to beta blockers. 'If you take one of these,' he told me, 'your heart can't race too fast, so you won't have a heart attack.'

It was a game-changer. A racing heart and the subsequent fear of keeling over while clutching at my chest had been a big thing with me. But if I took a beta blocker I knew that even when I felt panic start to overwhelm me, nothing *really* bad was going to happen. As a result of which, of course, the vicious circle was broken, and I stopped panicking.

For the first two weeks I was rehearsing with Sarah Brightman, whom I loved. I mean, she's absolutely mad as a box of frogs, so of course I loved her. During rehearsal, I was supposed to carry out this beautiful dance move, which had been worked out by my predecessor, Steve, along with Sarah, who's a wonderful dancer, and the choreographer Gillian Lynne.

This dance move had lifts.

I'm going, 'Okay, is now the time to tell you that I invented a heart condition at drama school, so I don't know how to dance at all?'

'We'll be fine,' they said, and so I had to try. I'd find myself walking Sarah around the stage, dumping her around, but loving it and actually, in the end, not being so bad that we had to change it. As I said, Sarah was going off to Broadway so by the time of going into her final fortnight on the show, we'd forged a good relationship and were working well together. One of our big songs was 'All I Ask of You', which involved us going into a big dramatic dance spin and then holding each other's hands to sing, *'Anywhere you go, let me go too.'*

Sarah would sing, *'Anywhere you go, let me go too / Love me, that's all I ask of you,'* looking straight out front, as though addressing some unseen person in the audience. Which struck me as odd.

'Sarah,' I said, 'don't we mean each other when we sing, *"Anywhere you go, let me go too . . ."*? Shouldn't we sing it to each other?'

Sarah smiled. 'I don't think so,' she said, with an unknowable air.

Okay, Sarah, whatever you say. And I left it there until

her last night, when we did the twirl. Only this time I took hold of her, gently held her face in my hands and gazed into her eyes as she sang, *'Anywhere you go, let me go too . . .'* while trying to twist her face away, cursing me with her eyes. We had a good relationship, and she found it funny, so I got away with that one.

Well, I think I did. I'll ask her next time I see her.

Chapter 11

After Sarah left the show, Claire Moore came in as Christine. The thing was that Claire and I had never rehearsed together, and the fact that our dress rehearsal was cancelled in favour of a photo shoot meant our first night was also the first time we'd performed together. (Not something that would ever happen these days.)

Happily, we clicked brilliantly, although it was a giggly partnership. For example, there was a moment about ten days into the run when we did the big spin on 'All I Ask of You'.

Now, that particular day, I'd told Claire my story about me and Sarah, and this being uppermost in our minds meant that when it came to that moment we were both gazing at one another, but *really* gazing, which became 'isn't this funny gazing', until suddenly it really was genuinely funny.

You could see it happening. How at exactly the same moment we both went from playing the character to thinking how funny it was, and we started to crack up.

The floodgates opened. After that, we couldn't get through the song without laughing, to the point where the Phantom, Dave Willetts, up in the Angel, could hear us laughing and couldn't sing his own bit. To be fair, most of the time, the audience wouldn't have known – we turned our corpsing into the joy of the scene – but even so, it had to stop, especially when we both got letters from management. But it took me back to the King's Singers. How the more you know you've got to stop, the more you're in pain trying to stop it.

But we did. We got a handle on ourselves and the performance was a laughter-free zone from then on. The 'All I Ask of You' bit, at least.

That is, until one night in the summer, when we did the spin and because it was so hot I was really sweaty, lost my grip and Claire slipped and flew off – literally sailed away as though sent across the stage by a human catapult and still, like a complete pro, trying to keep it all in the performance.

Now, I defy anyone not to laugh in a situation like that. Not a soul on earth could have kept a straight face. And so we pissed ourselves. I was literally uncontrollable with laughter. Claire the same. Trying to keep it professional. Failing spectacularly.

Oh, God, we had such fun in that show. You know the big moment in the second half, when the Phantom grabs the noose and puts it around Raoul's neck? A number of times the wire that held the noose didn't work, and I'd have to stand there, holding the noose up manually. But there was one particular night when he was supposed to go into the wings and fetch the noose but reappeared empty-handed. For some reason he couldn't get the noose. He was nooseless.

Eyes wide behind the mask he marched towards me anyway. In his hand was fresh air where the noose should have been.

I mean, it's a big moment. You need the noose. He was staring at me with a beseeching look in his eyes, quailing behind the mask but ploughing on regardless. 'Whaaaaarrr!' he roared, spooky Phantom, improvising a bit of scary hand acting at the same time. But all his efforts were in vain without the noose and so, with enormous presence of mind, even if I do say so myself, I flung myself on to the portcullis at the back of the stage and pretended that it was electrocuting me.

I yelled in agony, 'Aaargh!' but thinking, *If this is supposed to be electrified I have to keep this up all the way through the scene.* There I was spasming away, wetting myself at the same time, for the rest of the scene.

Then there was the legendary night when Christine went to unmask the Phantom, but his cufflink got caught and yanked her wig off. She's there with just a bald cap and the microphone taped to her head, looking worse than the Phantom, and he's desperately trying to shake this wig off his cufflink, and of course the wig won't shift, it's just hanging off his hand as he tries to get on with the rest of the scene, clasping his hands to his face, the wig bouncing around. It was absolutely hilarious. Fortunately, the audience thought so, too.

Other things would happen. At one point I was meant to jump through the stage on to a trapdoor, except this time the gondola got stuck. I was on the gantry really high up. Madame Giry says, 'He lives across the lake, monsieur,' and I say, 'Thank you,' and got ready to jump when a disembodied voice offstage goes, 'Don't jump.'

I stopped.

'Don't jump,' came the voice again.

I looked down to see that the gondola was stuck over the trapdoor. It was just lodged there, refusing to budge. If I'd jumped I would have smacked into it and broken a leg, for sure. Instead, I turned to the wings, called, 'Whereabouts *exactly* across the lake is he, Madame?' and then walked offstage.

If there's going to be a big change in the show, a cast swap, for example, then things get less than professional. All the performers are trying to mess each other up – without the audience knowing, of course. Matinees are another time reserved for general high jinks, my favourite being 'Slap Saturday' on *Chitty* where a member of the company was drawn out of a hat and every member of the cast had to find a way to slap them during the show. I remember getting beaten half to death after a particular performance of 'Me Ol' Bam-Boo', when everybody ran up to 'congratulate' me, as well as getting a smack in the face from Brian Blessed when I popped out of the box during 'Doll on a Music Box'. Great fun.

On *Aspects*, meanwhile, we had 'Kiss Saturday'. Same principle but with kissing, except that during Pride we did same-sex kissing, during which I managed to snog the priest officiating at the wedding of George and Rose as well as Jamie Bogyo, who played Alex.

But the most memorable was on my last matinee of *Phantom*. I remember Rosemary Ashe, who played Carlotta – and who is also in the new *Aspects*, funnily enough – had her rings tied together with wire; another time, they put a big gorilla teddy in box five, which Raoul visits during the show, so I had to perform sitting alongside the gorilla.

Meanwhile, I had decided to come out of the lake wearing a

ripped shirt, with 'Raoul for Christine forever' tattooed on my arm, and then, in the final scene, when we sail across in the gondola and the Phantom's having his breakdown, I was going to put on a chest wig, medallion and be holding a Cornetto, just like in the TV advert. Brilliant!

I was on with Jan Hartley-Morris, Claire's understudy, who took two shows a week for her. I clambered into the gondola waiting for Jan, in full Bee Gees chest wig, with a Cornetto dripping in my hand, ready to spring my surprise. Knowing what was about to happen, everybody in the company gathered in the wings, waiting. I was going, 'Buzz off, you're going to give the gag away,' ushering them away and then clambering into the boat, facing away from Jan.

The line she sings is, *'Say you'll share with me, one love, one lifetime,'* after which I'm meant to turn and sing, *'Say the word and I will follow you,'* except on this occasion I'd be holding a Cornetto.

I heard her sing, *'Say you'll share with me, one love . . .'* but the voice was coming from the side. Surprised, I looked up to see Jan in the wings. She was mic'd up and singing her part but not in the gondola. Now I looked down, and sure enough, instead of her in the boat, it was Claire Moore. Her hair was all over the show, and she wore skull earrings, a unibrow and a fake moustache, as well as a huge pair of buck teeth and massive sticky-out eyelashes. I was there with a dripping Cornetto in my hand in a chest wig, supposed to sing, but it was all I could do not to fall over laughing – until we got across the lake when we absolutely dissolved with laughter.

We got to the end, went out, did the applause and everything. I had friends in that night and they came back afterwards. 'Well, you could tell it was your last day,' they said.

I went, 'Really?'

They went, 'Yes. The emotion in that last scene, you could hardly sing, could you? It was so beautiful . . .'

Terrible, really. But that was a perfect onstage gag. We used to do things like it in *Les Mis* all the time. Terrible things. It was often the fault of David Burt, who played Enjolras. David is an illustrious stage actor and practically a resident on the West End where he's been in far too many shows to mention – all of them, basically. He loved a bit of onstage mischief, and in me he had a willing accomplice. One time he came up on the barricade and handed me a little fluffy squirrel. 'For God's sake take care of the squirrel,' he said, with total sincerity, and then left.

I realised that was the game, and after that it went round the whole company during the show. Staying in character, we handed the cuddly toy from person to person, whispering, 'Look after the squirrel,' until the end when Enjolras was dead and the revolving stage, aka 'the revolve', turned, and we had the dead Enjolras with the fluffy squirrel on his chest. We got a fan letter for the squirrel after that.

David Burt – honestly. There was another thing he instigated: 'Orgy Up the Bishops' he called it. This was in the prologue when we, the mob, catch Valjean trying to escape after stealing candlesticks from the bishop, and return him for justice. So we'd all gather round and Orgy Up the Bishops would begin, which involved us trying to remove the clothes from whichever luckless cast member it happened to be. On one notable occasion, we stripped Keith Burns completely naked on stage.

Another of his was 'Hunt the Banana'. He and I played arresting officers who come to take Fantine away, and during one performance he whispered to me from the side of his mouth, 'Hunt the banana.' I knew what he meant, of course, and looked high and low for that banana, knowing that he'd hidden it somewhere on the set. Until at last I spotted it – sticking out of his tricorn hat.

While I'm here, Ian Calvin was also in that show. I remember him with so much affection. Ian was what you might call an ageing chorus boy (that's how he described himself, I should add) and very camp. We used to have to wear bandanas and in his case the bandana, added to the head mic that he wore, would slowly lift his toupee – which to be honest was pretty ill-fitting to begin with – upwards and, inevitably, almost completely off. We didn't have the heart to tell him. Even David Burt didn't invent a game around that one.

One time we were all on the barricades, muskets are blasting away, explosions going off, with Ian flinching the whole time, visibly wishing he could be anywhere else but there, and he turned to me, and said, 'Well, this is all very well, but I'm more of a *Hello, Dolly* person myself.'

A sad end to that story is that Ian was one of the first of my acquaintances to die of AIDS. He actually died during the run in February 1987. Went very quickly after he was diagnosed. Alun Armstrong gave the eulogy at his memorial and it really was quite extraordinary – one of the funniest and most poignant eulogies I've ever heard. This seemed to mark the beginning of a very strange and difficult period during which concern about the spread of the virus was uppermost in our minds. If ever you got sick, you thought, *Oh my God, have I got something?* We all knew people who were dying. We were losing huge talents. Our industry was absolutely decimated by AIDS. It also played into that whole time when I was ill. Obviously you got tested, as I did, of course, but waiting for the result could be very traumatic.

On that note, the other great thing about that whole *Phantom* period was that any lingering remnant of my stage fright disappeared. Suffering terrible tonsillitis I'd gone to the doctor who said, 'Okay, you'll have to have your tonsils out or your illness is going to keep recurring, and you'll poison your system.' He told me, 'You'll be out of the show for six weeks and when you go back, start with two shows a week and then work your way up.'

But Cameron went, 'No, I think you'll find you're off for four weeks and you come straight back to eight shows a week,' and I thought, *Yeah, that's exactly what I'm going to do*, and that's what I did, and it was absolutely fine. Thank goodness.

So psychologically, I was able to attribute what had happened to me in *Les Mis* to the physical illness of tonsillitis, while also knowing that my beta blockers would keep any palpitation issues under control. I'm happy to say that other than a few isolated incidents, I've been fine ever since, although I remain conscious of the tricks the mind can play, and the devastating effects of depression.

Chapter 12

According to Andrew, *Aspects of Love* 'bubbled around for about ten years. But the book always came back to me, partly because I knew a little about that world [as in, that ex-pat, South of France, Bloomsbury Groupesque world in which *Aspects* is grounded], but also because, having done *Phantom*, the one thing I wanted to do was to write a piece about far more . . . how can I put it? Well, just, I won't say, *ordinary* people, because they're not, but more *real* relationships.'

He continues. 'The thing with writing is that sometimes you want to do something that's a total antidote to what you did before. *Cats* I wrote because I wanted to set poetry to music. *Starlight* was just fun. *Requiem* was for other reasons and *The Phantom of the Opera* was because I'd always wanted to write a high romance. Because, frankly, if you look at the story of *Joseph and the Amazing Technicolor Dreamcoat*, *Jesus Christ* or *Evita,* there ain't a lot of high romance in them.

'And also because I have more than one side to my personality:

I'm just as proud to have produced what was voted the 13th worst number one of all time, "Itsy Bitsy Teenie Weenie Yellow Polkadot Bikini", as I am of having written "Pie Jesu".'

Incidentally, I sang one of those compositions at Andrew's wedding to his third wife, Madeleine – and it wasn't 'Pie Jesu'.

The second passenger to board the *Aspects* train was Trevor Nunn. Trevor remembers that Andrew had come to him years prior to *Phantom* – around the time of *Starlight*, in fact – talking about a novella that he wanted to adapt: *Aspects of Love.*

'We began to discuss various song and lyric possibilities,' said Trevor. 'Andrew provided me with several melodies that I thought were richly wonderful. Ripple dissolve to many years later, and they all became as world-famous as the score of *The Phantom of the Opera*.'

Wow. That was news to me. Apparently 'The Music of the Night' had started life as an *Aspects of Love* song called 'Married Man'.

Meanwhile, there came a tour of America with *Cats*, when Trevor and Andrew sat in a hotel room 'exchanging ideas and possibilities' for *Aspects*. Trevor then became involved with *Les Misérables*, and after that went into talks regarding *Miss Saigon*. For reasons he'll no doubt reveal in a future autobiography, Trevor and *Miss Saigon* were a marriage that never happened, and Trevor was still reeling from the shock of the separation when Andrew rang, saying, 'I've heard a rumour that you're going to be free after all?'

'Yes.'

'Well, you know that thing we were talking about over the years and starting to work on, *Aspects of Love* – shall we do that?'

To Trevor, this was a lifeline, and he was happy to plunge into what was – after *Cats* and *Starlight Express* – a third collaboration with Andrew.

Remember: many of the tunes suggested during their previous talks had been used for *Phantom*, so they had to start again, something Trevor found exciting. Like Andrew, he was drawn to *Aspects*' spider's web tale of human relationships, partly because it represented an exciting change of pace from the likes of *Phantom* and *Les Mis*, and partly because that whole Bloomsbury Group scene seemed so ripe with dramatic possibility. After all, he said, *Aspects*' characters are 'redefining what love and loyalty can mean: the love affair, the long-term-love relationships, the difference between love and marriage, the memories of love that continue to influence your life and your expectation. But then, extraordinarily, two women becoming incredibly bonded. And although the show never finally expressed it, the love story between Rose and Giulietta when, at the wedding, Giulietta steps up and kisses Rose on the lips as best woman.'

(That kiss would end up worrying us when the Queen came to see the show, but we'll come to that.)

'*Aspects* takes it one stage further than that,' added Trevor, 'because you've then got a marriage happening but an affair going on with a previous lover; you've got the new relationship with Giulietta. But then, more complicated than all the rest of it, you have a 15-year-old girl saying, "I'm a grown-up and I've fallen in love with a 32-year-old." I mean, David Garnett was standing everything on its head at that point. Yes, D H Lawrence had done some pretty extraordinary things with love stories, but Garnett was really pushing at the limit, wasn't he? And I just thought it was completely fascinating that Andrew wanted to explore that.

'He was always wanting to be at the frontier. I mean, *Jesus Christ Superstar:* we're going to do a rock score on the story of the Passion of Jesus Christ. *Evita*: we're going to do a musical about a dangerous political woman who becomes the president of her country – let's celebrate what women are now capable of in this second half of the 20th-century world. *Cats*: what are you talking about? Children's poetry by T S Eliot? No, no, I won't invest in it; it's the worst idea I've ever heard. The only way that that show got on was that Andrew mortgaged his house and with the mortgage money, *Cats* opened at New London Theatre – and it ran for 21 years.'

Together, Andrew and Trevor are a musical force. Trevor, for instance, wrote the lyrics to 'Memory' for *Cats*, and together they could no doubt have written the entire book, music and lyrics for *Aspects* themselves. Even so, they decided they wanted a bigger team involved – and so turned to Charles Hart.

Chapter 13

Charles is a lyricist, primarily. He's been nominated for an Oscar, won two Ivor Novello Awards and been nominated twice for a Tony, the first of which was for writing *Phantom*, the second for *Aspects*. Like me, he's a reformed smoker. Charles is a reformed lots of things, having somewhat lived it up in his youth.

And guess what? I spoke to him for this book, a long, freewheeling conversation, during which I discovered that not only did he once sit next to a chap smoking crack on a commercial flight, but also that he considers himself not as posh as Andrew.

I don't know about crack, but for the record, Andrew *is* probably the most posh – in a kind of befuddled, genius-like way. If Charles is posh – and I think he might say not – then he's the louche kind of posh.

'Andrew likes taking risks,' said Charles, louchely. He was referring to the point at which he was still only in his mid-twenties and was hired by Andrew to write lyrics for *Phantom*, which was, according to Charles, 'an amazing piece of audacity. Because Andrew likes showbiz being taken into real life. I mean, they'd approached other lyricists and they were, for one reason or another, unavailable. Tim Rice was tied up with *Chess*. So I was a last resort.'

Because Andrew had mentioned Garnett's novel, *Aspects of Love*, Charles went out and bought a copy. 'I promise this wasn't a ploy. I was just curious. But Andrew spotted that I had it in my briefcase and said, "Come down to the South of France," which is where it's set, of course. He used to have a house there and was having a love affair with that part of the world, so we started working on it down there. We were both drinking rather a lot in those days, I regret to say.'

A few months after that, Andrew invited Don Black to contribute.

I wanted to know: did that invitation put Charles's nose out of joint? After all, initially he was on board as the sole lyricist for *Aspects*.

'Well, you want it to be your own project first and foremost,' admitted Charles, 'but Andrew's very savvy about these things, and to some extent, it was a relief to have somebody else working alongside me.

'Still, it was a very odd thing to do at first, both for Don and me. Particularly for Don, because being much more experienced as a lyricist, he wasn't used to working alongside other writers.'

Charles and Don would convene at Don's kitchen table in order to chew over the *Aspects mise en scène*, consider Andrew and Trevor's vision for the show, absorb Andrew's lush instrumentation and, ultimately, come up with some words.

'We'd be sitting there, me chain-smoking, and we'd be expressing the first thing that came into our heads, which initially was quite painful and embarrassing, because you have to expose your worst ideas first.'

From Charles, I learned that 'Anything But Lonely' was first intended for *Cricket*, a short and rarely spotted musical that Andrew did with Tim Rice, which featured Prince Edward among the cast. '*All I ask of life is to play my part / Let them hurl their worst at me / None can break my wicket or my heart.*'

'Love Changes Everything' was another one that had been written many moons before. 'Oh God, yes,' said Charles. 'Andrew was talking about putting it into the American production of *Starlight.* Trevor wrote a lyric that went, "*You are my America.*"'

And you know what? As soon as Charles said that, I could well imagine the song going that way. Sing it with me: '*You are my America / my brave new world.*' See?

Added Charles: 'And Tim Rice wrote a version that ended with the line, "*If this isn't love then I don't want to know.*"'

For the record, 'Love Changes Everything' was Don's title. One thing that we can all agree on is that Don is a real champ when it comes to titles. Prior to that it was called 'Love Anthem'. That's the magic touch of Don for you.

Now, Don Black, just in case you don't know, is an absolute legend. He penned the lyrics to Bond themes such as *Thunderball*, *Diamonds Are Forever* and *The Man with the Golden Gun*, as well as literally hundreds of other movie songs, many written with John Barry. He won an Oscar for the title song of *Born Free.* He wrote 'To Sir With Love', a huge hit for Lulu, and 'Ben', an even bigger hit for Michael Jackson. He has a list of stage credits almost as long as his film one, and added to all of that, he wrote a superb autobiography, *The Sanest Guy in the Room* which, as well as talking about his life, his incredible body of work and his love of the 'Great American Songbook', also chronicles his grief over the death of his beloved wife Shirley from Covid in 2020.

He's also a great friend, and was also generous enough with his time to grant me an afternoon. I can't tell you how illuminating it is to sit down with these guys – the likes of Don, Trevor, Charles and Andrew – just to really quiz them about how they got involved with *Aspects* and each other, because even though I count them all as friends, it's not like we've ever done that before, that 'talking about the past' thing; really waded into the reeds like that. I ended up learning things I never knew about them and especially *Aspects*, despite having starred in it.

For example, Don and Andrew had first got together after a show Don had done, called *Bar Mitzvah Boy*.

'It didn't do well,' said Don, 'but it got great reviews. I'd got two telegrams on opening night. One was, "Best lyrics I've ever seen on a West End stage", and that was from Hal Prince. And the other one was, "Impeccable work", and that was from Michael Bennett. Two absolute giants. They then told Andrew about it, and he phoned me.'

At the time, Andrew was planning a one-woman show but didn't know what road to take. Don suggested something about 'an English girl in America, because I'd known so many had gone to America to find themselves', and the pair of them got together to write the show that eventually became *Tell Me on a Sunday*.

'Andrew played this lovely tune,' said Don. He's got a distinctive London growl. 'And I thought, *Where do you start, with no story?* But I came up with a title "Come Back with the Same

Look in Your Eyes", which was the first thing I wrote with him. Andrew likes titles. A good title gets him going. "Capped Teeth and Caesar Salad" was the next one, and then I wrote "Tell Me on a Sunday". What was fun was that there was nobody else but just us two songwriters around a piano. It was so lovely, just the two of us. "Oh, this is very funny, Don," he'd say. He used to nod, you know?'

For *Aspects*, Andrew put Don together with Charles because 'he thought I wrote very emotional songs and Charles was very posh.' (Or, alternatively, as Andrew put it, because Don was a commercial lyricist, capable of coming up with memorable, catchy titles, while Charles was more of a librettist).

During our meeting, Don showed me alternative lyrics to 'Love Changes Everything', altered in an eventual rewrite.

'*Love, love changes everything / It's amazing, but it's true / Love had never crossed my mind / Now my mind is full of you / Ever since my eyes met yours / Every moment has more meaning / Yes, love, love changes everything / Every start and every street / All I think about is when will our lips meet.*'

According to Don they wrote tons more lyrics. In the end it's just a case of alighting on which one you as the songwriter thinks is best.

'*Love, love changes everything / It's as if she waved a wand / All I seem to think about / Is forever and beyond.*'

That was another one that didn't make the final cut.

'*Love has changed everything / All I think about is the love I have for you. / Since I set my eyes on you / I draw you on serviettes and dusty windows too.*'

Perhaps they don't all scan. But you get the picture. It's a fascinating snapshot of a work in progress and, for me, a glimpse of what might have been.

Chapter 14

Andrew Lloyd Webber's most famous property is Sydmonton Court in Hampshire, right next to Highclere, where they film *Downton Abbey*. It looks at Watership Down (which I think he now owns), and not only is it a very nice pad set in 5,000 acres of land, but it's also the base for Andrew's Sydmonton Festival. This annual shebang first started life in 1975, when he began inviting hand-picked guests to hear works in progress, enjoy gourmet food and drink and various other cultural and culinary delights. If you get invited to Sydmonton, you go. If you're asked to perform . . .?

'Do you want to appear at this year's Sydmonton?' was the question in 1988.

'Does Dolly Parton sleep on her back?' was my answer. I knew about the festival, of course. I knew that virtually every Lloyd Webber production had been workshopped there. I knew that Andrew was working on his follow-up to *Phantom*.

I was still playing Raoul at the time when Andrew came in one afternoon. With a show like *Phantom* that's up and running, you rarely see any of the big bosses. Andrew was mostly in New York overseeing the Broadway run, so we didn't see him at all, and in all the time I was on the show I met the director, Hal Prince, exactly twice. They'd appear occasionally, just to make sure we were all doing our job (our job being to ensure the show's continued success), but that was it.

So for Andrew to come in caused great excitement among the cast. *Bad luck, he's here to see me, suckas!* His people set up a keyboard in one of the boxes next to the stage. I became an audience of one as Andrew talked me through his new work, *Aspects of Love*, a show he'd been working on with Trevor Nunn, Charles Hart and Don Black, and then played me 'Love Changes Everything'.

'Do you like it?' he asked.

Well, it's one of those instant, earwormy songs that as a singer, you just *know*.

For the Sydmonton workshop – which would be made up of highlights – we'd have Susannah Fellows playing Rose and Dinsdale Landen as George. All they tell you is that you're doing the workshop. There's no offer of a job; you have no idea what happens next. You just look at the roll call of previous Sydmonton workshops – *Evita, Cats, Starlight, Phantom* – and you keep your fingers crossed. And if you're me, and the part comes with a song like 'Love Changes Everything' attached, you cross a few more things besides.

It was at the pre-Sydmonton sessions that I really started to work closely with Andrew. We'd meet in a little rehearsal room to learn the music and rehearse, him working on the sound, figuring out which instruments we could fit into the tiny space; me just trying to look like I knew what I was doing.

Trevor was there, too, as were Don and Charles, who would watch me going through the songs and suggest lyrical changes on the hoof. We marked out a space with gaffer tape. We mimed the doors and used a chair for the railway carriage. As we worked, we thought mainly of the invited audience to whom we'd be performing, knowing that whatever we produced didn't need to be a highly polished and finished work, but at the same time had to be as good as we could make it. Andrew, Trevor, Charles and Don – they knew Sydmonton for what it was: a chance to canvass the opinion of a rarefied audience of family and friends, movers and shakers. 'This is a new work by Andrew Lloyd Webber. Does it work? Is it going to fly?'

I had two shows off *Phantom* for the performances. Arriving in Hampshire, I was shown around the main house, which was like an art gallery – everywhere you looked, a masterpiece – and featured an incredible wine cellar. I quickly learned that only a select few of the inner circle actually get to stay in the house. The rest are farmed off to people who live nearby. I don't remember much about my quarters, only that I came down the stairs on the day of the performance to be confronted by the politician John Selwyn Gummer, who was wandering round the kitchen in his pants. I'm pretty sure he was a fellow guest. Let's hope so.

Recently, I told Andrew about the 'Selwyn Gummer in his pants' episode. 'I'm surprised you got over that,' he said.

'I'm not sure that I have, you know.'

'Has that explained some of the issues?'

'So many. So many.'

Sydmonton operates as a mini-festival, including speakers, wine tasting and fabulous food, but the main attraction is the 'new works' bit which we were to perform in a small, converted church in the grounds, a couple of hundred yards from the main house.

Personally I didn't get to enjoy the wine or the sampling menu. Our job as performers was to preview Andrew's new work and then make ourselves scarce. That cuts you down to size, I can tell you. Shining star of the West End I may have been. But at Sydmonton? Merely the hired help.

As an aside, Don Black tells a great story about Andrew's habit of inviting esteemed guests to hear his work in progress. Having just finished *Aspects of Love,* Andrew said to Don, 'I think it might be a good idea to ask a few mates over to hear the score.'

'Who are you thinking of?' said Don.

Andrew replied, 'Margaret Thatcher, Michael Heseltine, Geoffrey Howe, John Selwyn Gummer, John Major, David Frost . . .'

'What good will that do?' said Don.

'Well at least we'll find out what Joe Public thinks of it,' replied Andrew.

Anyway, on the day of the main event, Andrew gave a short introduction. 'This is a preview of our new show *Aspects of Love.*' I think Trevor did, too. 'Enjoy these extracts.' And that was it. We went on and did our stuff.

The reaction was fabulous – although I suppose you have to take that with a pinch of salt. I mean, honestly, who's going to turn around and go, 'You know what, Andrew? It's shit.'

On t'other hand, I'm sure that there are people within that set-up who are honest with Andrew and Trevor but do it behind the scenes. Don and Charles were there, so I bet they had their say. I can't remember if Cameron was there or not, but he would have given honest feedback. Either way, I certainly wasn't privy to it. My job was to present the work to the best of my ability and then return to work on *Phantom*, which was what I did.

Chapter 15

The business of auditioning is a road filled with potholes, to say the least. That thing you see in films where a bunch of people sit behind a desk while a nervous Nelly does their prepared song? It really is like that.

As I got bigger and became the national treasure you know and love today (stop sniggering), I've had a little more say on casting, and for the national tour of *Hairspray*, as well as *Mack & Mabel*, I took my place behind the desk, resisted the temptation to act like a demented Joffrey in *Game of Thrones* and had my say on the audition process. I did this for *Hairspray*, in particular, because I knew I was going to be on the road with these people and, having done the show in the West End, I knew the requirements exactly.

Thus, you would think that with *Aspects II* being very much my baby, I would have taken even more of a hand in deciding the casting.

You would be wrong. I left all (okay, *most*) of that to our director, Jonathan Kent, and Andrew. I mean, I had my say. I might have said, 'Why don't you try so-and-so?' I may even have said, 'No I prefer not to work with such-and-such,' perhaps because I've worked with them in the past and would prefer not to do it again (for whatever reason, personality clash, a dynamic I don't think will work, something like that). But mainly I preferred to stand back, leave it to Andrew and Jonathan, and thus be able to truthfully say to cast members, whether they be approved, potential, rejected or somewhere in between, 'Nope. Nothing to do with me.'

I know about auditioning, though. I know about it from both sides. In 1991, I was up for Andrew's production of *Sunset Boulevard* in the role of Joe Gillis, the one played by William Holden in the movie. And by 'up for it', I mean in both senses of the phrase: really, really wanted the part, was being groomed for it, had workshopped it, even did 1991's Sydmonton in the role.

By the following year, however, I was out of the picture and Kevin Anderson was named as Joe Gillis, a part he retained for the 1993 West End opening.

Now, I'm not going to lie. That one hurt. I mean, if I touch the bruise now it still smarts a bit. Not only because I was . . . well, I was 'Michael Ball' by that stage. But also because I'd done all of the prep. The trouble was that in the end, and despite the fact that I'd released the theme song as a single, and despite the fact that I counted Trevor Nunn, Andrew Lloyd Webber and Don Black, who was writing it, as friends, I wasn't the person they wanted. As they say in *Jerry Maguire*, it's not show friends, it's show business.

I mention all this because of Sydmonton in 1989, and

those *Aspects* workshops with Susannah Fellows and Dinsdale Landen. Now, if you know anything about the original *Aspects*, you'll know that the part of Rose, played by Susannah at Sydmonton, was eventually filled by Ann Crumb, while the part of George, played by Dinsdale Landen, was eventually filled by Kevin Colson.

Point being that the parts they'd workshopped and presented at Sydmonton were taken by others. Just as I was later invited to take a left turn off *Sunset Boulevard*, so Susannah and Dinsdale were no longer prospects for *Aspects* (although Susannah did go on to play Rose at a later date).

Gutting for them, of course. And I know exactly how they would have felt. They would have been thinking that their chances were better than good at not only starring in the new Andrew Lloyd Webber musical – and don't forget, Andrew could not have been hotter at this very moment in time – but originating the role; they were so close that they'd even been invited to do it at Sydmonton. Only not to be offered the role.

I feel qualified to comment because of my *Sunset* experience. It's awful. Andrew, if you're reading, it's awful. They would have been thinking, *What did I do wrong?* They might even have been wondering, *Is that it for me?* In time you're able to move on and rationalise it. You say to yourself, *That's their decision, not your choice, nothing you could have done.* You might even begin to think, *Hey, their loss. Forget them.* But yeah, it takes time.

So that was Susannah and Dinsdale. Out. Unfortunately.

As for me? Well, having come to the end of *Phantom* in London, and with Sarah finishing on Broadway, we embarked on a series of concerts together, co-headlining 'The Music of Andrew Lloyd Webber', and given that the show included two of the new songs from *Aspects*, I was beginning to feel a little bit more confident that the role was mine.

I remember those concerts well. It was around the time of the Duchess of Windsor's jewellery sale when Andrew had bought Sarah some items. We'd do these gigs and she'd come on for 'Don't Cry for Me Argentina' wearing a Cartier leopard bracelet and choker. Me, I got paid £4.20 and a bag of chips. But trust me, I wasn't complaining.

One time at the Queen Elizabeth Hall, my head mic went down and so I went to the back-up, which was a handheld. No problem. I was using that, backed by a full orchestra, having the time of my life, when suddenly that one went down as well, and with no other choice, I had to scuttle off for maintenance, just as Sarah, wearing an amazing Emanuel gown, came centre stage to sing, using a head mic.

'Test the channel,' I told them as we worked to repair my mic at the side of the stage. 'We need to make sure it's working.'

I was fretting because what I really wanted to avoid was the last-ditch option of two performers having to share one mic. No turn wants to do that. I was, ahem, 'making my feelings clear on the matter' just as they tested the channel – except that they tested it out front, and so from Sarah's mouth came my words, which were, 'Because I'm not sharing her microphone for all the fucking tea in China.'

That'll teach me to be a potty-mouthed diva. An awkward moment that took me a while to live down.

Our encore featured those two songs from *Aspects* – still only in their infancy, remember – with me singing 'Love Changes Everything' and then Sarah coming on to finish the show with 'Anything But Lonely'.

During rehearsals for 'Love Changes Everything', the way it had ended was on the *'love will never, ever let you be the same'* line, which was okay lyrically, just that I wasn't happy about the delivery. I was going, 'That's not much of an ending, is it? Why don't I go up at the end?'

'Well? Can you?' asked Andrew. 'What? To B-flat?'

I don't read music. I don't know what my range is. I mean, really, I'm just blagging this whole thing. Still am. Don't tell anyone.

'I don't know,' I told him brazenly. 'Let's have a go.'

So we tried it, and I hit the note.

'Well that's going in,' said Andrew, and there you have it, an ending was born. The money note; the one that gets me a round of applause every time I sing it (and, often, *before* I've sung it).

So that was the intended arrangement, after which Sarah was supposed to come on to sing 'Anything But Lonely' and, being the bigger star, close the show.

The problem was that you had the audience going mental for my big 'Love Changes' note, and that's the place you should really finish the show.

They *ummed.* Perhaps they even *ahhed.* Until they came up with what they thought was a solution. Just as I was hitting my note from 'Love Changes Everything', Sarah would appear from the side of the stage and undercut my applause by beginning her song. This was sold to me as being like a mini version of the musical.

Only . . . look, I'm sorry, but this was my big note, a great note, and I just wasn't into the idea of sacrificing the moment. Trying to persuade Andrew and Sarah to change the order was pretty much out of the question – they were married at the time, whaddya do? – so instead I took a different approach. As the song ended and Sarah wafted on, I didn't come off the note as I was supposed to. I just held it. Let the applause happen and . . . well . . . milked it basically, much to Sarah's chagrin.

There you go. That's showbiz.

But still, I stayed alive. And nobody's nose was yet out of joint. Which was lucky, because final casting for *Aspects* had yet to be decided.

And here's the thing. *Aspects* wasn't the only project I had on the go. I'd been working with a writer, Joe Brooks, on a musical version of *Metropolis*, the 1927 Fritz Lang movie set in an urban dystopia of the future, one of the first-ever science fiction films.

Brooks had made a fortune writing chart hits, especially 'You Light Up My Life', which had been a smash for Debby Boone, and that was enough of a financial buffer for him to embark on a passion project like *Metropolis*.

Joe Brooks was, well, let's just say an 'interesting' character. If you go to his Wikipedia page you'll see that he ended his life rather than face charges of raping or sexually assaulting 11 women. Far be it from me to say if he was guilty or not, but I guess the fact that his assistant was jailed for aiding and abetting him tells its own story. That darker side to him was never apparent during our work on *Metropolis*, I'm glad to say, but he was certainly what you'd call a handful. A bit nuts.

Brooks was keen for me to play the lead in *Metropolis* (told you he was nuts) and I'd been working with him on the score. But at the same time *Aspects* was going from a slow simmer to a fast boil. I mean, I wanted to do *Metropolis*. I thought it was a good show; there was a lot of buzz around it, and I would have been working with Brian Blessed. In short, I would have been crazy to turn it down.

By which I mean that I would have been crazy to turn it down for literally anything other than the lead in Andrew Lloyd Webber's follow-up to *The Phantom of the Opera.*

It's a nice problem to have, but at the same time a really tough one.

So, some 'shit or get off the pot' conversations took place. 'Do you want him for *Aspects* or not?'

In the end, my agent got a call from Biddy Hayward, who was running Really Useful Productions at the time. They wanted me. Amazing. The negotiations began. I'd been on £900 a week on *Phantom* but for this they were going to give me £1,500 a week, which was big money. Not stratospheric – there would be other members of the cast commanding the 'bums on seats' money – but decent. When you consider that I'd got £200 a week on *Pirates.* And I was 26 years old and it was 1989. Pretty bloody good.

Oh, and *Metropolis* tanked, so I dodged a bullet there.

Chapter 16

Whether Sarah was considered for a part in *Aspects*, I don't know. She later played Rose on Broadway, so it's not like there was any resistance artistically. I don't know. Not information I was privy to. All I knew was that Sarah wasn't involved, making me the only confirmed performer.

Although it was incredibly exciting to be in at the ground floor, and a great learning experience, I was aware of a slightly heightened tension around the team: Trevor was still smarting from his *Miss Saigon* experience, and Andrew was going through some personal turmoil. Added to which, the extraordinary success of *Phantom* and *Les Mis* had created that 'tall poppy' syndrome, with people waiting to cut them both down to size.

It's funny. I sometimes think that Andrew always hankered after the critical success of Stephen Sondheim and the reverence with which he was held by the intelligentsia, while Stephen probably wished he'd made as much money as Andrew.

Maybe. Maybe not.

As for Trevor. Well, the same. *Les Misérables* got a terrible reception in the UK, and although the Broadway reviews were mixed it got a real battering from Frank Rich. We'll be hearing more about the critic they call 'the Butcher of Broadway' in due course, but there's no doubt that he didn't like the British takeover of Broadway, which of course put Trevor in his sights.

To me, though, Trevor is huge. A massive figure in my life and career.

The first time I ever met him was at that audition for *Les Misérables*. He knew how terrified I was but put me at my ease. It's one of his particular talents. The force in him is strong, and I'm telling you, the force needed to be strong on that occasion. I was like a star-struck kid, desperate to be in *Les Misérables* and desperate to work with this great director and creative talent. The whole thing could have been overwhelming, but he didn't allow it to be. He was just down-to-earth Trevor Nunn, exactly the same Trevor Nunn you're picturing now. I mean, if there was a 'Legends of British Musicals' action-figure range (and there should be – come on, sort it out!) then Trevor's figure would have longish hair, a goatee, and be wearing jeans and a denim shirt, which is exactly how he rocks it, every day. It's how he looked during my audition for *Les Misérables* in 1985, and it's how he looked when I interviewed him 38 years later for this book. It gets so that you'll see him at a do wearing a tux and not recognise him.

Back in the *Les Mis* days he had two denim shirts that he'd rotate. You could tell which one it was, because one of them had an iron mark on the back, so he'd wear that one day, another the next, and then the iron mark would return the following day.

The other thing about Trevor is that he's 'huggy'. Very tactile. Everyone says, 'Have you been Trev'd?' which is when he hugs you and it just goes on that bit too long. Not in a spooky way, just in 'what do I do now?' kind of way. 'When will this hug ever end? In fact, *will* it ever end? Will I stay like this, being hugged by Trevor Nunn forever?'

What I soon learned about working with him is that although he's great at making you feel comfortable (hugs apart) he also knows when to be tough, but most of all, he's very articulate; there isn't a question you could ask about character, motivation, idea or the journey, to which he won't have the answer. With him it's never just a case of 'come down-stage, turn, smile and deliver', even when that's the kind of direction a performer wants. No, everything's got to be rooted in truth. It's got to be consistent with the character and story.

What else? He always comes in prepared, but is great at adapting on the hoof. He's intensely creative, but knows when to abandon a bad idea. Oh, and he's really good at creating a collegiate feel where nobody is more important than anybody else. This was most apparent in *Les Misérables*, which was an incredibly tight company. You went from me, who had very little experience, up to Patti LuPone, who was a huge Tony Award-winning, Broadway star. You had leading lights of the RSC, Colm Wilkinson, Roger Allam and Alun Armstrong. You had people who'd worked with Trevor before, people who hadn't – a real scattered, disparate bunch. But he brought us all together. There were no star moments with him. No diva-ish outbursts.

All productions have a 'first day at school' when the team meets properly for the first time. The cast may have got together as a group for photo shoots and press work – we did exactly that on *Aspects* in 2023 and it was a lovely 'getting to know you' session – but that 'first day at school' is where you really knuckle down to work and do so with the entire creative team present: the musical directors, stage management, wig department, costume department, lighting, sound, all the actors, producers, writers. You do a mingle – 'Darling, I haven't seen you for ages,' (now what the hell is her name?) – and then you sit around in a big circle and do first-day introductions. 'My name's Michael, and I'm going to be playing Marius.' And that's when you start to get an idea of people, the sort of baggage they're bringing, or will bring, to the production. Who wants to be centre of attention? Who prefers to take a back seat? It all bubbles up during those early moments.

After that, you promptly forget all the names.

Having taken your seats, you get a talk from the designer, who will usually have a mock-up of how the stage will appear, one of those three-dimensional models so beloved of bank robbers and Derek Zoolander. You'll gather round to look at the model as the director and designer talk you through how the scenes change, how it's going to work. This is where the orchestra is going to go. There will be stairs here. There's going to be an entrance here. This is how it will all revolve. They might show you the lighting state as well.

After that, the director will talk.

And if the director is Trevor Nunn, then he'll talk.

And talk.

The first day at school for *Les Misérables* was a huge event. You know *Les Misérables*, don't you? I mean, if you don't know *Les Mis* you're probably reading the wrong book. It's a huge production. There were hundreds of us in the room sitting around in a circle. All the little Gavroches were there. All the little Cosettes and Éponines. Everybody.

Trevor starts talking at, let's say, 11am.

At 1pm, he was still going, and we hadn't even got to Act II. That super-prepared state I'm talking about taken to the *n*th degree. A knowledge of the work that was both encyclopaedic, incisive and insightful.

And yes, also, exhausting.

I mean, it's impressive. Absolutely no doubt about that. But my goodness, it goes on a long time. I found my mind wandering, wishing we could get on with it, until, at last, he said, 'Right, I think we'll break for lunch there.'

There was an almost audible sigh of relief from the assembled company. Thank God for that. Thank God he's finished.

'Are there any questions?' he said.

Don't anyone dare say a word, we're all thinking, *because if you do, we'll be in here for another half-hour.*

At which point one of the little boys playing Gavroche put up his hand, and everybody looked at him daggers, thinking, *What?*

'Yes,' said Trevor, 'you have a question?'

'Yeah,' said the little boy. A pause. 'What did you say again?'

And . . .

Trevor pissed himself. We all pissed ourselves. The whole company falling about thanks to this 11-year-old boy. And, possibly as a result of that, the second half of the talk was a little bit more succinct.

It was during those early days of *Les Misérables* that Trevor's love of character development came to the fore. At his behest we'd play trust games like, 'Be your favourite cartoon character,' things like that. I was Sylvester the Cat. I could do his voice and could be heard declaiming 'suffering succotash' around the rehearsal room with the kind of confidence and style for which I am rightly famed.

I'm joking of course (a bit) but the fact is that these kinds of exercises are important. They're important for any show, but particularly a big one like *Les Misérables*, so that when you have these big moments where the stage is full of performers, you can look at an actor who's not doing anything particular but know that they're in it, they have something going on. Not just that they're staying in character – that's something that my dad taught me all those years ago. But that they're giving the character a reason to be doing what they're doing.

Trevor, of course, had had months of meetings with the production team before that first day of school. He and the designer, John Napier, had worked together on *Cats* and *Starlight Express* and together they had such a bold vision. Those structures that started life as twisted bits of metal at the side of the stage, but then came together to mesh and to make a huge barricade? That was all them. Nothing like it had ever been attempted or seen before. Then more simple ideas, like creating the sewers using an uplight through the grill combined with dripping sound effects in order to give the impression of a life going on down below.

In the Astoria theatre, they built a mock-up of the huge double-revolve that they would eventually use in the show itself, another first for the West End, as far as I know. We needed the revolve because *Les Misérables* was so long that we had to keep it moving by having one scene blend into the next. Later, we would achieve the same effect in *Aspects of Love* – both iterations – using travelators, those moving walkways you get in airports.

Even so, when we first opened, the show was, I think, over four and a half hours long. I distinctly remember performing the first matinee previews, and as we were coming to the end of the finale, we could hear, 'This is your half-hour call, ladies and gentlemen, half an hour,' coming through the tannoys backstage. We literally had 30 minutes to get ready for the next performance. Absolutely insane.

That's when the cuts started coming in. They cut a chase through Paris and one of Cosette's songs. They also cut a song called 'Little People', which featured in the Barbican run and was even on the cast recording album, a big *Oliver!*-type production that everybody hated because it was so completely at odds with the tone of the show (but had mystifyingly been a chart hit in France).

Even with the edits it was still over three hours, and they were getting worried, Cameron especially, because if you exceed three hours you have to pay overtime to the orchestra and costs begin to soar.

Cameron was saying, 'Well, we could cut "Empty Chairs",' which upset me enough to raise an objection. 'Look, if you do that then Marius is just a prat who hasn't learned from his experience. There's no personal growth for him. He has to have a moment to show where he's moved to.'

Luckily, the writers, Alain Boublil and Claude-Michel Schönberg, agreed. The boy with the cello in his throat, was what Claude-Michel called me. Fortunately Trevor agreed. So they kept it in.

Can you believe that? We nearly lost 'Empty Chairs' from *Les Mis.*

A time like that, it raises the question of who really has the power in the show. If you hit a complete impasse, who's the one who gives in? Is it the producer? Is it the director? Is it the writer? It certainly isn't the turn.

Anyway, my point here is that just as he had done with *Les Misérables*, Trevor had done an awful lot of prep work on *Aspects of Love*.

What, exactly? Let's ask him, shall we?

Chapter 17

So, when we last left him, Trevor was just getting involved with Andrew's initial ideas for *Aspects of Love*. Together they did some 'doodling' for *Aspects*, but the unimpressive results had convinced them to call Charles Hart, who in turn was joined by Don Black, and the 'kitchen table sessions' began. Their job, to take Garnett's source material and turn it into a book (as in a musical 'book').

It was then that Andrew said something Trevor found tremendously exciting: 'I want this to be a small theatre show,' he declared, at which point Trevor was fondly imagining an intimate space, something like the Cottesloe at The National. He was envisaging a small chamber piece, quite different to the spectaculars for which they were both famed, and as work continued and design exploration began, that was the thought uppermost in his mind.

Ah. But then Andrew started talking about needing an orchestra of 70. 'I'm not going to use synthesisers,' was his mantra. At the same time, according to Trevor, other voices were being heard. Stuff like, 'Come on, you can't have a new Lloyd Webber at a 400-seat theatre,' until they were proposing the Prince of Wales as a venue. Capacity: 1,183.

As an aside, I think that this push and pull between the intent of the original low-key vision of *Aspects of Love* and what it eventually became, which was something really quite grand, is another key to understanding why I wanted to revisit it. Our latter-day production of *Aspects* at the Lyric was by no means small (capacity at the Lyric is 915), but a reduction of scale was certainly something we kept in mind during early talks and rehearsals – that desire to bring it back to something more intimate and therefore slightly more characterful than it had been before.

Andrew himself agreed that it should make a slight return to its more low-key roots. 'The more chamber idea probably suits it better,' he told me, adding, 'but I'm very much of the view that Jonathan should be allowed to do the production as he sees it. I don't think that me fussing over it is going to be a real help.'

'And how easy is that for you to do – to take a step back?'

'It's much easier for me now.'

'Why?'

'I guess because I'm a lot older, and I can stand back and say, look, that was something I did nearly 40 years ago.'

I put it to him that the process of restaging *Aspects* in 2023 (actually, the process of staging any work) naturally involves a desire to honour its author, i.e. him.

'I think, looking back over my career, there have only been three productions of which I could say, "I don't think anybody could have ever done any better." One of them would be *Phantom*, of course, and then I think the original *Cats* and probably Hal Prince's *Evita*, which were all extraordinary.

'For *Aspects*, I suppose I wouldn't be totally happy if it was like that thing with opera sometimes, where it's set in a totally different time and in a different way. I've seen *Tosca* set in Nazi Germany. You say to yourself, "Why?" Or modern-dress versions of Shakespeare. And with *Aspects* it's very much of its particular period and involves a particular type of person who perhaps we don't really see today, those emigrating Britons who went to Europe.'

He needn't have worried, of course. In 2023 our version takes place in France and Italy between 1947 and 1964, just as it did in the 1989 incarnation.

Talking of which, the next of the main personnel to come on board for the original *Aspects* was the production designer Maria Björnson.

Maria is one of the many gold-plated, stone-cold legends involved in this story. Sadly no longer with us – in 2002 she died of an apparent epileptic seizure aged just 53 – her career began designing sets and costumes for the Glasgow Citizens Theatre in the early 1970s. By the end of that decade she was working with the RSC, the Scottish Opera and the Welsh National Opera, while in 1986 she embarked on her most famous production, *The Phantom of the Opera*, for Andrew and Hal Prince.

You've heard of the *Phantom* chandelier – one of the most famous set pieces in the history not just of musical theatre but of all theatre? That was Maria. It earned her a Tony Award among various other plaudits.

Of course I knew Maria through having worked with her on *Phantom*. She'd styled me on that so may have been responsible for the atrocious wig I wore – a wig so bad that even now I can't bear to look at pictures of myself wearing it. Why did I even *need* a wig? Most of the time you need a wig to hide the mic, but I've never had that problem. Steve Barton, my predecessor, had thinning hair, but even though mine's fine ('great' some might say) they gave me an identical syrup, which looked shite.

Anyway, that's apropos of nothing. Let's give Maria the benefit of the doubt and say it was her day off on the day of the wig discussions, because in every other way, she was a genius. Lovely, funny, dry, very imposing. An extraordinary lady who loved what she was doing and did it brilliantly. I mean, come on, just look at the staging for *Phantom*. It's a work of art. Take the costumes. You can't see unless you're close up, but the detail on them was incredible, which when you're a performer and you're wearing something that's proper, not just a cobbled-together bit of old tat, really helps with the performance.

And as for the chandelier. Not only was it a gasp-inducing bit of theatre, but the secret brilliance of it – indeed, all of the staging for *Phantom* – was that it didn't rely on modern trickery. No word of a lie, *Phantom* could have been put on in the Victorian era, because other than the radio-controlled boat, which was the prop that messed up most, it was all done using the original theatrical methods of pulleys and trapdoors, and all from original designs. That unbelievable moment when the candelabra come up through the stage and the *Phantom* is rowing the boat through the dry ice. Nothing like that had ever been seen before; it was incredible, absolutely incredible. It was all done the old way. And it was all Maria.

Trevor and Maria hadn't worked together prior to *Aspects*, but the two discovered that they were practically neighbours.

'She lived by the river, just a few blocks from here,' said Trevor, 'so I used to walk from my place, under the underpass, go to a little coffee bar, buy a couple of coffees, ring her doorbell and then we were at work. It was magical.

'We decided, after a while, that we needed to research, so she and I set off on a journey to the Pyrenees in the very south of France. We then came back to Paris and by reading the original novella we found exactly where George's apartment was. That was thrilling. That, for us, was it completely coming alive.'

One feature of *Aspects* is that it has a lot of scenes and situations, many of which are quite short. I say 'features'. Trevor says 'headaches', especially when 'the notion of the railway station platform at the beginning arrived relatively late on in the writing. But Maria did a wonderful job.'

I remember there being a problem with getting things to flow so the scenes transitioned into one another, while staging constraints meant that more bits had to be written to cover up scene changes.

For Trevor, further inspiration arrived at Sydmonton, where seeing extracts from *Aspects* made him 'hugely, hugely excited.

'One of my many pompous utterances was that I wanted musical theatre to be capable of being true, real, genuine, emotional and three-dimensional. I would always say that there's a connection between Shakespeare and musical theatre in that with Shakespeare we're abiding by a huge number of rules of the beat, the emphasis, the rhythm, the pause, the change into prose, then back into verse, the half-line – all of those things. But while we're presenting all that, our task is to make it totally real and true and as three-dimensional as Shakespeare wanted it to be.

'It's the same in music. There's a beat, a back-phrase, a hold and it's fortissimo at this moment, and so on. Here in *Aspects* was something that was very, very sophisticated and real. So, I thought that was a wonderful challenge.'

As for casting, Trevor was looking for 'people who I knew could be capable of that third dimension. There was only one worry I had, which was a guy called Michael – Michael Ball . . .'

Now, you may think that this is one of his little jokes, but in actual fact he's being at least semi-serious. Up until *Aspects*, I hadn't been required to do anything out of my comfort zone, acting-wise. I mean, yes, of course, Marius was challenging. But the role of an idealistic young man who goes through this dark event and becomes a man was mirroring who I was at the time. It fitted me. Raoul is a Disney prince and I can do that, fine.

But *Aspects* was a whole different ball game. Obviously we'd done the Sydmonton workshop, but it wasn't the whole thing, and so Trevor suggested a couple of masterclasses – just me and him in a dance studio owned by Wayne Sleep.

I went with trepidation. I was thinking, *He's trying to see if I'm a good enough actor to do this.* Which led me to thinking, *Am I a good enough actor?*

Classic imposter syndrome stuff. I felt confident in musical terms; the music itself fitted me like a glove. But I was teaming up with a legendary theatre director who had worked with the greatest actors, and I was not that. Would I be up to snuff? Would I be what he wanted?

The only thing I could do was learn, and during those sessions I was like a sponge, soaking up Trevor's suggestions, trying everything he asked as he worked on enabling me to analyse a character, how to make the character come alive, and how to make interesting choices when reading. It was an intensive two days, interrupted only by Wayne coming in to reminisce about *Cats* every now and then. We took a speech from *Romeo and Juliet* and analysed it, line by line, word by word. What function does the speech have in the text? Why this word and not that word? Why is the rhythm like it is? Just me and the greatest director of Shakespeare ever (and no, I haven't forgotten about Peter Hall, who is amazing, but I still think it's Trevor). And it was revelatory.

Those workshops ended up having a huge effect on me. I came to understand why I loved Shakespeare, and how it was because of that musical quality. I also started to focus on delivery. When do you hold a note? When do you come off a note? How do you make a rhythm? How do you throw in a spoken word in the middle of a song to give it impact? It was about approaching every song from an acting perspective. What information am I trying to impart? What emotions am I feeling? What's the meaning behind this? Who am I talking to? I was finding the language of musicals, making bold choices. It was brilliant.

'I just wanted us to be on the same page and be ready for the first day of rehearsal,' said Trevor.

And of course, he got me there. What's more, because things were moving so fast I didn't really have time to dwell on my stage fright issues at all. I was so totally vibing on this whole idea of sitting around in workshops talking about character and doing 'proper' acting that I had no time for the kind of self-reflection that would have sent me back to the dark place. Thanks to the guidance of Andrew and especially Trevor, I didn't find it at all overwhelming. I felt looked after by people in whom I had the utmost confidence and who, crucially, had the utmost confidence in me.

I also knew by then that I was able to do something with my voice that wasn't common in the West End, and whatever it was, it really interested Andrew and brought a new dimension to his music. Trevor had seen me create the role of Marius, so he knew I could do that, given the right help. In other words, I had the right tools for the job.

Also – and I do think this is important – I know how to conduct myself in rehearsals. I'm positive, I can be funny, I can take the piss and have the piss taken out of me. I'll crack on and work hard, I'll take direction, I'll offer ideas but only when they're welcome. And that really, really helps in my business. If you can be someone that people want to work with (i.e. not a pain in the ass) then that's half the battle won.

It was a strange feeling. When I was first cast in *Aspects*, I definitely had that imposter syndrome thing. I felt as if I was going to get 'found out' and told to bugger off. It's not as though the feeling ever leaves you completely, but by the end of those sessions with Trevor I felt like I knew why I was there. As though I'd earned my place on the team.

PART THREE

'Bumholes Back'

Chapter 18

So I'm in *Aspects*. I've workshopped with Andrew Lloyd Webber. I've done masterclasses with Trevor Nunn. What could possibly go wrong?

Nothing, is the answer. Sorry if you're waiting for my leg to fall off, or a tragedy of similar proportions, but as far as this particular period of my life is concerned, it's pretty much all plain sailing, beginning with being chosen for *Aspects* and continuing with the next step, which was recording the single of 'Love Changes Everything'.

It wasn't the first time I'd entered a recording studio. That came either for the cast recording of *Les Mis*, or for a concept album I did called *Rage of the Heart*. However, it was the first time I'd travelled in a helicopter or a private jet, and that's not something you do every day. Andrew had said, 'Right, we're going to record the orchestra in Vienna and you should come and do the guide vocal.'

This meant, firstly, boarding a helicopter, which I did with eyes on stalks, trying to be nonchalant, like I commuted by helicopter on a daily basis, when in fact it was my first time ever, and inside I was screaming, *Oh my God, this is so cool, I'm in a helicopter.*

And that wasn't the end of it. Oh no. The helicopter ride was just the first leg of the journey. It was taking me to – wait for it – Andrew's private jet – a jet that when not in use by Andrew was regularly leased to Michael Jackson – which then took me to Austria. There, I sat in a studio and listened to an orchestra play a song as I sang along, and then returned and recorded the proper vocal in Air Studios in Oxford Street.

The single came out at the beginning of 1989, by which point we'd started rehearsals on the show. As I've already mentioned here, and indeed as I mention several times a day to random passers-by, the single reached number two, a huge hit by anybody's standards. It wasn't like the charts nowadays, where a single goes straight in high and then drops down. Back then, a song would 'climb the charts'. First we're at 42, then we're at 20, and it was going up every week, getting more traction the nearer we got to the show, gaining me more recognition. Until it came to Mother's Day when they advertised it with the tagline 'Take Michael home for a Mother's Day treat', the idea being to give it that final push and get us to number one.

By midweek it was indeed at number one, and I was thinking, *We're going to do it,* and we would have done if not for Jason Donovan, who absolutely nobody calls JaDo, who had appeared in a TV series, *The Heroes,* in which (spoiler alert) his character died, and then released 'Too Many Broken Hearts'.

And because the world was having its JaDo moment, everybody went out and bought his single, and there was one extra broken heart, mine, because he got the number one and not me.

So there's that happening. I'm performing the song on *Top of the Pops* and *Wogan*. Life was getting unrecognisable. Just over a year prior to that, I'd been mouldering in my grotty flat, worried about panic attacks and wondering about signing on the dole, and now I was practically a household name. Providing it was a household that watched *Top of the Pops* and *Wogan*.

Like I say, I had a profile already. I mean, I even had my own stalker back in *Les Mis*. She would write to me and turn up at the stage door, and on one particular day she turned up and pulled a knife on security. 'I need to see Michael now,' she apparently said, 'He's the only man who will understand me.'

It was a matinee and my folks happened to be there. Usually, I'd go to the stage door to meet fans and sign autographs, but on that occasion I was told to take my parents and leave by the side door, and the police were called to escort her away.

However, it turned out that she followed me to my agent's office where she put her hand through a window trying to get in. All very upsetting, as you might imagine. People joke about having a stalker, but it's not in the slightest bit funny; mostly it's just very traumatic for all concerned.

It was definitely during that period that the whole fan thing started. I developed a little band of admirers who would be waiting for me at the stage door, first at *Les Mis* and then at *Phantom*. Thing is with me, I'll chat and stop for pictures. I like to think I'm pretty approachable.

When it all went bonkers in that *Aspects* period, my merry band of admirers told me they thought they might lose me somehow. But they didn't, and I like to think I've stayed true.

It was around that time that Gill and Maureen, who run the fan club – and I'm proud to say I count as friends – came into my life.

But after the single, things really kicked up a gear. People were stopping me in the street, invitations were coming in, everybody wanted a little bit of me.

I was cushioned to a certain extent because I was part of a company, and you know what it's like. They'd take the piss, keep me grounded. So I never lost sight of what the job was. Even so, there was no getting around the fact that all of a sudden I was around 40 per cent pop star.

Trevor sat me down. 'You're going to have to make a decision. You're at a bit of a crossroads. Do you want to be a serious actor or do you want a showbiz life?'

A showbiz life, eh? Refusing to do stairs. M&Ms with all the brown ones taken out. Scented candles in the dressing room and a brand-new toilet seat every day. Sounded great.

'Well, why can't I have both?' I said.

'It doesn't work like that,' he said. 'You have the potential to be a respected serious actor and you could also pursue a successful career in more mainstream showbiz. But you can't do both.'

But guess what? As he now freely admits, he was wrong about that and years later ate a bit of humble pie, saying, 'One of the greatest visits to the theatre I ever had was seeing you in *Sweeney Todd*. There you were inhabiting one of the most difficult roles in any form of theatre, and doing it so brilliantly, and I knew that you wouldn't have been able to do that if you hadn't had the commercial ability to have that show put on.'

Which was true. My involvement with *Sweeney* went back

to 2006 and a visit from Cathy and our friends Callum and Michelle McLeod while I was appearing in *The Woman in White* on Broadway. Callum's my musical director and has been since my first-ever concert in 1988. He and Michelle are great friends and regular holiday companions – in fact, they were there in Majorca when I had the idea for *Aspects II.* So anyway, while in New York, they and Cathy went along to see *Sweeney Todd: The Demon Barber of Fleet Steet* – to give it its full title – a revival starring Patti LuPone as Mrs Lovett and Michael Cerveris as Sweeney. They came out giddy with it, particularly Cathy who up until then didn't really count herself as a Stephen Sondheim fan.

'You *have* to play Sweeney,' she told me later.

It was a role I'd never considered. I didn't know if I'd be any good, or if I was even capable of it. And who would cast me anyway?

Still, Cathy was insistent and so I took a closer look under the bonnet of the show, finally getting to understand how brilliant it was. I called my agent who agreed it could be a good project for me and suggested we try somewhere 'out of town'. Chichester, say. It sounded like a good idea. But who should play Mrs Lovett?

At his time – by now 2008 – I was appearing in *Hairspray* and had just started my Radio 2 show, where an early guest was Imelda Staunton, promoting whatever show she was doing at the time.

Before she came in, somebody had told me, 'Did you know that Imelda's got six fingers on one of her hands?'

The usual number of fingers is five, so I was like, 'Woah. Really?'

'Yeah, really. It's one of those things that everybody knows. Like, David Bowie's eyes are different colours. Imelda Staunton has an extra finger.'

'It must make wearing gloves a problem.'

'Yeah!'

I spent the first bit of my interview with Imelda trying to see her spare finger. When I couldn't find it, I began looking for a scar where the extra digit might have been removed, still with no success, until we broke for a record, and off-air I said to her, 'Imelda, I was told you had six fingers on one hand.'

She howled. She hadn't heard that one before. It definitely wasn't 'one of those things that everybody knows'. It was just a weird rumour that had somehow become fact.

Any road up, that broke the ice and Imelda and I got on so well that as another record played, I said to her, knowing her extensive background in musical theatre, 'Would you ever play Mrs Lovett?'

'I'd love to.'

'Would you play it with me as Sweeney?'

'I'd love to. Are you serious?'

Yes, I was, and with Imelda on board, I went to Jonathan Church, the artistic director at Chichester Festival Theatre, who was keen, found us a spot for the following year, and we played there for six weeks or so, before later transferring to the West End.

Basically, to cut a long story short, Cathy bullied me, and was right – as usual. Thanks to her I'd instigated the show, knowing I'd never be cast as Sweeney otherwise, and in doing so, I'd thought back to my drama teacher telling me, 'You won't work until you're 40, and then you'll be doing character roles.'

Well, of course my teacher was wrong about the first bit; I worked plenty before turning 40, but even so, I got to a position where I was then able to do the character roles to which I'm probably more suited. I made the leap from fluffy leading man / pop star into doing more left-field character stuff like *Sweeney* and *Hairspray*, and I was able to do that because I'd built up a more commercial name for myself, partly as a result of releasing records. I think I made the right choice.

Chapter 19

Anyway. Deep breath. Back on the subject at hand, which is *Aspects of Love*, where I was getting to know others who were on board: Mike Reed, who was the musical director, and who had conducted, orchestrated and arranged for more West End shows than you can count; Andrew MacBean, who was the assistant director, and Gillian Lynne, the choreographer.

Gillian is yet *another* of those genius figures who appears in this story. She choreographed *Cats* and *Phantom* and many, many others.

Now, most shows need a choreographer of sorts. For *Sweeney*, and indeed for *Aspects II*, we had a movement director, Denni Sayers, who was in charge of general stage traffic, ensuring that the performers moved around each other in an aesthetically pleasing way. There's choreography involved in the fairground scene in Act I of *Aspects* and again for the song 'Hand Me the Wine and the Dice' in Act II, but Denni's task here – and one she fulfilled brilliantly – was to bring a storytelling element to the dancing.

Gillian Lynne, on the other hand, was very different. You don't get Gillian Lynne, hot off *Cats* and *The Phantom of the Opera* to do what are relatively subdued dance scenes. Gillian's thing was routines. Big, spectacular song-and-dance showcases. And for 'Hand Me the Wine and the Dice' in 1989, we had an instrumental interlude and a solo dance routine from Sandy Strallen (the head of a performing dynasty that also includes his daughters Scarlett, Summer and Zizi Strallen). It was . . . well, it was certainly *something*. But it definitely ran contrary to Andrew and Trevor's initial desire for a smaller, low-key production.

It was a similar story with Maria. You can see why Andrew would bring these guys on board. They were trusted, celebrated figures, gargantuan talents in our world, and having them on board took just a little bit of that enormous pressure off his shoulders, knowing they would bring their A-game. But for the likes of Gillian and Maria their A-game is played at Wembley. They go big or they go home. Maria Björnson isn't going to follow up her *Phantom* chandelier by plonking a candle-dripped wine bottle on a table and saying, 'Look, everybody! Paris!' She wants to flex her creative muscles.

And she did. We had a wall at the back that would part in order to give you a view of the Pyrenees; we had travelators carrying us from one side of the stage to the other so that performers would look as though they were gliding around the stage. You thought we were simply light on our feet? Oh no. We had mechanical help.

The other thing was the car, a Rolls-Royce, which appeared in Act II, and among its many faults was that it had malfunctioning windscreen wipers. Obviously it wasn't a real Rolls-Royce. Using a real Rolls-Royce would have been cheaper though, because this was the most expensive – and the most shite – prop in the history of expensive shite props. It looked great, but most of the time it just sat there, stuck, taking all of the audience attention away from the story, music and performances.

When they removed the car, they couldn't get it out of the theatre, so it had to go up into the rafters for the entire run, hanging over our heads like a big symbolic symbol-like thing.

Saying that. I take my hat off to directors who see something, realise it's shit and take it out. Like in *Phantom*, there was a horse that came down from the rafters. The horse was fake but it had real birds, which were supposed to be pigeons, but for some reason turned out to be doves that were painted grey. The idea was for these birds to flutter off towards the light, which they did, but the wrong light. Instead they flew to the exit light and stayed up in the rafters for days on end, shitting on everything.

On *The Woman in White*, we had a rat. Now, on one occasion I accidentally chopped off the rat's tail. It sounds worse than it is – it got caught in a glass container I was closing. The rat wrangler went mental at me. Quite understandable. We had to have an understudy rat, and that one just sat in my hand shitting on me.

Regarding Maria – and before I open myself to accusations of tarnishing her legend, which I would *never* do – I should make the point that she would have been working to her brief; I very much doubt that any upscaling was made at her insistence. Again, I was just the turn. Not privy to those kinds of conversations. All I know is that there was a certain expectation that we should be eliciting gasps of awe and wonderment from the audience, and as a result the show just grew and grew, moving away from being a chamber piece into something that had to fit the stage at the Prince of Wales.

Like I say, ours not to reason why. We actors just work with what we've got. A very good example of that was the rat. Yes, *another* rat. If you recall, in *Aspects* there is an entire scene in which Rose and Alex are in the bedroom and hear something that they think is a rat – but turns out to be a shoe. It's an odd scene to say the least. Nobody could really work out what it was doing in the show, or why a shoe might sound like a rat, but it was in the book, so it had to stay.

For the scene we had a little trapdoor, which was supposed to flip and reveal the shoe, but it was so erratic that eventually we just pretended it was there. Mind you, Ann gave me a plastic rat on the first night as a present, and I think we may have used the rat on at least one occasion.

Meanwhile, we were supposed to be naked for the scene, but Trevor allowed us to keep our underwear on. Being body-conscious, the idea of appearing on stage in just my pants was bothering me, but I put it to the back of my mind. Having rehearsed it fully clothed we got to the first costume tech run, when Trevor, who like everyone else in the company knew I was in a bit of a tizz about it, said, 'Michael, it's the moment. You're going to have to come on the stage in your pants.'

God knows what I had to worry about. I mean, I was young, I looked pretty good actually, in a 'no abs', reasonably fit kind of way. These days, I'd have every reason to feel the terror, but you know what it's like: we carry our troubles with us and I wore mine on my sleeve.

I asked to see the lighting state and was relieved to see that the way they planned to light it was with a little tunnel of light so to all intents and purposes, I'd be silhouetted; you'd hardly see me. Feeling somewhat comforted, I came on, and . . .

The bastards.

Every spotlight and light in the entire building went on me, picking me out on stage.

It was just a wind-up, of course. But actually, it was the best thing they could have done, because suddenly I got over myself. *This is me, in my pants. Have a look everybody.*

That aside, I've never really lost the body consciousness. Like I say, you carry your troubles with you. Put it this way, don't expect to see me in *Oh! Calcutta!* any time soon.

© Clive Barda / ArenaPAL

Aspects of Love then and now. Just add a beard, cravat and two stone (otherwise, not aged a day).

© Johan Persson / ArenaPAL

Above: My first-ever stage appearance in amateur panto at Droitwich Theatre, singing 'Do-Re-Mi' with a black eye and upstaging everyone.

Below: Prep school at Plymouth: I'm the adorable one third from right.

Top: Second-year summer holiday, driving through France. We crashed and came home on the third day.

Below left: My first headshot.

Below right: Headshot for *Aspects*.

Right: Legendary swordsman (not remotely camp).

Left: With Paul Nicholas and Dilys Laye in *Pirates of Penzance*.

Right: With Kevin Webster, aka Michael Le Vell, fighting over a girlfriend in *Corrie*. Gran would have been so proud.

Top left: With Rebecca Caine in *Les Mis*.

Top right: In *Phantom*, complete with dodgy syrup.

Below: With Claire Moore and Dave Willetts in 'The Final Lair'. Luckily the noose worked that time.

Right: Andrew announcing my casting as Alex.

Below: 'Take Michael Home as a Mother's Day Treat.' Not enough people took that advice and I stayed at number two.

Below: The dream team, Andrew, Charles, Trevor and Don doing, um . . . whatever they're doing.

Rehearsals for *Aspects*: in my bloody element.

Above: My favourite picture: relaxing after the show on *Aspects'* opening night.

Below: My role as Alex really changed things for me, and Ann Crumb was a divine co-star to have by my side.

Chapter 20

Aspects of Love has a great roster of songs. Proper great. I mean, we always pick out 'Love Changes Everything', but honestly, there are so many highlights, real 'bring down the house' numbers, especially in the second half.

'Hand Me the Wine and the Dice' is one of those. It's begun by Giulietta, who having already had a dalliance with Rose – at her wedding to George, the hussy! – is now flirting with Alex. And then, as Giulietta sings a song about letting the chips fall where they may and living for the moment, she is joined by the rest of the company for a rousing climax that underlines the show's entire theme. George's creed is that love changes everything, but at the same time none of us have a say in how or even what love changes. Ultimately, it's all in the fates. It's got so that I say it at times of indecision or fateful turns. *Hand me the wine and the dice.*

As I've said, our original choreographer, Gillian Lynne, built that song from being a big number into an even bigger one – a major hubba-hubba showstopper. We scaled it back for the *Aspects II* version, but even so, it remained a big ensemble moment. Why? Because that's what the song deserves.

Andrew and I got talking about Gillian and what a hard taskmaster she was. Just how hard was she? Put it this way, if you worked with Gillian you had to expect that at some point, your feet were going to bleed.

'If half the cast of *Bad Cinderella* had been working under Gillian they would have run for the hills,' sighed Andrew, and with that we got on to the subject of 'work ethic'. In other words, the lack of it.

Believe me when I say that it's a perennial topic of conversation among us oldies, because the trouble with so many – not all, but a percentage big enough to comment on – of today's turns is that it's all about *getting* the job, rather than *doing* the job. The first hint of a bit of *discomfort*, shall we say, something somewhat on the *challenging* side, and they're pulling a duvet above their ears. You've heard of the expression 'the show must go on'? Not for this lot. It's all, 'The show must go on, but can someone else do it? I've got a poorly toe.'

I had one like that during *Hairspray*. 'I'm not feeling well . . . my throat . . .'

'Well, you already did the first half.'

'Yes, but I don't think I can do the second half.'

They're not thinking about the ramifications. It's not just the audience you're letting down. It's everyone else – it's wigs, costumes, make-up, everything. None of these guys are prepared for this. 'Look, surely, you can get through to the end of the show?'

'Well, I could, but I'm worried about the effect on my mental health.'

I fixed a smile. 'But how will your mental health be if you get a reputation and struggle to get more work?'

My words had no effect. They didn't come back for the second half.

I had another one on the *Hairspray* tour. She phoned in sick, so I gave her a call. 'What's the problem, darling?'

And she went, 'I'm just really tired.'

'Are you?' I said. 'Are you tired?'

'Yeah, I'm really pooped.'

I said, 'Aw, well, don't take the day off . . . take the week off . . . matter of fact, take the contract off, or . . . how about instead get in and push through. What about that? I promise you'll feel better if you do.'

And she did. She came in, did the show and felt better.

Perhaps my behaviour then might be seen as being a bit bullyish, but it's not – it's just being professional. It's asking people to fulfil their commitments. I mean, come on. *Tired.* I ask you.

It happens a lot with cast changes. I've been in shows where the original cast worked their arses off, morning, noon and night. But then we had a cast change and a bunch of kids fresh from drama school came in, and they were so unreliable; they'd be off at the drop of a hat.

'People sometimes seem to forget that we're a service industry,' sighs Andrew.

Post-Covid, things are probably even worse. Everyone's more worried about putting strains on their mental health. Rightly so, of course, because as I know better than anyone, being in this business takes its toll on you, it really does. You have to be a certain mentality to get through it. But at the same time, you're in a West End show for God's sake; you have a responsibility to yourself, to the audience, to the rest of the company. During *Hairspray* I had emergency root canal treatment which didn't finish until midday. I ran in for the matinee and had so much anaesthetic in my mouth I was playing Edna but dribbling. Not only that, but they'd accidentally sewn my gum to my cheek, and I still went on. 'Don't worry, I'll make it part of the character.'

Still, those performers (*a minority*, he hastens to add) who slack off tend to get a name for it. That casting process I was talking about before? I've pointed out people. 'Not that one there.' But of course, it works the other way, too. We had a guy on *Aspects II*, Vinny Coyle, who played Hugo, and was the understudy for Alex. He'd been in the Dream Cast production of *Les Mis* and was not only a great company member but got thrown on to play Enjolras one time and just . . . did it. Absolutely threw himself into it, not a word of complaint. True pro. And as a result, in my role of unofficial casting consultant to Jonathan and Andrew, I'm going, 'Vinny's who you want, somebody like that, who gets the ethic.' It's a small business, you get a reputation really quickly, and it works both ways. Sometimes the best advice is just 'to crack on'.

As I say, it feels like a bit of a modern phenomenon, maybe even an 'only since Covid' phenomenon. Put it this way, it wasn't something we had to contend with during the original *Aspects*.

Chapter 21

So, casting for *Aspects I,* then, and our Rose, the character around which so many of the romantic entanglements revolve, was to be played by Ann Crumb.

I'm sad to say that Ann lost a battle against ovarian cancer in 2019 and died at the age of 69. Up until she retired from performing, she was an in-demand actress, having made her Broadway debut in the original cast of *Les Misérables* in 1987. Also on Broadway, she had been in *Chess*, which was directed by Trevor.

Most of the cast I met at that 'first day of school' I mentioned, but I'd bumped into Ann beforehand, at a fitting, and liked her right away, which was great, firstly because my character had to fall head over heels in love with her (after which almost every other character also falls in love with her), and secondly because, well, because I was going to be spending a lot of time with her.

Although she was innately funny, she was also very serious

about her work and could be quite fragile at times. Like many a performer, including yours truly, she liked a lot of reassurance, but being American, and fitting the stereotype perfectly, she maybe needed it more than most. The thing was that she'd been in a number of productions and had paid her due. But even so, to originate a role in a Lloyd Webber in the West End was a big deal for her, and all the pressure and insecurities of that would occasionally bubble up, and of course she was relocating from New York.

Hardly surprising. Rose is a tough, demanding role, what we call a rangey role. You need an actress who can play young but also go up in age. You need an actress with incredible charisma, who also has a fabulous singing voice. The other thing is that although the action seems to revolve around Rose, the show's not really about her, and I think that dynamic may have affected Ann. I think she may have seen what was happening to me, with the chart hit making me the focus of attention, and felt as though she should have had that sort of impact. I could be wrong. She never said anything. But I think that was probably it.

I remember also that she obsessed with her dogs. In those days if you brought dogs into the UK, they had to stay in quarantine for six months and she was desperately upset about that; she used to go and visit them as often as possible. Perhaps that had an effect on her. There were also rumours that, as an American, she was cast as part of an Equity agreement, which was untrue. As Trevor told me: all casting was done on the basis of vocal talent and acting ability. Still, she might have been stung by that.

As for me and her, she probably considered me a little . . .

ahem . . . 'immature'. And of course, I probably was. Probably still am. [Farts].

This is absolutely not to say that there was anything wrong with Ann's performance. Far from it. Nothing she had going on in terms of doubts or insecurities made it to the stage. 'Ann had that wonderful ingredient of being a brilliant actress as well as a brilliant singer,' said Trevor. She had an exotic, entrancing quality which made it entirely plausible that all the male characters (and at least one of the female ones) would be metaphorically prostrating themselves before her. Our Rose in *Aspects II*, Laura Pitt-Pulford, did an incredible job, and in Ann she had a very hard act to follow.

Kevin Colson ended up playing George (and no, I haven't forgotten about Roger Moore. If you could bear with, he's got his own bit coming up). Kevin had an interesting history. He'd acted when he was younger and had been a bit of a fixture in the West End, including a stint in *Cabaret* with Judi Dench at the Palace Theatre. Then, in 1969, he gave it all up and went to work in the oil industry for a spell, unsuccessfully, before returning to acting in 1985. There followed roles in *Follies* and then in the West End production of *Chess*, directed by you know who, and then . . . us.

Kevin is no longer with us, sadly. He died in 2018, aged 80. But you know what? He was a great George. I thought so. Trevor thought so. The people who nominated him for a Tony Award on Broadway thought so, too. He was very tall, beautifully spoken, handsome, elegant . . . all the things that George is supposed to be.

Which begs the question, how could I possibly improve on Kevin as George? The answer is that I approached it in my way, which is to say, 'The character of George is the character of George.' His journey, his life and his relationships are on the page, and it's down to how I interpret those.

It's the same as doing anything, the same as playing Edna in *Hairspray* or doing *Sweeney Todd.* I've seen other people play the role before playing it myself. I saw Harvey Fierstein do Edna and thought to myself, *I'd kill to play that,* but even then, when you really admire what's gone before, you mustn't think about it. You can't. You need to make it yours. Besides which, it's only when you get into rehearsals and you're working with the company that you really find your interpretation, and the chances are that it's different simply by virtue of it being you combined with that particular group of people and that director. Some aspects of the performance might stay the same: the moves might be similar, the notes are definitely the same. But your physicality, how you're interpreting the songs, the way you're coming across and what you're bringing to the stage is very different.

I guess what I'm saying is that there can never be a definitive performance of a character. It's all down to interpretation and that interpretation is informed by a host of different factors.

For the free-spirited Giulietta in *Aspects II*, we cast Danielle de Niese, an opera singer who's absolute dynamite. She withdrew from Glyndebourne just to be with us. Back in 1989 she was played by Kathleen Rowe McAllen, who won a Theatre World Award for the Broadway production. This was a real feat, actually, because Giulietta in the show is not quite as involved as the central trio of Alex, Rose and George, but she was great and a really engaged member of the company. Ann had her fella with her in London, but Kathleen, another American, was alone, so she was keen for us Brits to show her the sights, which we did. When the show transferred to Broadway, she reciprocated, and oh, the fun we had.

Chapter 22

Diana Morrison was the last major member of the cast back in 1989. She played Jenny, by which I mean the controversial, dare I say 'problematic' Jenny. I was with Diana when I had one of the strangest experiences of my life, which was making the music video for 'The First Man You Remember', the follow-up to 'Love Changes Everything' (number two in the charts, kept off the top spot by JaDo, don't you know).

In the show, 'The First Man You Remember' is performed by George and Jenny and is a song about the relationship of a father and his daughter. For the single they wanted me to sing the George part, so it became a song of two lovers, a fact that was reflected in the video we then shot.

I remember exactly when this was, funnily enough. We had opened and performed two shows, so were just coming out of that 'exhausted doing rehearsals' period and going into that 'exhausted doing the show' period. The thing about the show is that you stay knackered. You never catch up on yourself. Me,

I tend to arrive at the theatre at about 4.30pm, for a 7.30pm start, and I'll always try and get an hour's kip if I can, just so I'm as fresh as possible. Even so, it always feels as though you're chasing your own tail in terms of physical and mental fatigue.

Back then, of course, I was a much younger man with, I hope, a little more stamina. But still, my world was absolutely rooted in work. You can't party hard when you're doing a West End musical because you're not going to turn up the next day – or you're going to turn up, but just not 'turn up', if you know what I mean. And there's always something to be getting on with. You're doing rehearsals for new people going in, you're helping an understudy get up to speed, you're making an album or shooting footage or doing an interview. After a show you grab a bite to eat and then it's home, sleep, repeat.

So anyway, back to my video story. We'd been open two nights; the cast recording album had been released and reached number one, and so we had some kind of celebration dinner. This might have been fun except for the fact that Diana and I had this video for 'The First Man You Remember' to make, and helpfully, it was to be shot at a country house miles out of London.

Thus, when the celebration dinner was over, the pair of us were decanted into a car and driven for hours, arriving at our hotel about two in the morning, and then, about four hours later, called on set for a 6am start at the country house. And . . . action.

This video. Have you seen it? If not, go to YouTube and watch it. I'll wait.

Back? I know. I'm so sorry. Your poor eyes. Firstly, did you spot Bruno Tonioli off *Strictly Come Dancing*? He's the guy twirling Diana around the floor as I'm coming down the stairs. Gives me daggers. Did you spot the voguing people? Yes, this was of course 1989, and voguing was all the rage, but – and I've literally just checked this – we actually beat Madonna's 'Vogue' to the punch by a good few months, so at least we were ahead of the curve.

The stately home in which the video was set had been hired to us by the owner. I can't remember exactly where it was located, but I do know that during the 26-hour period we were there – yes, you read that correctly, we were there for 26 wide-awake hours – it got fairly comprehensively trashed. I remember Andrew arriving in a helicopter and frightening the poor woman's deer. Not only was there, let's just say, 'a party atmosphere' to the whole thing, but just look at the video. See all that stuff in the house? That's not CGI. That's actual stuff. And it got everywhere. I still shudder when I think of the mess we must have left behind when at last the shoot / marathon / endurance test was over. I think they were trying to give the video a kind of decadent, Gothic feel, perhaps a reference to its Lloyd Webber / *Phantom* roots. I don't know. Who cares? As far as I'm concerned, they mainly gave it a feel that said, 'This video could not have been made in any decade other than the 1980s,' but at the time, I was far more concerned about my own discomfort and, being a gentleman, that of young Diana, just 19, me as chaperone trying to steer her clear of the worst of the hedonism. She and I had to do a lot of filming outside, and it was freezing cold. We had to dance in a pond. Actually *in* the pond.

We were of course the Lilywhites who were never led astray because we had to do the show the next night, so it felt as though we were simultaneously participants and observers doing what we were told by the director – Jack Bond, it was. He did a bunch of Pet Shop Boys videos as well – and was probably thinking, *God, this is shit, isn't it?* The filming went all through the Sunday until about 9am on Monday morning, at which point we had to go back to London and do the show that night.

And after all that, the single reached the grand heights of number 62.

So, yes, filming that video was definitely one of the weirdest experiences of my life. And that's quite something when you consider that I've worked extensively with Alfie Boe (joke, Alfie) and once represented the UK at the Eurovision Song Contest. Thankfully, Diana was great company, partly because she is one of life's great corpsers.

Yes, corpsing. Now, as I think I've said, I'm a great fan of the art. The key to a good corpse is that firstly, it should be spontaneous and completely organic, and secondly that it should be successfully concealed from the audience. That second bit? That's the real trick.

As for the source of the corpsing? Well, it can be anything. It can be something almost metaphysical, like that moment in *Phantom* where Claire and I both realised that we were thinking the same thing at the same time. Or it could be that we're triggered by, I don't know, a lamp falling over. Or the best one: farting.

And with that said, it's at this point in that I introduce the promised Favourite-Ever Corpse. Ready?

So, there's a pivotal moment in *Aspects* where Jenny's in bed, Alex is in the room and she sings a cappella, '*Alex, let me hold you, I've got so much on my mind.*'

At first Alex turns away, but then he gets into bed, whereupon Jenny clings on to him, and sings, '*I want you here forever in my arms and in my life, to belong to you completely.*'

On this particular night, I was a bit windy, and as Diana pulled back the bedclothes, singing, '*Alex, let me hold you, I've got so much on my mind,*' I turned.

And as I turned, I emitted the biggest, loudest fart in history.

Diana said, 'Oh.'

It was that one word. *Oh.* It was her look of surprise, her obvious internal conflict at trying to stay in character, but at the same time needing to react to a fart that was so loud they'd clearly heard it in the audience; heard it in the wings; heard it in the orchestra. I mean, the guff itself was funny – I'm yet to meet a fart I didn't think was worth a chuckle – and maybe I could have held it together if it had just been that. Just the fart. It was the reaction, Diana's 'oh', that pushed things into the realm of the uncontrollable.

The bedsheets shook as I clambered into bed, trying and failing to keep the scene moving. Diana was laughing, too – so much so that she couldn't sing or speak, and nor could I, meaning that our sing-through musical had temporarily turned into a mime show.

Kevin came on for the scene where George has a heart attack and dies, and of course he was affected by the corpsing, so he had his heart attack shaking with laughter, as I tried to give him CPR, unable to stop laughing myself.

It was awful, and yet simultaneously brilliant. Diana was so upset afterwards, but I told her not to worry (which was very gallant of me, considering that I'd started the whole corpse thing by reacting to her character's entreaties with a fart) and that it was the best time I've ever had on stage, and I meant it.

Which reminds me, there was another time, just before the shooting scene, when Ann had gone off to do the quick change, as Alex is singing, '*Where is she, where is she?*' and she was meant to come back in, singing, '*What are you doing here?*'

Except that she'd fluffed up the quick change. Some problem with her wig, which meant that she had to do her lines offstage behind the door, singing, '*What are you doing here?*' except not on stage. So, there I was performing to an empty stage until finally she burst in with her boobs hanging out, trying to hold up her dress and her wig all askew.

Well, I mean, honestly – how was I supposed to keep it together?

I didn't, is the answer.

So, yes, Diana was great, and it was a shame that she couldn't transfer to Broadway when the time came (which definitely *was* for Equity reasons). Recently she came to see *Aspects II* and sent me the loveliest card afterwards. She'd loved it, she said. It had brought back so many memories for her. A great actress, a fine singing voice and a champion corpser.

Chapter 23

For the most recent *Aspects*, the casting process began almost as soon as the green light went on. As with most productions, it was a case of, firstly, announcing it to the industry, and secondly, creating a breakdown of the characters and the kind of performers we were looking for to fill those roles. We had a casting director, David Grindrod, who having been briefed by us, was in charge of canvassing agents who in turn would send him CVs of possible talent, after which we had a casting call.

At that particular moment in time our director, Jonathan, was editing *Long Day's Journey into Night*, a film he'd been making with Jessica Lange and Ed Harris (it's an adaptation of the Eugene O'Neill play that Jonathan had directed on Broadway in 2016), so we had to wait for the physical auditions to begin. It's not a big company for *Aspects*. The story is centred on four or five characters who have 90 per cent of the dialogue, and there isn't really much for the ensemble to do, which means that we weren't looking for the usual musical theatre turns, actors who go from show to show, but neither were we looking for kids straight out of drama school. We wanted character actors with unique voices, people who had a unique special something that, when they're on stage, come across as individuals with backstories and inner lives, whatever characters they're playing.

Casting is a really, really important part of the process. If you get it wrong, you don't have a great show. And when I say 'you', I don't mean you. I don't even mean me. I mean Jonathan, in whom I had absolute trust, because I know how brilliant he is and how right he is for the piece, and Nick Skilbeck, our musical director, who knows way more than I ever will about what's required musically from these people. At the casting call they'll be working to firstly spot the actor's potential, and secondly, be satisfied that they can respond to direction.

Other factors involved can be quite idiosyncratic. You'll see someone at audition and there's something about them that is absolutely right, something indefinable and they're about to be cast but then, oh, there's somebody else who's also perfect, and so you have the thing where there are two really great actors but only one role, and so you have recalls, get people back and work with them on different scenes and with different performers, at which point you're trying to ascertain whether they're the right fit. It's why I didn't want to get involved in that process with *Aspects II*, because it can be down to granular things like the performer's height, a timbre in their voice that isn't right or doesn't mix. It's never personal, but Christ, it feels personal.

The creatives got it right on *Aspects II.* Our Alex, Jamie Bogyo, has a tremendous voice. I dragged him on to the Radio 2 Piano Lounge in order to show people just how bloody good he is. Obviously, it was important to Jonathan that Jamie had chemistry with Laura Pitt-Pulford's Rose, so he worked with them a lot to ensure they had the right dynamic.

I had a bit of veto, of course. But only because I needed to answer the question: do I want to spend six months with these people? I had a great lunch with Laura and knew that we were going to have a good time; ditto Jamie, who's just fabulous. He's bright, a great actor, amazing singer, keen to learn. And if I was worried that having initiated the production and being so closely associated with it, people might start off being a little bit wary of me and find it difficult to relax, then I needn't have done. On any show you get a three-day period, starting with that 'first day of school' onwards, where you get the measure of people. How they're going to operate in that environment. How you can make them feel comfortable and how to feel comfortable with them, because, in the rehearsal room, the most important thing is to develop a rapport and develop trust, so you have the freedom to be a prat, or experiment with line readings and character choice, without feeling self-conscious about it. You need that. You're actively pursuing it. It's why companies form a very close almost familial connection. You're spending more time with these guys than your own family, and they're seeing you at your most exposed, so it's inevitable that you create this incredible bond.

And yet, here's the sad thing: it's a bond that doesn't last. The bald truth of the matter is that very few of them will stay in your life afterwards. Ask me six months later, I might not even remember all their names, and that's not just me, everybody's like that, which is where 'darling' comes in. 'Darling, my lovely, how are you?' Because your brain doesn't work quickly enough to place them in context. Who are they? When did I work with them? What's their bloody name?

Which is absolutely not to say that the original bond is anything but genuine and sincere. I guess it's just that we've only got enough bandwidth for a certain number of those relationships in our life, so we have to free it up occasionally.

Of course, the casting process throws up mistakes. Usually, one mistake per production, because it's well known that every company has the 'Company . . .' well, I can't say the word, not in a family publication like this, but let's just say it's an alliterative four-letter word that rhymes with 'seafront', and the story goes that if you're part of a company and you don't know the identity of the Company Seafront, then it's you.

I'm not talking about actors who are a little bit eccentric. Rosie Ashe was in *Aspects II*, and she is one of the true eccentrics, a real grande dame of the theatre, and I absolutely adore her.

No, I'm talking about the members of the company who act as a slightly poisonous influence. For example, if you're in a company where the leading roles are played by people who don't get on, it's a nightmare. It creates a culture that filters down and affects everyone. I've been in situations with members of the company behaving badly towards wig people and dressers and the younger members of the crew; I've seen people playing married couples who literally can't look each other in the eye, and when they go in for the big kiss turn away and you think, *That's a lack of professionalism*, because if you're in a situation with somebody you don't get on with, it has to stop the second you walk on the stage.

And you really don't want to be the Company Seafront, because part of getting any job is to make sure you get another job after that. And you either have to be extraordinarily talented, a big, big money-spinner, or just unhinged to gamble with that.

For one reason or another, you often get a bit of musical chairs during the lifetime of the show itself, oftentimes because people are ill or indisposed. As a result, you need understudies for the principals, while if minor cast members are unavailable then they're covered by someone else in the company in the form of 'swings'.

A swing is, without question, the hardest job in the theatre because you're basically being an understudy for a number of other actors, gender and age allowing. Not only does a swing have to learn all of the relevant lines but also 'the track', which is the movements on and off stage, the costume changes and choreography, and you learn it for every member of the ensemble, so that if anybody drops out, you can replace them at a moment's notice. If a principal is off, the understudy comes out of the ensemble and the swing goes in and covers them. If a member of the ensemble is off, then the swing goes in and covers them. Occasionally – as happened during Covid – you get the principal *and* the understudy off, in that instance the swing is going to have to somehow amalgamate several different parts, and you have a frantic rehearsal to try and work out how you're going to do it.

What about when a performer leaves for good? Well, that's very rare. Except, of course, that it happened to us on the original *Aspects*.

Chapter 24

So, at some point, possibly even before coming on board, it became apparent to me that despite my number two single, I wasn't the biggest star to appear in *Aspects of Love*. What? Who could possibly be bigger than me? Surely not Jason Donovan?

No, not Jason Donovan. In fact, that honour went to Roger Moore.

To say that I was pleased or excited about the fact that Roger Moore would be joining the production to play George would be seriously understating things. I'm a big Bond fan, not, 'I quite like a bit of James Bond', but proper Bondage. Ask me who directed *On Her Majesty's Secret Service*. Go on. I'll tell you. It was Peter Hunt, who had previously edited *Dr No, From Russia with Love* and *Goldfinger*. Ask me another. No, actually, don't. The point is that I ain't no plastic Bond fan. What's more, my favourite James Bond isn't Sean Connery. It's not Daniel Craig. It's not Barry Nelson (the first actor to ever play James Bond on screen). It's Roger Moore who, if you've been paying attention, you will remember stars in my favourite Bond movie, *The Spy Who Loved Me*.

Roger Moore.

When did I first realise I would be sharing a stage with my childhood hero? Not sure, but it was Andrew who told me, and typically he underplayed it. He said, 'Oh yes, and we're talking to Roger Moore about playing George.'

'I beg your pardon?'

Not just because it's Roger Moore, of *The Saint*, *The Persuaders*, *Gold* and *Shout at the Devil* fame. But also because it's Roger Moore of the 'not really a stage actor' fame. Roger Moore of the 'has he ever done a musical, like, *ever*?' fame. Robert De Niro has done a musical, *New York, New York*; Marlon Brando did *Guys and Dolls*. Even Clint Eastwood did *Paint Your Wagon*. But Roger Moore?

I mean, could he even sing?

'Oh yes,' Andrew assured me. 'We were down in the South of France. I played something to Roger, and he started singing. He's fantastic, and he's a perfect George.'

These are the kinds of circles in which they move. I asked Andrew, Trevor, Don and Charles how Roger was invited on board *Aspects* and none could remember exactly, just that it had, erm, something to do with being in the South of France, and, erm, Michael Caine might have been there. Oh, and Leslie Bricusse and, erm, something like that. One thing they could all agree on was that it had come through Andrew. Another thing was that Roger would always pick up the bill at lunch. Don remembered that well, adding, 'Roger used to call me "Scaremonger" because I wrote *The Man with the Golden Gun*.' Don is of course rightfully proud of his many credits writing Bond themes.

'They looked at a lot of possible Georges,' remembered Charles Hart, who went on to say that for a while they were considering Albert Finney, and during that period they set the action in Albi because they thought it would be funny to have Albert in Albi. Perhaps you had to be there. Either way, Albert Finney turned them down.

Nicol Williamson. He was another one they considered. As was Michael Gambon and Robert Stephens.

I'm sure they would all have been great, but for me Roger was ideal. The idea of just meeting him, let alone working with him, was incredible on so many levels. First of all, it's Roger Moore, it's James Bond; secondly my showbiz head is thinking, *Roger Moore in an Andrew Lloyd Webber Musical*, it's brilliant, it's going to get everybody talking, it's a phenomenal idea. There was no downside in my head, absolutely none. Okay, maybe I was worried that he might be Billy Big Bananas, big movie star and all that, because however nice they seem, and even if they have a good reputation, well, you're always hearing stories, aren't you? And I know from personal experience that such-and-such who seemed so nice turned out to be an arse. (Me? I am of course 100 per cent genuine, all the time, never a cross word nor a diva moment.)

And so it came to the first day of school, where all my excitement about meeting the cast and crew paled in comparison to the excitement of meeting Roger Moore.

What had I been expecting? An advance party of minders asking us not to make eye contact with Mr Moore? Perhaps a glamorous PA complete with headset and clipboard, tapping her watch meaningfully? Who cares, just as long as he's not an arse. *Don't turn out to be an arse, Roger. Don't be an arse.*

He wasn't. And what we got was Roger. Just Roger. Casually but elegantly dressed in a jumper and open-necked shirt, his George-beard just beginning its journey from stubble to full growth, working his way around the room in order to meet every one of the assembled cast and crew. 'I've seen you in action in *Les Misérables*,' he said to me. 'I only hope I can compare.'

'Well, I'm sure . . . I mean, I'm sure that . . .'

'Well, we'll have a go, shall we?' he said. 'Have a bit of fun at the same time, perhaps.' Just *so* Roger Moore. You know the way you hope and expect Roger Moore to be? Yup, exactly like that. He doesn't *say* stuff, he *twinkles* it.

But although he worked the room – and by the end of the day knew everybody's name – and was exactly as charming as you might expect him to be, it was also obvious that he was a bit nervous; in fact, probably very nervous. After all, he knew what a big casting decision this was. It was him, Roger Moore, who a mere four years ago had still been playing Bond and was deeply embedded in what is famously one of the closest-knit operations in the movie world, being asked to lead the cast of the new Andrew Lloyd Webber musical. To say he was out of his comfort zone is putting it mildly.

On the other hand, he must have thought he could do it. And of course, Andrew would have had every faith in him. As Don reminded me, there were many mutterings of surprise when Michael Crawford was cast in *Phantom*. Everybody was like, 'How can the "Ooh, Betty" guy do a Gothic musical?' but that turned out okay. Could Andrew do it again, that was the question? Could he make Roger Moore into an unlikely musical theatre star?

Chapter 25

Roger being out of his comfort zone was something that became even more apparent the next day, when Gillian Lynne stepped up for her morning warm-up.

I'd worked with Gilly before, of course, so I knew exactly what to expect, which was . . . well . . . let's just say that Gilly had an idiosyncratic way of delivering instructions, so instead of saying, 'Push out your chest,' for example, she'd say, 'Nipple juice.' And instead of saying, for instance, 'Thrust your hips,' she'd say (and please excuse the language), 'Push cunty forward,' meaning that a typical instruction might go, 'Nipple juice, nipple juice, nipple juice! Push cunty forward and . . . come!'

Oh, God, they broke the mould when they made Gilly Lynne, they really did. She used to get so carried away giving directions on stage that she'd regularly fall backwards off the stage and into the pit.

Roger knew all about the morning warm-up, and so he'd come correctly attired in an immaculate, never-been-worn tracksuit – exactly the kind of thing that James Bond might wear if he'd been sent by M to the Shrublands health resort in order to recuperate after a dangerous mission.

'Shall we go down to the front, Michael,' he said, sorry, *twinkled*, and of course, I was eager to comply. Not only did I want to be bezzie mates with Roger Moore, but I was secretly keen to watch him do the whole 'nipple juice' routine. This, I thought, should be good.

So it started up. 'Nipples to the stars, bumholes back.'

It swiftly became apparent that Roger wasn't one of life's great dancers, and of course neither am I, so instead we grovelled around on the rehearsal room floor as Gilly watched us disapprovingly, knowing that she had a right pair of wallopers in us.

The next day Roger arrived in a considerably less enthusiastic frame of mind, and this time, we didn't go to the front. Like kids on a school trip, we scuttled to the back of the bus, and once again I had the secret thrill of watching Roger Moore experience the world of Gilly Lynne.

'Flaps to the side, flaps to the side. Nipple juice, nipple juice. Cunty, cunty bumhole. Arse!'

Roger's patience, having been stretched on day one, snapped on day two. We were on the floor with our legs splayed, pushing cunty forward and he said, 'This woman's fucking insane. I'm James fucking Bond. Why the hell is she making me grovel on the floor like this?'

But he stuck it out. And if that tiny temperamental outburst makes him sound at all like a petulant prima donna, well, nothing could be further from the truth. Right from the start there was never any pulling rank, no big-star stuff. Because

'Love Changes Everything' had been such a big hit there was a lot of attention coming my way, and while there are plenty of big names who would have bristled at that, not him.

At the same time, he had other battles to fight. At the age of 61, having been a movie star for well over two decades, Roger, let's not forget, was making his West End debut. I think that at the beginning of his career he'd done a bit of theatre, but nothing on this sort of scale, and certainly never a musical. As you can imagine, that put an enormous amount of pressure on him. He seemed to deal with it, though – at least at first.

I've made the point that the atmosphere in the rehearsal room comes from the top. A niggly, bitchy lead makes for a niggly and bitchy company, while a generous, unselfish and inclusive lead creates a mutually supportive atmosphere.

I learned that watching Roger. He made everyone feel loved and special and he let us know that he felt as privileged to be working with us as much as we did with him. We were rehearsing at this place called Alford House, which is in Kennington and is inevitably known as Awful House. Back then, Kennington was a fairly run-down area, with just one dodgy café in which to eat, and so that's where we went. Because it was the only café, it became a running joke. 'Now, dear boy, where shall we eat today?' People in there would be goggling at us. Roger Moore with that boy off the telly who sings 'Love Changes Everything'. We'd eat there every day, often just the two of us, sometimes a bigger crew. But as Don says, no matter who was there, Rog always paid the bill, and he always did it before the issue of the bill came up, so that the matter was settled; there could be no argument.

He was also great at playing George. That much became clear

in rehearsal, where he truly flourished in the creative freedom given him by Trevor and Gilly. When you're in rehearsal, it's just you and whoever else is in the scene, as well as the director and the accompanist. Musically, you learn the tunes first. The pianist is there to help, to give you a tempo and help with where you need to breathe, your inflection and so on and so forth. There's a real freedom and security within that set-up. If you get it wrong, they tell you and you try again until you've got it.

Rog learned it very quickly. As far as anybody could tell he was pretty secure with his words and as for his delivery, his singing was lovely. Really tuneful. No, you wouldn't mistake him for a singer, but he was definitely an actor who could sing, and the thing was that his voice, whether by accident or design – I'm sure the latter, though he was too self-deprecating ever to admit it – really, really suited his interpretation of the character somehow. It acted as a foil to his characterisation, which was nigh-on perfect. He was just the epitome of the attractive older man. As you know, Rose initially takes up with Alex, who is besotted with her, but then moves on to George. Alex is a lovely guy – he was, after all, played by Michael Ball – so it has to be believable that Rose might clap eyes on George and make the move. George has got money, and I'm sure that's part of the attraction for Rose, but there needs to be something else. Some kind of especially charismatic gene that persuades Rose to trade up.

Roger had that. He had that absolutely. You could absolutely believe that Rose was going to choose Roger Moore over Michael Ball, much as it pains me to say. That sense of wisdom and worldly experience and sophistication – all of those George qualities, Roger had in spades. (I would of course get my revenge by waiting 34 years, casting myself as George and having Rose choose me over Jamie Bogyo, mwah-ha-ha.)

If all this sounds like I'm gushing, then it's my book and I'll gush if I want to. I adored Roger and we got on like a house on fire. Like me, he had a self-deprecating sense of humour.

I remember one time, Trevor was doing his usual intense and quite elongated explanation of a character moment, talking about how George is seeing the relationship develop between Alex and Jenny. 'So, Roger,' he said, 'this is a pivotal moment for George and you're really going to have to think about the nuance of this and how we express that to the audience.'

Roger looked at him. 'It sounds like a very important scene, Trevor,' he said.

'It is, Roger, it is.'

'In that case,' said Roger, 'I think you'll be requiring *both* eyebrows.'

Brilliant. Absolutely brilliant. He had us all falling about, just as he would when he told his brilliant stories. I mean, he had worked with everybody that I idolised. David Niven, for God's sake. He'd starred in *The Wild Geese* alongside Richard Harris and Richard Burton. He'd worked with Lee Marvin.

I mentioned that Roger had always been so good regarding the amount of press attention I received thanks to the 'Love Changes Everything' hit. He once said to me, 'Let me give you one piece of advice. May I?'

'Yes, yes of course,' I said, eager to learn from the master. Call me SpongeBob.

'Tell people very early on that you're a liar.'

'What do you mean?'

'When you're giving interviews, say, "I'm an awful liar," and that will mean that you never have to tell the truth ever again in an interview. Tell them you were brought up by wolves in the Avignon. Say your mother is Lucille Ball. Tell them anything and they won't ever get to know you and they don't need to. Always keep yourself private. Never let it all out. Because it's nobody's business unless you choose it to be. I never worry about lying in an interview.'

I was thinking, *but that's so not me*, and although I agreed with him to be polite, at the same time I was thinking that it just wasn't something I'd ever do. I mean, I understand. You don't have to share and all that. But still.

But, yes, they were great tales. He'd drop them in all of the time. Just the funniest man. And it was just glorious, absolutely glorious, hearing these brilliant stories. Oh, we had a magical time, really magical time.

Until . . .

Chapter 26

Nothing about Roger's relationships with me or the rest of the cast and crew changed. He was still our leader sending good vibes down the line; he and I still used to enjoy our lunches at the café; he still picked up the tab, however much we tried to insist that it was our turn.

Just that the early promise of his performance seemed to slowly evaporate.

Just a tiny bit, one day at a time, hardly noticeable but noticeable enough. It wasn't the whole performance as such. It was the singing. I remember that one day he came in with a cold sore and thinking that it seemed somehow to symbolise what was happening to him, an externalising of inner anxiety. You could almost see his confidence slowly drain away.

I think the problem was that, having started well, he was failing to progress. As though the potential he had shown, musically, wasn't quite being realised, and that was an obvious source of anxiety for him. He would stay on pitch, but he was finding it more and more difficult to find his notes. There's one bit, where the quartet is singing, which is very difficult musically, lots of interposed and different vocal lines coming in and out and singing over each other. He was really struggling with that, couldn't get it. His shoulders started to drop a little.

We were there for him. We had his back. But at the same time, I think that it had started to dawn on him. The reality had set in. He was going to have to do eight shows a week of this, every week, for months.

It's a very exposing thought. And it's certainly one thing being pretty good when you're accompanied by a pianist in a rehearsal room, quite another when you're standing on stage in front of 1,183 people accompanied by a full orchestra expected to deliver the goods.

If there was a single straw that broke the camel's back, then possibly it came during the sitzprobe.

Now, I can hardly believe that we have got this far into the book before I brought up the subject of the sitzprobe. 'What's one of those?' you ask. In real, simple terms, it's a rehearsal stage when the performers all sing with the full orchestra, the idea being to hear what they sound like together. It's the first time this will have happened because previously performers and orchestra will have been rehearsing separately. It really is a special moment, because it's that happy, glorious, uplifting moment when all the work you've done in the rehearsal room, and all the work that the musicians have done in their music room comes together. Before that, we've heard nothing. We only heard the lone pianist. Before that, the orchestra has heard no voices, just a guide vocal.

But now – now we're hearing the full score, all the orchestra playing, and they're hearing our voices, singing with them, and we're saying to each other, *This is what we're going to sound like. This is what the audience will hear.*

Oh, it's amazing. Always, on every production I've ever done, a truly life-affirming time, when whatever difficulties you've had in the run-up, whatever arguments you've had, any grievances, all those other bits and pieces of daily life that intrude, just fall away and all you have is the music. That's the business we're in. The business of musical theatre.

The word sitzprobe is derived from the German, meaning 'seated rehearsal' so, we're all seated, although you stand up when it's your turn to sing, and it's slightly amplified so that you can hear yourself, so that you're singing it like it would be in the theatre.

For this particular one, we did it in a place near Westminster, a conference centre opposite the Houses of Parliament. We started out, and I, as usual, was loving it.

Sitting next to me was Roger, and gradually I became aware that things were not great in the world of Roger. For a start, he was shaking. Actually, properly trembling. Next, he was forgetting lines. He was out of pitch. A couple of occasions we had to restart because he fluffed it up.

Looking back, I assumed that I was on the same page as everyone else in my thinking, which was that it didn't really matter that things were going wrong with Roger because everything else was going so right. It didn't matter because we'd get there in the end, everything would work out fine. And I'd be lying if I said anything other than, I loved that sitzprobe.

But no, I wasn't on the same page as everyone else. There were clearly huge question marks over his performance, and no one was more worried than Roger himself.

Chapter 27

Shortly after the sitzprobe, there came a knock at my door, an envoy from the Dorchester where Roger was staying, with a letter for me.

'Darling nephew,' it opened. Well, of course, I knew at once it was from him. It went, 'I hope this won't come as too much of a shock, and you don't hate me too much, but I have decided to withdraw from the production. I'm only dragging all of you down. I don't feel I'm up to doing it, and this show is yours, and I want you to take it and fly with it and have a wonderful hit and never think too badly of me. I wanted to tell you this in person, but the news is about to break, and as an old hand, I know the hotel is going to be surrounded by the hounds and it would make life impossible. Will you please explain everything to the cast from me. I love you all.'

That's probably not it exactly. But pretty much.

And of course, it broke my heart. What a lovely man, what a lovely letter. And, actually, what a brave decision.

On top of that, what a shock. Like I say, I'd been (maybe, in retrospect, naïvely) optimistic about things. Me, I was buoyant, things were happening for me, and not just the press attention, but something else too, something we'll come on to. I'd assumed that whatever problems Roger had, he would see things through, and the more I'd got to know him the more I became certain of that. And, what's more, I really, really wanted to share a stage with Roger Moore. I knew that I was going to get a kick out of it, and I was pretty sure so would the audience.

Roger mentions *Aspects* in his autobiography. He begins by telling of how he appeared on *The Dame Edna Experience!* show, during which he performed a song-and-dance routine – '(You've Either Got or You Haven't Got) Style' – with Les Patterson. According to Rog, Andrew Lloyd Webber saw the show and called him, saying that he wanted to discuss a role in his next production, *Aspects of Love*.

Thereupon, Roger joined the 'lovely cast, headed by young Michael Ball' and seemed to enjoy his experience, which he said was 'like being in rep again'. His recollection is the same as mine, which is that early rehearsals were good, but as opening night loomed, he had started having nightmares about forgetting his lines and having to sing 'without a note to keep me in'.

This was something that had been apparent to all. Roger was confident with an accompanist present to play a note, but had real difficulty finding it himself. As he says, this caused him to feel jittery until a 'final run-through', by which I assume he must mean the sitzprobe, and he 'sensed Andrew wasn't happy'.

There is a bit of audio on YouTube where you can hear

Roger singing 'Other Pleasures' and I will leave you to make up your own mind about it. As for Andrew's reaction to the sitzprobe, I don't recall. Possibly I was like the village idiot at this point, *Aspects*' very own Pollyanna, thinking everything was fine when it clearly wasn't.

'The long and short of it was that Andrew didn't want me to open in the show,' says Roger in his book, adding that although he was disappointed and sad, it was agreed to issue a statement in which he said that he was backing out.

Andrew, meanwhile, told me, 'I think it was Trevor who felt it was not going well. I mean, we all did, but it fell to Trevor to say it. And it was a great shame, because Roger doing "The First Man You Remember" would have been absolutely lovely.'

And so to Trevor, who told me, 'Roger made the plot work perfectly because, yes, he was an older man, but he was a charismatic, handsome, attractive man. So that everything Garnett was writing about just makes wonderful sense.

'I tried with him,' he continued, 'but I think the crisis was to do with the orchestra playing different notes from the singer in order to accompany and present the voice. But Rog was hearing that note and not the note he thought, and then got confused and kept coming in in the wrong key.

'I did say that Rex Harrison found himself in a similar situation when he was rehearsing *My Fair Lady*. I thought that some of it could be semi-spoken.'

It was of course to no avail. As to who made what decision when, I guess you could say there are slightly differing accounts of exactly how Roger came to bow out of *Aspects*, but the bottom line is that whoever decided he wasn't good enough, he wasn't good enough, and he withdrew.

Personally, well, I hope that Roger wasn't fired in the way that he suggests, but if so, then how typical of the man to fall on his sword and take the blame, leave with dignity and in a way that didn't greatly impact the show. A typically classy move on his behalf. That's one way of looking at it. Another way is that he didn't want anyone to know that he wasn't good enough and that Andrew Lloyd Webber had fired him, which would have been slightly embarrassing. We shall probably never know.

Now, for *Aspects*, we had an eight- or nine-week rehearsal time and that sitzprobe took place seven weeks in.

What normally happens after the sitzprobe is that you do a tech rehearsal for Act I, run Act I, then do a tech rehearsal of Act II, run Act II, then run the show again and again, iron out bits that don't work, after which you do the dress rehearsal fully frocked, fully orchestrated, everything done, and then you move into the preview period, which is a set of shows that happen before the press night.

During the previews you're seeing how the show lands with an audience, what works, what doesn't, where the applause points are, where you need to take your foot off the gas and where you need to apply it. What happens is that you do your preview and then go into the next day's rehearsal, making changes and redoing technical rehearsals, but you can't apply any changes you make, because there isn't time for them to be fully orchestrated, which means that you're going on that night to perform an older version of the show while rehearsing a newer version during the day.

And if that sounds confusing to you, then I promise it's not because I haven't explained it very well. It's just because it is in fact very, very confusing.

So although he'd run the show through many times, Roger missed all that (lucky him, in some respects – the tech rehearsals are interminable). He missed the last two weeks of run-in before the opening.

And we, of course, were left without a principal.

Chapter 28

Roger withdrew over the weekend. On Monday we turned up for technical rehearsals and were gathered together. Having had the letter, I knew, of course, as did Trevor and Andrew, who explained the situation to the rest of the company.

Trevor did his best *Henry V*. 'Roger has decided to leave, and though it's sad, we rejoice in the wonderful things we saw him doing, the incredible things we learned from him, and the impact he's had on the show.

'But luckily we have, waiting in the wings, Kevin, who is fully prepped, fully supported and will be ready to step into Roger's shoes as George.'

Yes. Thank God that throughout this whole period, Kevin Colson had been shadowing Roger.

The idea had always been that Roger would have what we call 'walking cover'. Walking cover refers to an actor who is not in the show and is only used when the person they're covering – almost always a principal – is either off for any reason, taken ill, or otherwise indisposed.

So for example, in *Aspects II*, I had my Radio 2 show to consider, and so it was decided that I'd do seven shows a week, not eight, and that we'd get walking cover for me, a performer who would be guaranteed the Monday night show as well as being on call should I be unavailable for any reason. Dave Willetts, my old *Phantom* friend, took that on for us (after a search that went down to the wire). Meanwhile, Dani, who plays Giulietta, wouldn't be doing eight shows, because she's an opera singer and they have to protect their voice – plus she had other commitments – so she also had a walking cover, Soophia Foroughi, who had previously been my backing singer on a number of shows, and is fabulous.

If being a swing is the most difficult job in the theatre, then being a walking cover is the most thankless. You don't get to rehearse with the other turns, you just have to sit there, keep your mouth shut and take notes, being sure to memorise all the moves, listen to Trevor's direction and so on and so forth. Bit of a chore, like I say, but one of those that is essential to get right. You might sit there looking like you're not participating, but people are soon going to know if you spent the hours doodling on a pad and daydreaming about beach holidays.

Kevin Colson didn't have that problem. Kevin was not only talented, he was diligent and engaged. Put it this way, if you really have to lose your principal two weeks before opening, pray you've got someone like Kevin Colson as walking cover.

On hearing the news of Roger's departure, a wave of shock and sadness had swept through the entire company. I don't have to blow smoke up Roger's arse because sadly he'll never read this, but he was absolutely adored by each and every cast and crew member, and everybody wanted to see him on stage and in some cases share it with him. We all wanted him to have the theatrical triumph he so richly deserved.

Even so, it didn't turn into a pity party, because in all honesty, we didn't have time to mourn. We had to get on with things.

Was there ever any talk of cancelling or postponing? No. I mean, what would stop a show going ahead? A strike, perhaps. Maybe if Andrew suddenly decided that he wasn't happy with it and didn't want it performed. Even then it would only be a postponement.

But a turn pulling out? No way. And in our case, we had Kevin. The quiet man, who for weeks had sat barely speaking a word to anyone, was about to step into the spotlight.

Everybody gathered around Kevin to reassure him, 'We've got your back. Anything that you need to be able to do this, we can help you with.' And like the fickle luvvies we are, we moved seamlessly from 'we love you, Roger Moore, it's all about you' to 'we love you, Kevin Colson, it's all about you'.

And Kevin really needed that. He needed as much support and encouragement as existed in the world because his was a truly uphill battle. Firstly, he was stepping into the shoes of Roger Moore, the top-billed artist, James Bond; secondly, although he'd done all his work and knew the role backwards, he still wasn't as drilled as he needed to be, as well rehearsed as Roger had been. Not only did he need to work with other members of the cast in a way that he hadn't been able to up until then, but he also needed to put his own stamp on the part. Kevin was a true pro, so there was no way he was going to step into Roger's shoes and simply do a carbon copy; he knew that he had to have ownership and play George how he saw it, the way that he wanted the part to be played.

Remember that cold sore? Kevin had his own version. A painful tooth abscess that developed close to opening night that, I swear, was a manifestation of the exhaustion, nervous energy and panic he was feeling. Ever the trouper, he was dosed up on every medication known to man, and didn't miss a rehearsal.

The whole Roger-out, Kevin-in situation affected the company in a variety of different ways, but maybe the most profound was a sense that suddenly everything became real. Sitting in the rehearsal room with Roger Moore had been great, but it always felt a bit bonkers, like, *Is this really happening?*

Now there was no Roger and with just two weeks to go, and we were suddenly acutely aware that we were no longer playing and fooling about and basking in the reflected glory of Rog and his Kennington café visits. We had a show to put on. In two weeks' time, an audience would be filing into the auditorium to watch the fruit of our labours – an audience who'd each paid a lot of money to watch Andrew Lloyd Webber's new show, who would be hopped up on advance publicity and tabloid hype and even a number two hit single (and in short order a number 62 chart flop).

No doubt about it, a situation like that has the effect of sharpening your thinking. We became a more solid company. Kevin, after all, was an accomplished musician and had been in musicals, so he understood what we do. He knew the language. He had an innate understanding of the creation of character through song. That gave the rest of us security that we hadn't had under Roger – a knowledge that we were no longer having to carry someone who lacked our musical theatre experience, someone who needed help finding the note. Out went the sheer charisma and star power we'd been enjoying before, but in came a new creative energy, a new dynamic. Kevin went from being diligent but basically invisible to welcomed with open arms by the rest of the company, and he responded by being a brilliant company member and, ultimately, a superb George. I mean, Roger had brought something extraordinary to the role, simply by dint of being Roger Moore. But what you got with Kevin was a brilliant all-rounder, and he turned out to be literally faultless in the role.

He was a very tough act to follow.

*

I didn't see Roger for a while after that. He didn't come to see *Aspects*, and of course I don't blame him for that; it would have been very hard for him. But we would phone and we wrote Christmas cards and emails, and he sent me the most beautiful letter on opening night. I think the next time I saw him in person was at the opening of *Sunset Boulevard*, which would have been about two years later.

After that, we stayed in touch. He talked to me about his autobiography. 'You're in this, is that all right, dear boy?'

'Of course it is, Roger, I'm thrilled.' (And I was.)

He called me nephew, and to me he was always Uncle Rog. His work for UNICEF was legendary, and he got me doing some stuff for them, narrating kids' stories. It was around then that he emailed to say he was a little poorly – 2017, this would have been. Not long after, his death from lung and liver cancer was announced. He was 89, so a grand old age and, boy, what a life.

As for me, I was proud to have known him and proud to have called him a friend. For those few weeks at the beginning of the *Aspects* rehearsals we were joined at the hip and I'll treasure the memory of our morning sessions with Gillian, and our surreal visits to the Kennington café.

You know what it's like in this business, you're best pals but things end, and everyone goes off to do their own thing. It was pretty much the same with me and him, but I always thought very, very fondly of him, and I'm pretty sure that he thought fondly of me. Or I like to think so anyway.

*

Meanwhile, another thing that happened in the wake of Roger's departure, I became the focus of the show so I can't really complain. But at the same time we were conscious that many of the audience would have been hoping, expecting, and indeed *had paid* to see Roger Moore. Fortunately, I think that a lot of the disappointment was mitigated by the fact that 'Love Changes' had been a hit so there was still a bit of a star factor going in, and sure enough, in Roger's absence, I stepped up to the plate to handle even more of the press duties. Thankfully, I didn't get a grilling every time I sat down for an interview. Like everybody else, the press adored Roger, and there was so much goodwill towards him that they didn't really go after him. There was no sense of wanting to sniff out the big story.

The problem for me was workload. Stepping up to the plate meant that I was constantly in demand, and I could feel myself becoming isolated. I had mates from drama school. Still my best mates, actually, Ben and Phil. I had friends that I'd made from *Les Misérables* and from other shows. There was Sarah and Tracey, flatmates who were also in *Godspell* with me. I was seeing less and less of them, and when I did see them, I would be, like, 'Life's great. I'm riding the crest of a wave, what could possibly be wrong?' Because the last thing the world needs is somebody whingeing about a number two single and life as Lloyd Webber's new protégé, when the truth was that I was struggling a bit.

The experience of my breakdown was always uppermost in my mind, of course. It sat there sometimes, like a dark spectre, reminding me how catastrophically wrong things could so easily go.

Luckily, help was about to arrive. Help, and much more besides.

Chapter 29

The reason I'm writing about the life cycle of *Aspects of Love* – and at least part of the reason I ended up revisiting it – is because it was so momentous the first time around. There are so many reasons that *Aspects* changed my life, and chief among them was that at the same time as becoming bezzies with James Bond, something else was happening. I was meeting the love of my life.

'We've had a request in from *Newsroom South East*. They want Cathy McGowan to interview you.'

The call had come in early in rehearsals for *Aspects*. I knew Cathy, of course. Wait, no. I knew *of* her. I knew that she was Cathy McGowan – the ex-presenter of *Ready Steady Go!* who now helmed a weekly showbiz spot on *Newsroom South East*. But I said no. There was too much other stuff going on, I protested. Not enough time.

I still don't know why I turned it down, to be honest. Roger was still in the show at this point so though I was busy, I wasn't run ragged just yet. Probably I was a bit intimidated. Firstly, I thought, she's Cathy McGowan; she's going to be a piece of work. Secondly, I knew the grade of guest she normally had on her show, people like Elton John, Paul McCartney, Anthony Hopkins and Roger Moore, of course . . . I mean, a proper high calibre. Not Michael Ball. I pictured myself saying yes, going there like a lamb to the slaughter and being the subject of a hatchet job. No, thanks.

The next thing was that I found myself at Wayne Sleep's studio, which marked my return for the first time since my momentous masterclasses with Trevor Nunn, and, possibly in unconscious celebration of that fact, I'd gone for the double denim – jeans and a denim shirt – as well as a blazer.

Cathy was there, too, filming a piece on *Aspects* with Andrew and Don. Andrew introduced us, and it was such a positive atmosphere that I agreed to do an interview with her and sing a bit of 'Love Changes' accompanied by Mike Reed on the piano. We didn't stop laughing the whole time.

Cathy was also scheduled to do an interview with Roger as part of the production. She said to Roger, 'Why don't we get Michael to come in on it as well?'

Most interviewers, having landed such a big fish as Roger, couldn't ask that of the catch. But most interviewers wouldn't have known what she knew, which was that Roger would be more than happy to budge up and share the limelight.

'Oh, what a lovely idea,' he said, 'let's make it a lunch,' before offering to call his great friends Lorenzo and Mara Berni, owner of San Lorenzo, a beautiful classic Italian restaurant in Beauchamp Place in London.

Roger asked San Lorenzo to deliver some food to Awful

House, so it was just the three of us, with Roger using the interview to big me up and promote me, something he did all the time, turning his opportunities into mine.

Meanwhile, my workload issues were intensifying. My life at that time was just *insane*. You know how I said that you never catch up on yourself? Well, that's true – it's true even if you're not Michael Ball in 1989, and in 1989 I was very much Michael Ball. I appreciated it, don't get me wrong. But at the same time, I could feel my life slipping a little, as though it were being taken out of my hands. Like I was handing responsibility to others. That weird video, for example. A song in the charts. Constantly having to field requests for press. As my friends receded and my sense of self decreased, the spectre grew.

Meanwhile, having got on so well at the lunch, Cathy and I had become what you might call 'phone buddies' and were speaking more and more frequently, sometimes late into the night. She became my sanctuary. She was the lighthouse steering me away from the jagged rocks, and as a result, I clung to her a little. Because she was covering *Aspects*, she understood exactly what I was going through, so I was able to talk to her about it and learn from her. Roger, bless him, with his 'always tell lies in interviews' advice paled in comparison next to Cathy. Truly she had the wisdom born of experience. God knows what I brought to the Cathy McGowan party. Probably nothing, apart from a love of toilet humour and a bunch of unsold CDs of 'The First Man You Remember'. But what she brought to the Michael Ball party was beyond measure. She was a source of strength, a person with whom I could have a lot of fun but who also knew exactly – better than anyone not directly involved in the show – the sort of pressures I was under.

My problem was that I wasn't being selective enough. The guys at Really Useful wanted to promote the show, that was their job, and as far as they were concerned, the more publicity they got, the better. 'Will you come to open an envelope?'

I'd be like, 'Yes, of course, my lovely. Where is the envelope? Should I bring my own envelope-opening equipment? Would they like me to sing "Love Changes Everything" while I open the envelope?'

Real people-pleasing stuff. These days, of course, we'd go on about it being bad for my mental health. Back in 1989 we called it being fucking knackered.

It was one of the first pieces of advice that Cathy ever gave me, but by no means the last. 'Don't say yes to everything. Value yourself. Understand that everyone will want a piece of you. Everyone will try and get whatever they can from you, but you need to know that you're worth more than that. Don't just be fodder.'

Oh my God, that was freeing. Just to be given that ammunition: *you can say no.*

So, yes, my sanctuary. A godsend.

Chapter 30

As though being the love of my life wasn't enough, Cathy has been tremendously supportive in my career.

Back in 1992, riding high on the success of *Aspects of Love*, I was given the opportunity to record what would be my debut album. And with something like that, you're as excited as a puppy bringing the ball back to its owner, tail wagging, desperate for praise. *Look, I've made a new album, what do you think?* And because it's your new album that you've spent ages slaving to make, you of course think it's bloody ace, and you expect your loved ones to think so, too, except . . .

'Shocking.'

That was her verdict. 'It's really shocking. It'll end any hope you have of a recording career. You need to redo it.'

I asked her, 'Do I need a good agent?'

She said, 'No, you need a good lawyer.'

She told me that I'd recorded the album as though I were performing a musical. Projecting. Emoting. Forget what you know, she said, a whole different skill is needed for an album, and with that in mind she introduced me to a producer, one of her best friends, Mike Smith, who had been the main singer and writer with the Dave Clark Five. He and I got on like a house on fire and thanks to his guidance and Cathy's advice, I learned what needs to happen in a recording studio. I learned that you don't need to belt it out. I learned that there are certain songs best kept for the stage, certain songs that work well on albums. I spoke to my label, Polydor, and we scrapped that first attempt, agreeing that I should make another, this time with Mike.

That was the time that Eurovision was offered to me. I had an idea to get the record company behind me by going on *Wogan* every night to perform a different song from the album, with the nation voting on which song should represent us at Eurovision.

Now, Eurovision is a poisoned chalice, or can be, but I wanted to take a risk and thought it would be a good way to promote the album. Sure enough, 'One Step Out of Time' was chosen, I did Eurovision, came second, really credible – well done the public for choosing that song – released the album and embarked on my first solo tour.

The album got to number one. I sold out the Hammersmith Apollo, and my career went on a different trajectory.

And all of that happened thanks to Cathy giving me unvarnished advice, good advice. Introducing me to Mike, being a sounding board, not a 'yes woman'. I knew by then that I didn't want to be a jobbing actor in the musical theatre stable. I knew that the only way I was going to make a mark and capitalise on the success that I'd had early doors was to diversify. So, an album. Eurovision. Then a TV series and more albums. I guess you could say a move into a more light entertainment sphere.

As a career path it has occasionally had its downsides. Remember the advice Trevor gave me, how I couldn't combine the two? He wasn't 100 per cent wrong. I recall desperately wanting to do *Carousel* at The National, the Nick Hytner production, and they wouldn't even see me. Wouldn't even audition me because, they said, I brought too much baggage. That was a bit of a blow. Not getting *Sunset* in 1991 was a bit of a blow (I should point out, however, that I did eventually get to play Joe Gillis).

The knock-backs sharpened my thinking a little. And with Cathy's help, I've been able to take the wheel of my own career, use that 'baggage' to my own advantage, so in the long term the records, TV and my radio show have allowed me to make a name for myself in the wider world. And in fact, seven years after *Aspects of Love*, I received a letter from the producer Bill Kenwright who'd just seen Stephen Sondheim's *Passion* on Broadway and on his ticket had written, 'Get the rights and Michael Ball.'

And that was what he did. He obtained the rights to stage *Passion* on the West End, and then he got me.

So that was cool. Rather than my theatre career being dead and buried, the first thing I did going back to the West End after *Aspects* was a brand-new Stephen Sondheim musical. I felt that it wouldn't necessarily be a commercial success, but it was credible, and not only would I have my name above the title, top billing, but that simply being in the show would bring people into the theatre, fans who wouldn't normally have come to see a Stephen Sondheim. That's baggage. But a good kind.

Still, there are times when I wondered if the rug had been pulled out from under my feet. I thought that I might have to wave a reluctant goodbye to the world of West End and Broadway, but I've been lucky enough to always find something, a new direction and do something that people weren't expecting. *Sweeney Todd*, *Hairspray* and, of course, *Aspects II*. And I swear that the reason I've been able to do that, the reason I've had the strength to do what was needed and the advice to do it right was because I had Cathy, and the knowledge that if she thinks something is a good idea, it probably is. And if she thinks that something is shocking, well, then she's probably right about that, too.

Chapter 31

'Stephen Sondheim used to hang around a lot, didn't he?'

So said Charles Hart when I interviewed him. ('Michael, did you use your Dictaphone?' 'No, I used my finger like always.')

He was referring, not to anything untoward, but to those times when the writers of a production haunt the rehearsal process. Some do, Sondheim being an example. Some don't.

I was asking if he remembered whether he and Don spent much time in rehearsals when we first did *Aspects*. Personally, I couldn't remember seeing much of them at all. Trevor was there all of the time, of course. Andrew was there an awful lot as well, although he also used to spend time with the orchestra. Gillian and, later, Maria. But Don and Charles?

'No, I don't think so. Well, hardly at all. I don't think it's proper, really. It's useful only in so far as you learn how to improve the show, and of course Stephen was a restless soul, wanted to tinker all the time, but I think for the rest of us you try and get it as right as you can when the script is printed. You want to give it to the actors and the director as a finished thing and let them try and make it work. If they can't make it work, they come back to you. I think that's probably the better, happier process, otherwise it gets heated.'

It's also a point worth making that in plenty of shows the writers are on a kind of hierarchical level with the performers. They're hired hands. That's how it was with *Aspects*. Steering the ship were Trevor and Andrew.

'Oh yes, we're quite low down the pecking order,' agreed Charles. 'But we do something a lot of people can't do, so they have to come to us, which I like. I like the fact that we're specialists.'

There was quite a lot of work done on *Aspects* at the workshop stage. It was Don who told me that the best lyricists are the ones who are economical, who find the right three words, not the right 17 words, a philosophy to which Charles also adheres. Now, one thing we know about Trevor is that he is very much not a person who uses three where 17 will do. One can only imagine how those sessions must have gone. Another thing I know about Trevor is that he does like to change the words – or at least try to. He couldn't do that with Shakespeare, of course. Chances are the frustrated lyricist in him would have wanted to go to town on the work of Don and Charles.

I'm hypothesising, of course. I'm sure that the workshop process was a time of great diplomacy and mutual working together stuff.

Mind you, Don and Charles must have spent *some* time in rehearsals. Together we remembered that there was a song added during this period, 'There is More to Love', an Act II number sung by Kathleen as Giulietta. Up until that point, Giulietta had plenty to do in Act I, but after ice creams slightly fell away. She took the lead on 'Hand Me the Wine and the Dice', and that was it. Andrew, who quite rightly felt she had slightly disappeared in Act II, brought her into it that way. It's a beautiful song, and as Charles said, beautifully orchestrated, a way of reminding us that what we are watching is part way between a West End musical and an operetta. Fitting, then, that our opera star, Dani ('Opera's coolest soprano,' according to *The New York Times Magazine*) should be singing it in *Aspects II.*

Back to 1989, and I guess you could say that the final stages of rehearsals went about as well as they could, considering that we'd lost our principal. Shortly after the sitzprobe we left our rehearsal rooms at Awful House, waved a fond farewell to the Kennington café and moved to the Prince of Wales Theatre in London's glittering West End. There we'd have two weeks of tech rehearsals before opening for previews. That was the plan anyhow.

Now, tech rehearsals. Without question the easiest time I've ever had doing a tech run was *Hairspray*, because it had spent five years on Broadway, been on the road and was fully bedded in. Everybody knew exactly what they were doing. We came in, did our first technical run-through, and it was seamless. So seamless, in fact, that they said, 'We'll have a day off. After that, come in, and we'll do an open dress.'

An 'open dress' meant that we would perform in front of friends and family and various invited people. I remember it so well. The audience was gagging for it. Couldn't wait. And from the moment that the overture started the show was absolutely immaculate.

So if you've got *Hairspray* on one end of the scale, our *Aspects* tech rehearsals were over to the other end. Waaay over. And as those 'two weeks' of tech rehearsals went on and on, everything that could go wrong did go wrong, from the smallest thing (that trapdoor) to the biggest, where the pitfalls of the ambitious, widescreen staging of the piece became apparent. It'd be like, okay, start. Something goes wrong. Stop. Fix that thing. Start again. Something else goes wrong. Stop. Fix. Start. Stop. Repeat till fade.

And because of that, we never really managed to catch a wave with the rehearsal. There was no flow to what we were doing. It's a situation that creates a domino effect. Because things go wrong, you can't create impetus. Because you can't create impetus you start to lose sight of everything you've done in the rehearsal room. All that stuff you worked on to deal with character and story, about bringing Andrew's beautiful music to life, doing justice to Don and Charles's lyrics, executing Gillian's moves perfectly, realising Trevor's vision. All of that, it all goes, reduced to, 'How do I do this quick change?' 'Where are we going next?' 'Where do the chairs go?' 'Who's bringing that on?'

And mostly, 'Why isn't this bloody thing working?'

We had actors not making it back on stage because of costume changes, props not being in the right place, everything grinding to a halt because the technology wasn't working, travelators failing to come on. We had these massive, slatted screens all the way across the stage that were meant to go on and off and even revolve, but they just didn't work. Like *This is Spinal Tap* the musical theatre version, you're there trying to perform while stagehands are working to get these slatted screens to work, and you keep on going, trying to do your thing, until they give up, yell, 'Cut, stop, stop, we can't leave until this works,' and it takes hours to reset these things, hours to get them to work.

And then, of course, that bloody car. Half of it stuck through a wall. Windscreen wipers going. Oh, it was bloody awful. We just couldn't get a run of the piece.

At times like that, it gets very tense, very pressurised, and tempers can get frayed. You've got the previews looming, when actual people will see the show. You feel as though you're never going to be ready. You start to seriously consider the possibility that you might fall flat on your face. That you might just *fail.*

Chapter 32

Things going tits up is bad for everyone. I mean, you all have something riding on it; the success or failure of a show reflects on every member of the company. In our case, none so much as Andrew. He was, well, he was Andrew Lloyd Webber, the *Phantom* man. The composer with the golden touch. But it's that tall poppy thing again. You've got half of the country rubbing their hands with glee at the prospect of you messing up; you've got the other half of the country to whom you represent something important, a cultural moment, a great British export.

Back then, of course, I was way more wrapped up in my own particular set of problems, but I asked him recently how it felt to be in that position. 'The thing that one has to remember about musicals, and this is the most important thing that people don't remember, is that it's not just me,' he said, 'I'm the music, of course. But it's the words. It's the choreography. It's the direction. It is the performance. It's the set. The lighting. All of these things coming together and, actually, if you look at musical theatre over the years, the number of times in my lifetime that all of these things have come together I could probably count on one hand. I mean, the really great ones, when I think of, in my case, *Evita*, *The Phantom of the Opera*, definitely. But elsewhere, you think of *The Lion King*, you think of *Hamilton*. Very few where almost every single aspect comes together. So when you're looking at something and it's not quite working, well you can be sure that the score is working but you're not sure why the other things haven't quite come together.'

Philosophical and laid-back though he sounds here, I hope he won't mind me mentioning that I've seen Andrew very, very frustrated when things haven't been going well. It's the perfectionist in him. He lives by a code, hates cutting corners and despises seeing bad theatre. It was one of the reasons that he moved into production with the Really Useful Group – a frustration with seeing things done badly. 'One of the things one has to try and remember – and something that some people in the theatre forget these days – is that we don't have a divine right to be on stage, or have our work on stage.'

You've got to work for it, in other words. You can't coast.

And he's passionate about that – passion that can occasionally boil over. There was one occasion during those fraught *Aspects* tech rehearsals when Mike Reed was conducting and things were going badly, when suddenly we heard a scream from the back, 'Stop, this is shit,' and Andrew came storming down the auditorium, grabbed the master score from Mike as though it was a baby in need of protection from a marauding grizzly bear, and said, 'We're not doing this. We're not doing this.'

That's when it gets scary. Forget Roger Moore leaving.

When the composer starts threatening to pull his score is when you really start to worry for the future of the show.

But with Andrew he burns hot and quickly. Whatever it was that provoked his outburst – cold feet, fear, sheer frustration – things got quickly sorted and we moved from a state of authorial dissatisfaction to problem-solving mode. Okay, so we have these problems, what can we do to resolve them? Again, you can draw a comparison between tech rehearsal problems and Roger leaving. There's a moment of worry, a collective gulp, and then it's gone and you move on to dealing with it. The mark of a good company is not so much how well you operate when things are going well, it's more how you work when the shit hits the fan.

I'm lucky. I'm not the shouting, 'ejecting toys from prams' type. I get incredibly positive and funny and chipper and try to keep people going. Pollyanna again, that's me. 'There's nothing to worry about,' I'll chirrup. 'Things are fine. Hello sky, hello grass . . .' I might be dying on the inside – and was – but that was my way of dealing with it.

Anyway, it was a tech rehearsal. They always go wrong. Virtually every production I've ever worked on, the tech rehearsal was terrible. And this was no different. Just maybe a bit worse.

During the tech period, the performers were working from 10am until 10pm every day, but stage management, stage crew, Trevor, lighting and sound would be in at 8am and not leaving until midnight, later maybe, practically living there. Everyone was getting tired, everyone's judgement was becoming skewed. The producers were concerned about budgets but nothing much was getting sorted. People were literally saying, 'Guys, we have to open at some point,' which is really not what you want to hear.

So the first thing we did was delay first previews. You don't want to do that. You really don't want to do that. It's like telling the world that something is rotten in Denmark. The next thing we did was put back the opening night. And you don't want to do that, either.

The press loved it, of course. If they'd been almost uncharacteristically laid-back about Roger leaving, well, now they started making up for it with stories that implied *Aspects* was if not a sinking ship, then a ship that was listing badly.

At this stage, huge changes were occurring, scenes were being cut or rewritten or restaged. Now we were doing that juggling act of not knowing which was the old version and which was the new. Scenes would come out and then be put back in. Things that had worked suddenly stopped. Costumes, for example.

So, yes, we worked like Trojans and, having delayed those first previews, everything shunting back a bit, we got there at last. We finally had a tech run-through which, while not perfect was at least most of the way there.

After that, what usually happens is that you undergo ten days of previews, during which you have that confusing period of rehearsing a 'new' show during the day while you're still performing the old one at night. The preview shows themselves can be quite chaotic. The audience knows that the show isn't locked; it's not unknown for things to stop while something is worked out. I can't remember if that ever happened during *Aspects*, just that we had to delay previews by at least a week to work out the millions of technical issues. Make the changes that needed to be made. Oh, and at some point somebody mentioned that the Queen was coming along to one of the previews. No pressure, then.

Chapter 33

After previews, you go on to the press night, which in the UK is also the opening night. On press night a show is locked, which means it's now the show that you're prepared to unveil to the public, the one you'll take forward.

It's also practically the last time you'll see the top-line creative team; they're not needed any more. The show is frozen. Left behind is a resident director whose job is to ensure that everything runs smoothly, but as for the likes of Trevor and Andrew, it's 'lie down in a darkened room' time. They'll need it, especially after the sheer trauma of the opening night. Why? Because traditionally, the opening night is the worst night of the run. Yes, you've got through previews and you have your show, but still, there's a hype and a pressure to it, which inevitably affects the finished product.

Which means it's something of a pity that you have press night so early on in the run. That's the nature of the beast, I'm afraid. You need that initial publicity explosion. We can have all kinds of conversations about the importance of reviews (and to let you into a little secret, by the end of this book we will have done exactly that), but you need your reviews, or it is certainly *believed* that you need your reviews – in order to get the audience in.

Saying that, it's interesting that they do things differently on Broadway. There, the critics come over two nights of previews prior to the opening night. The advantage of this is twofold: firstly, the critics can form a more balanced opinion by basing it on two performances rather than one very stressed and pressurised night; secondly, the opening night itself is just a straight-up celebration and thus a lot more civilised for the performers.

Our system in the UK makes the press / opening night a doubly weird event because of the audience demographic. You have friends and family of the company, all willing you to succeed; you have the business, who are far more interested in who else is there and where the after party's happening than they are in what's happening on the stage; and you have the critics who will sit sucking lemons. And when the show is over, they literally run for the exits, not bothering to applaud – very rude – just focused on getting their review in for the next day's edition.

So, very weird, and not the best atmosphere in which to stage what – in theory – should be the best show you can manage. (But like I say, usually ends up being the worst.)

Meanwhile the company is absolutely exhausted. We'll have been in since ten that morning, rehearsed right through the day, put in whatever changes needed making and then opened in the evening, gone to the party afterwards, normally just for a couple of drinks, making the rounds etc., and then having to do it all again.

Oh, the second night. Absolutely horrendous. Purgatory, darlings. You've had all that adrenaline coursing through you from the opening night and then, with no time off at all, you have to do it all again, added to which you'll no doubt have more press to contend with.

The good thing is that the show keeps improving. It's all about rhythm, about understanding the whole process, making the show's runtime as smooth as it can be and, invariably, getting better and better.

Occasionally one of the creatives will pop in. You'll hear from the resident director that 'Trevor is going to be in tonight taking notes', or 'Andrew is popping in', and afterwards those notes will be relayed to you. If you're a principal then Trevor or Andrew will pop back to your dressing room in order to give you the notes in person, otherwise they might gather the company together on the stage or even make an announcement over the tannoy (that is, if it's good news).

Chapter 34

So, with *Aspects* the previews started off quite badly, and we were still battling tech problems at the same time as making changes to the show itself. One of the major alterations during that period was placing a reprise of 'Love Changes Everything' at the end. If you saw the first few previews, and my apologies if you did, you may remember that the show ended with a reprise of 'Hand Me the Wine and the Dice', but while that's certainly an ending, and for the story, may be the *right* ending, it wasn't working. It was as though the finale was too abrupt, and the audience were looking at one another thinking, *Oh? Is that it?* And then going into this slightly delayed applause.

Now, what happened was that my two fan club ladies, Gill and Maureen, who have been with me since *Phantom* days, actually approached Don Black in the foyer and said to him, 'You have to end the show with Michael singing "Love Changes Everything". You do know that, don't you?'

They love to tell me that. They go, 'I don't know if it helped change everybody's mind, but the next time we saw it, and you were finishing with "Love Changes Everything", we sort of knew.' Personally, I'm marking that one up as a Gill-and-Maureen win.

At the same time, we were still beset by various technical issues – the car, the screens, the bloody trapdoor – while looming was the knowledge that we were due this visit from the Queen, some kind of gala charity night just ahead of the opening.

This had put the cat among the pigeons for several reasons. Firstly, the Queen. *She is the Queen.* Or was. Secondly, the show was still very hinky and ragged around the edges; we hadn't even opened to the press yet. Thirdly, we had a same-sex kiss between Rose and Giulietta. We were like, 'Should we cut the lesbian kiss?' 'Are we going to get in trouble for allowing the Queen to see the kiss?' 'Should we contact the Palace and warn them what's in the show?'

After which we came to our senses. 'Nah, she's probably seen far worse in the stables.' And, indeed, if she was at all shocked then she certainly gave no sign of it when we were presented to her afterwards. Nobody was dragged off to the Tower; Andrew still got his knighthood.

That reminds me, there was another gala charity night for The Variety Club of Great Britain. None of the performers were invited to the reception in the foyer afterwards; it was basically just so the great and the good could wear their very best bib and tucker, eat Ferrero Rocher and raise money for The Variety Club. Cathy was going, 'You've got to come.'

I said, 'But I can't, I haven't been invited, and anyway, I'm wearing dungarees.'

'No, they'll love meeting you,' she insisted.

So I trotted down from my dressing room to the foyer, wearing my dungarees, and it looked like I was making a political statement, like I was a member of Chumbawamba. Mortifying, at first, but I ended up loving it.

Anyway, the other funny thing about the Queen coming for the gala night was that her visit marked the very first time – *literally the first* – that the show went well.

'And I remember,' said Andrew, 'the word around town was that *Aspects of Love* was a disaster, but on the front page of *The Times* the next day there was a story, something like, "If you think *Aspects of Love* is a disaster, think again." Whoever had written it had been at the charity preview the night before and was saying it was a massively important musical.'

Then came the reviews.

A good number of them seemed to complain that *Aspects of Love* was essentially a critic-proof show. 'This is one time when reviews may well be irrelevant,' snarked *The Los Angeles Times*. 'Lloyd Webber, superstar, must be laughing all the way to the bank.'

They were right, to some extent: opening in April, we were fully booked for months ahead, right up until Christmas and beyond, so of course you might imagine that we were feeling a bit like 'bugger what the critics think, we're a hit anyway'.

But in truth, it doesn't really work like that. Show me a theatre person who doesn't care about reviews and I'll show you a liar. Andrew and Trevor claimed never to read reviews, which sounds like a deflection tool to me, something to rank alongside Roger's 'I always lie in interviews' spiel. I don't believe it, in other words.

Elsewhere, most of the critics found something to really like in the show, just that they didn't all like the same thing. Some of them thought it was Andrew's best-ever score, others found it anodyne and repetitive. Most seemed to agree that the story was flawed, that it depends on coincidences and never really gets beneath the surface of its subject matter, that it was asking too much of the story to span a period of 17 years and encompass more than 40 scene changes. Some really got into the expansive nature of it. Some really liked my poor performance, others thought I was eclipsed by Diana and Kevin.

I mean, you take them with a pinch of salt. You realise that the chap from the *Daily Telegraph* who thinks the show is 'certainly Andrew Lloyd Webber's best so far', is just as entitled to his opinion as Milton Shulman of the *Standard* who thought it, 'a mannered, rather precious operetta . . . Singularly lacking in real passion'.

At least most of the critics seemed to appreciate and admire Andrew's desire to do something a bit different, staging a much more human show than his previous spectaculars. As the guy from the *Guardian* said, it explores 'the human heart rather than the possibilities of high-tech scenery', although of course he added that it was 'a beguiling, fitfully pleasing musical, rather than a perfect one', while *The Times* seemed to sum up the general mixed-bag feeling by calling it 'a well-crafted show' that also suffered from having 'timid and uninteresting' music.

The thing is that *Aspects* – then and now – is a challenging prospect. Its whirlwind of love affairs are either dazzling or baffling, depending on who's watching (and maybe how receptive they're feeling when they watch it). The first thing it does is confound your expectations by not being Andrew Lloyd Webber's *Love, Actually*. Richard Curtis it most certainly isn't. After that, there's a certain amount of having to use your noodle, letting yourself be carried forward by events on stage and maybe even, at times, allowing yourself a little willing suspension of disbelief. Sometimes, when a critic or audience member doesn't quite get what they're seeing they'll take against it, and that's fair enough. Quite understandable, really.

Anyhow, although we had a couple of marks on the debit column, we had enough in the credit column to pull out some praise for the poster. Did the bad reviews affect us? I honestly think not. We just kept on keeping on.

Chapter 35

Tell you what was a challenge. Hitting that note at the end of 'Love Changes'. I had to do it eight shows a week, twice on Thursdays, twice on Saturdays. It's tough because you've done the whole show, you're knackered, and then you have to hit what I'm convinced is the hardest note in the history of musical theatre: the big B-flat.

In Act I the big ending to 'Love Changes' is in A-flat, but in Act II it's in B-flat, which to the layman means higher and harder. They're both long and loud, but the A-flat is comfortable, B-flat is opera, tenor territory, and I'm a baritone.

Tough, then. Added to which, I smoked a lot in those days, which is not the best idea when you have that note to reach every night. What happens is that you develop what we call your 'chops', which is when your voice understands what it needs to do in order to sustain the note, and thanks to that, I got it pretty much every night. Okay, sometimes it might have been shorter than others, if I was unwell or just super, super tired. But mostly, I nailed it.

Talking of those big moments. You know 'The Music of the Night' in Phantom? I was always terrified of ever being asked to sing that one. It ends with that line, '*You alone can make my song take flight. Help me make the music of the night,*' which as the singer you're supposed to start and then hold all the way through the orchestral phrase, but in a high, floating tone, not belted out.

At least one Phantom, who shall remain nameless, God love him, was so clever; he'd sometimes sing, '*Help me make the music of the ni . . .*'

His mouth would be open, he'd be doing the expansive arm acting, and you'd swear that you could hear him sustain the line. But of course he wasn't singing at all. You just *thought* he was. Genius. Absolute genius.

Sadly, I didn't have that option with 'Love Changes Everything'. It's the big full-throated final note whether you like it or not.

I didn't always remember the words during the run. On a wet Wednesday when you've been doing it for a long time you tend to rely on muscle memory; you're hardly thinking about what you're doing, and that's when things can go wrong. On one occasion I went out to start the show, Kathy Rowe McAllen was on stage, sitting with her back to the audience, and I could see her looking at me as I started singing, '*Love, Love changes everything, hands and faces, earth and sky,*' and then that thing happened in my brain, almost like a return of the dreaded panic attacks, where I went blank, and there were no words where there should have been words, and nothing else instead.

So I sang, '*Love, love changes everything. Hands and faces, earth and sky*,' again.

And then I sang, '*Love, love changes everything. Hands and faces, earth and sky*,' again, again.

And the words still wouldn't come, so I sang, '*Yes, love – love changes everything. Hands and faces, earth and sky*,' again, again, again.

All the time screaming inside, thinking, *What's the next line?* As though I was going to be stuck on the opening forever. Seasons would pass, governments would change, flared trousers would go in and out of style, and I'd still be here on the stage at the Prince of Wales Theatre, singing, '*Love, love changes everything. Hands and faces, earth and sky*.'

Seeking help from angels, I looked to Kathy. But she, *the cow*, just sat there laughing, watching me sweat. Oh, Christ, I thought. I'm done for.

'*Love, love changes everything. Hands and faces, earth and sky*.'

What saved me was a little old lady on the front row. She sat with shopping bags around her feet, evidently aware that I was stuck in Groundhog verse, and as I looked at her, she began mouthing the words to me. That was how I got the second verse, by watching her.

She saved my life, that lady. She really did.

Apart from that moment making a funny story and giving Kathy a good laugh, it also became a bit of a teaching moment for me. The thing with me is that I always come out with something; even when the words won't come, some noise will come out of my mouth. I'll invent a lyric or make something up.

In *Phantom*, there's a scene at the mausoleum where the

Phantom is firing fireballs at me and Christine. I was supposed to sing *'Angel of darkness seize this torment,'* but instead I went, *'Angel of snardar stum dum toilet.'*

Angel of snardar stum dum toilet!

Could they sing after that? Ho ho, no way. They couldn't sing another note. It just turned into another ballet. But the point is that something comes out – mostly.

What made that old lady moment different was me freezing. The sense that my performer's instinct had temporarily gone AWOL. And there had been a time when a hiccup like that would have been a real panic attack trigger moment that would have destroyed me, absolutely destroyed me. But because of these little beta blockers I thought to myself, *I'm not going to have a panic attack. I've just forgotten the words, that's all.*

Like reaching the cash machine and momentarily forgetting your pin. And then remembering. Like switching on your coffee machine in the morning and having a brain fart. 'How does this work again?' And then doing it.

It was just that. Nothing more than that. I was able to let it go, see the funny side and make it an amusing anecdote, rather than allowing it to be the beginning of a spiral into despair.

I no longer take the beta blockers – I stopped them quite early on in my career. But from that period has evolved my entire philosophy when it comes to freezing on stage, making mistakes and so on. It's not that I don't take it seriously, but at the same time I allow myself to understand that it's a live show and things can go wrong in a live show. Sometimes the audience will notice it, sometimes they won't. You'll notice it, of course. But you just move on past it. The show is a train, and if you're on it, you stay on it, you don't fall off it, it's not going to stop so you just put it away, look at it later, get yourself where you're meant to be and keep moving forward.

So that was a great lesson and funny as hell. I also knew that if the roles had been reversed, I would have been killing myself laughing, as I have done on many occasions when people have gone wrong. But thank God for looking out into the audience, and thank God for a little old lady with shopping bags around her feet, who knew all the words to 'Love Changes Everything'.

Chapter 36

In 1989, *Aspects of Love* in the West End was a real celebrity magnet. I remember the day that Eartha Kitt, who at the time was starring in *Follies* for Cameron Mackintosh, came to see us and sat in the front row. She was wearing one of those turbans that ladies of a certain age seem to like, and was looking quite dishevelled. I could see her as I came out to do the opening, 'Love Changes Everything'. I launched into the song, and as though triggered by some kind of Blofeld brainwashing experiment, her chin dropped and she fell asleep. And one thing I now know about Eartha Kitt. She snored. Loudly. She snored throughout the entire show. Well, we'd had worse reviews.

Another of our celebrity guests was Princess Diana, who never came in any official capacity but because she fancied seeing the show. It was well known that she was a *Phantom* fan and she must have taken to *Aspects* as well, because she paid us several visits, during which she'd sit in the second or third row but never come backstage. Far be it from me to say that she was also a Michael Ball fan, but just between us, I was told that albums I'd made were found in her record collection. Not boasting or anything. Yes, okay then, boasting.

I suppose you'd have to say that her visits were practically incognito. She would have phoned the office, or more likely asked a minion to phone the office, and was then brought into the auditorium and taken out afterwards. Not quite your average audience member, and it wasn't like she tried to disguise herself or anything. That famous Diana baseball cap never made an appearance, and it wasn't as though she could sit anonymously in the audience without being seen: as performers we were drawn to her, and so were the rest of the audience. It was like there was this glow in the audience. In fact, the only time I've seen anything remotely like that glow was when Paul and Linda McCartney came to *Les Misérables* and we in the cast basically projected the entire show just at those two.

'Diana was capable of being quite the groupie,' said Trevor when I interviewed him. 'She came to the Barbican on two occasions to see *Les Misérables*, and then on four occasions to see it when we were at the Palace. I'd get tipped off when she was going to be in the audience so I'd talk to her in the interval. She brought William and Harry to see *Les Misérables* actually.'

Although I never met Princess Diana on *Aspects of Love* duty, I was introduced to her at a couple of functions and the thing that everybody says about her, that effect she had on people, I can tell you was absolutely true. She was radiant and funny and did the old flirty-eye bit, and like everybody else who came into her orbit, I fell in love, just a little bit. She had the most incredible eyes. The Queen did, too, now I come to think of it.

Clear, piercing eyes. I may even have fallen in love with her a little bit as well.

Probably just as well that Diana didn't come backstage, really. It can be a bit of a lottery. To put it mildly some celebrity encounters are better than others. Personally, I absolutely love meeting a celebrity. Like Elaine Stritch, who because I wore a vest for most of the show said to me, 'You're like the young Marlon Brando, and I fucked him, so I should know,' and afterwards sent me a picture of Brando on which she'd written, 'Here's looking at you, kid,' and then underneath, in brackets, 'Watch your weight.'

I was, like, *'Watch my what now?'* Me, Mr Body Conscious. Was she saying I was fat? Was it something to do with Marlon Brando? I never got round to asking her, although we had one more memorable encounter when I went to see her in cabaret at the world-famous Carlyle Hotel in New York. This was in 2005, when I was doing *The Woman in White*. I was with Stephen Sondheim and had nipped out for a fag. As I came back, she was just getting ready to go on, and I said hello.

'Hello,' she barked back at me. 'Hold my drink,' and I dutifully took her glass of bourbon from her then watched as she removed a syringe from her handbag, jabbed it into her thigh, grabbed her drink back and said, 'I'm ready.'

(No, nothing like that. She was a diabetic.)

I had no words. The mark of a true legend. I rejoined Stephen and we watched her knock that show out of the park. Brilliant.

Howard Keel was amazing. He was still in *Dallas* at the time and was booked to do a series of gigs in London. I heard he was in the audience and got very excited, having absolutely worshipped him from those MGM musicals *Calamity Jane,*

Kiss Me, Kate and *Seven Brides for Seven Brothers*. I thought he was just everything the big Hollywood musical on Broadway star should be: fabulous voice, funny, great-looking, just amazing. He asked to come backstage afterwards, came in, and I wasn't disappointed. I was firstly struck by the fact that he was such a tall and dignified-looking man.

And secondly, that he was crying.

'Oh my God,' I said. 'What's wrong?'

He looked at me, his eyes glittering with tears, and said, 'I feel like I can pass the mantle of musical theatre's leading man to the next generation.'

Well, what a lovely thing to say. Not that it held up to much scrutiny. I mean, there were a few generations between me and Howard Keel when you think about it. And in retrospect it was probably just a bit of cheese from an old campaigner. But he said it, and that's the important thing. He said it, and it meant the world to me.

Chapter 37

There's some sleight of hand that goes on when celebrities want to come and see your show. 'House seats' are kept back by the theatre, and if it's a hot ticket, then someone from the celebrity's set-up will call the producer's office and ask for access to them. Sometimes they come complimentary, but usually they need to be paid for. The front-of-house manager will be told that they're coming and depending on their profile and how many are coming with them, they may get access to the VIP room where they'll be looked after and then escorted from their seats backstage to meet the turns should all parties so desire.

You do get to say no if you want. I mean, depending on who it is. Some performers really don't like it when celebrities want to meet them. Based on what you know, what do you think my position is on the matter? Correct. I love it. It's all great to me. What's especially fun is when you get two celebrities who come on the same night – and this gives me a nice link into one of my favourite stories, which took place when Joan Collins was appearing in *Private Lives* at the Aldwych at the same time as publishing another of her several autobiographies.

Cathy went along to cover the afternoon book launch, and I went as her plus one. Now, I love Joan Collins. Who doesn't love Joan Collins? So we were at the launch, and Joan approached, the first time I'd ever met her, and she was in full-on warm and welcoming mode. 'Darlings, aren't you simply lovely?' she said, looking and sounding like Joan Collins doing a Joan Collins impersonation. You remember those ads with Leonard Rossiter? Like that. 'Are you coming to the show tonight, to see *Private Lives*?' she asked us. 'Oh, you must. You simply must.'

'Absolutely we will,' I said, before Cathy could reply.

'Lovely,' purred Joan, adding, 'and do make sure you come back afterwards to say hello, won't you? It'll be simply *lovely* to see you.'

In what world am I *not* going to see Joan Collins backstage at the Adelphi? No world. So I'm already gearing up for a great encounter when Joan adds, 'Diana is in. Diana Rigg. You'll be sitting with her or near her.'

Now I'm like, *Diana Rigg and Joan Collins. Same day. Boom.*

So we went along to the show, which was possibly not the best version of *Private Lives* I've ever seen. It was *Dynasty* meets Noël Coward and trust me, those particular worlds should probably never meet. But still, it was fun. It was what it was. More to the point, we'd been invited into the VIP room, what I call the royal retiring room, and there we had a few drinks with Diana Rigg at the half.

Diana was knocking them back, being very indiscreet, saying things I couldn't possibly reprint here. The previous evening she'd been at some kind of Natural History Museum event. 'Well,' she said, very put out. 'They put all of us celeb women in a room to make an entrance called Birds of England. I ask you – *Birds of England*. So we marched in, but they'd only gone and consecrated the fucking podium, so we had to take our shoes and socks off to get up there.' She paused. 'Even Fergie.'

It was brilliant stuff. I was in my element just listening to her. Birds of England? Consecrated podiums? Didn't have a clue what she was on about but it didn't matter. It was Dame Diana Rigg with a glass of wine in hand holding forth. What's not to love?

We went back for the second half. More *Dynasty*-Coward mash-up. Afterwards, Cathy and I went to meet with Spencer, Joan's dresser. It's usually the dresser or assistant who has the job of hunting down the celebrity and escorting them backstage to meet the turn. Mine is a wonderful guy called Andrew Ross, whom I met in 2005 when I was doing a solo concert tour after the West End version of *The Woman in White* before going to America with the show, and needed an assistant to come with me on the road. I'd asked the wardrobe mistress if she knew anyone, and she told me about a guy currently dressing Christian Slater in *One Flew Over the Cuckoo's Nest*.

So I met Andrew, explained what the gig was, and although he'd never done anything like it before, he said he'd give it a go. Thus, his introduction to me was being on a coach touring the country with a live rat called Missy he had to look after. And he was just brilliant. So sensitive to moods and atmosphere, so efficient, got on with everyone and absolutely hilarious to be around. Seventeen years later, he's still with me.

Anyway, I digress. You want to hear about Joan and Diana.

Right, so we were met by Spencer. Diana hadn't arrived at that point, but Spencer said, 'Miss Collins will see you now,' and led us back through the theatre to Joan's lair. I mean, just that particular sequence of words. *Miss Collins will see you now.* I was practically levitating with excitement.

We arrived at her dressing room, and if it wasn't apparent from our afternoon encounter then it was now: Joan is not in the disappointment business. She is never not Joan. As we were ushered into the dressing room, she stood and wafted over, looking exactly as you would imagine Joan Collins to look. She wore one of those 1930s or 1940s black silk long negligée things, with a black silk housecoat over the top. Her hair looked amazing, and in one hand she held a champagne glass, in the other the bottle itself.

'Darlings, come in, come in,' she said. She poured champagne. We were saying all the right things, mainly how much we'd loved the show (there's an etiquette to going backstage and we'll come on to that in a minute), when there came a knock at the door.

In walks Diana Rigg. Imperious, haughty, slightly drunk. Peak Dame.

'Darling, darling.'

Everybody was saying 'darling'. Champagne was being poured, air kisses kissed. 'You know darling Michael and darling Cathy, don't you?'

'Yes, darling, absolute darlings.'

And then – beat. That post-introduction lull which we all know means that we're getting down to business. Dame Diana has to give her feedback.

'You my darling,' she said to Joan, 'were simply marvellous.

You came on to that stage, charisma personified, and owned it. You were just wonderful.' There was a pause. 'Just one note, though,' added Diana. 'Can I give it to you?'

'Yes of course,' said Joan, and I need hardly add that there was a touch of frost in that response. Enough to let Diana know that there was a line, and she was very much in danger of crossing it.

Me, I literally thought that all my Christmases had come at once. I was in a room where Dame Diana Rigg was about to give Joan Collins a note.

And what a note it was.

'Were you nervous in Act I?' said Diana with a flourish.

Joan's lips tightened. 'No, not especially.'

'Hmm, really?' Diana patted the base of her throat, just below the larynx. 'Lower register. Where was it? You were screeching, darling, absolutely screeching. I thought you must be nervous because it really was quite piercing, if I'm honest.' Again, tapping at her throat. 'Lower register, bring it down. If you can do that, you'll have us all eating out of the palm of your hand. Will you try that for me?'

And Joan went, 'Yes, well, we've got an old people's matinee tomorrow afternoon. I might give it a whirl.'

Brilliant. Absolutely brilliant. Easily among my favourite-ever celebrity encounters.

Who else came to *Aspects*? I remember that Judi – that's Dame Judi Dench to you – came to see the show with her daughter, Finty, and they were great, really lovely to meet and perfect with the etiquette.

Which brings me on to the etiquette. What you have to remember is that for the performer, the backstage encounter is like having to do another show, especially if the person coming back is unfamiliar with our world. If they are 'civilians', to quote Liz Hurley. These guys tend to just stand there not knowing what to say, and in that case then you're forced to do what is essentially an ad hoc performance just to keep everybody feeling comfortable and relaxed (well, you do if you're me and an inveterate people-pleaser).

But when other turns come back, they know the etiquette, which is this: you go in, you say, 'You were marvellous,' you have a drink, have a laugh, and then go. Ten minutes, max, if that.

I've been in both positions many times, of course, and the worst is when you have to go backstage for something which has been absolute shite. In those instances it's usually a good idea to work out what you're going to say beforehand and make it something specifically unspecific.

'What a brave performance.' That's a good one.

'You had them. As soon as you went on, you had them.' There's another one for you.

Roger Allam, who was in *Les Misérables,* reckoned he had the whole issue sorted. He said, 'It's easy. You go backstage, you knock, put your head around the door and go, "Bastard! I saw you!" and then leave.' Genius. Never tried it, but still.

Personally, I play it safe, which in this case means unleashing a Niagara of unqualified praise. Stephen Sondheim always used to say that the worst thing after a show has just opened was people coming up giving notes or offering advice. The show is locked. The reviews are in. Everybody's worked so hard, they're stressed, they're completely immersed in this thing to which they've given everything, and all they want to hear is 'fabulous, fantastic, just amazing, can't believe it, what a brilliant night'.

And that's a real friend. Not somebody who comes in and goes, 'Well, you know, I think you could do a little bit of this here,' or, 'Great, but things flagged a little in Act II,' or even, 'Lower register. Where was it?' You just don't want that. I'm not saying ever. Just that there's a time and a place, and backstage immediately after a show is absolutely not that time or place.

Chapter 38

My relationship with my leading lady, Ann Crumb, was an interesting one. It's always slightly more difficult when you're working with someone you have to kiss. There are those eggy moments of the first kiss, the drawing of lines between being a professional actor and a man and a woman in a room snogging, the no man's land between it being a mere technical kiss and it being something believable that the audience must really feel. It's a pitfall for so many actors that that love affair bleeds over into real life which is why everyone's knobbing each other all the time. That was never the case with me and Ann.

Me being so very fresh to the whole thing, I remember feeling as though we needed to make it very clear that ours was just a professional relationship, especially as I was single at the time – this being in the days before I met Cathy. Ann wasn't. She had a boyfriend who was staying with her in London, so I guess that added an extra dimension.

I think what I'm trying to say is that it was all a bit awkward, and though it was an easy task to act the 'falling in love' bit – Ann was stunning, after all, which made my job so much easier – there was some debate as to whether there was any chemistry between us. Some critics: yes. Others: no.

What do I think? I'm not sure. I do know that it's a new era, and our latter-day Rose, Laura Pitt-Pulford, presented a different kind of performance, a different interpretation, and it's been very instructive to watch her at work. I've seen the tweets. The audience literally crushes on Laura in a way that I never quite felt with Ann. Is it a charisma thing? Is it a performance thing? I've stood with both of them on stage, snogged one of them, and even I can't answer that. It's just an indefinable *thing*.

I do know this. Ann had an awful lot to contend with. She was away from home, missing her dogs, originating a role in a new Andrew Lloyd Webber show. None of which Laura had to deal with in 2023.

Oh, and let's not forget the intense press scrutiny, the fact that Roger Moore walked out. Again, none of which Laura had to contend with. Fair's fair, you've got to say that the circumstances were almost ideal for Laura to dig out the perfect performance of Rose, and in my opinion that's exactly what she did. Her performance is *free*. She totally inhabits the charismatic, sexy, bohemian sides to Rose and thus what her admirers see in her.

That, really, is key to the success of the show, because to a certain extent the audience should find all of the main characters appealing and attractive in their own way. You have to be able to understand their motivation for feeling the way they do, doing the things they do. The audience has to not only understand why they behave that way – often rather despicably, and in the instance where Alex fires a shot, almost homicidally – and then forgive them for it.

But look, I don't want you to come away from this thinking that I'm down on Ann's performance. I'm not. And at the end of the day, most of the architecture was in place: I needed to fancy the pants off her, and I did; I needed to have a good working relationship with her, and I did. Just that . . . Well, I've said it. She didn't have that *thing* for me, a factor not helped by the fact that she was uncomfortable going on telly and talking to the press, whereas I took to all that like a duck to water and, well, we know where all that went.

Things changed in the most horribly ironic way possible, because Ann did indeed make the headlines when she had an accident during a performance – one of the worst things I've ever seen on stage.

*

It was in September. In other words, about four or five months into the run, and it happened towards the end of a show. She'd just sung 'Anything But Lonely', and as that song finished we would go to a blackout, at which point Ann would step on to a travelator in order to be taken off into the wings for a change before the final number. As that was happening I'd be taking up my correct position on the stage, which is what I was doing when suddenly there came a scream. A terrible, blood-curdling scream. Like nothing I've ever heard, before or since.

I need hardly say that it was a genuinely terrifying moment, made more so by the fact that we were in blackout. I couldn't see anything; all I could hear was this awful tortured wail.

We play jokes on each other in the theatre. We fool about and corpse and pass cuddly toys. But not for one second did I think that scream was a prank. Not for a half-second did I think it was anything other than another human being in absolute agony.

'Stop the show,' I was shouting. 'Stop the show, *now*.'

The stage manager hit the emergency button, which stops all the automation on the set and freezes the action, bringing up the lights at the same time. Another button push brought down what we call 'the iron', the big safety curtain you see at the beginning of the show. It dropped, shielding us as I dashed over to the source of the scream.

It was Ann. And what I saw will stay with me forever. Her foot had become caught in the belt of the travelator and she'd been dragged across the stage to where it disappeared underneath the boards and had tried to take her foot with it, jamming it.

The only thing stopping the travelator moving was the bone of Ann's foot. The underside of it was caught in the mechanism. Blood everywhere, Ann screaming in agony. I was holding her, at the same time saying what was becoming obvious, 'We're stopping. We're not going to finish the show.'

Somebody rushed off to call an ambulance, but at the same time it was clear that we needed medical assistance more quickly, and so I did something you hear about – something you never in a million years expect to have to do yourself: I went out front to address the audience.

Still with Ann's blood on me, her screams from behind me ringing out, I looked out into the shocked audience and said, 'I'm so sorry, ladies and gentlemen, but as I'm sure you're aware, something very unfortunate has happened. We're dealing with it now, but I'm afraid that we will not be able to continue with the show – and, may I ask, is there a doctor in the house?'

There was. He attended to Ann, and together we were able to remove her foot from the travelator. Meanwhile an ambulance arrived and transported her to the hospital, where she was taken into surgery. The travelator had literally ripped off the sole of her foot.

Awful for Ann.

Awful, awful.

That first operation was the first of many, as Ann began a slow recovery process during which she was told that she might never walk again and probably would never be able to perform again.

On both counts the medics were wrong, I'm pleased to say, but there were some very traumatic moments in between diagnosis and final outcome. As a cast and company, we'd go backwards and forwards to see her at the hospital, and there's a great picture where we're re-enacting *Whatever Happened to Baby Jane?* with Ann in bed as Joan Crawford and me as Bette Davis. We made the best of it; in other words, we tried to do what we could for her, but no amount of visits could disguise what an utterly devastating event it was.

But of course, as we all know, the show has to go on. It isn't callous, it's just what it is, and stepping into the breach was her immediate understudy, Carol Duffy.

Carol was great. What a trouper. There was one night during the Act I scene when we're running through George's house exploring, and she got her blocking wrong. As I jumped on a box, my elbow smashed her in the nose. I heard it crunch, and turned around to see blood pouring from her nose.

This was at the beginning of the show. But she didn't stop. She'd almost been knocked out, but just went into autopilot, continuing to perform with blood pouring down her face until we got to the end of the scene, when she rushed into the wings and ice packs were applied and a sticking plaster slapped over her nose. She had to do the rest of the show with a huge plaster on her nose. Now, that's a trouper.

Carol stepped aside for Susannah Fellows, who if you remember had performed as Rose for the Sydmonton performance, and so was able to complete our run in London.

Ann's accident took place in September 1989. My run in London finished in January 1990. *Aspects* then transferred to Broadway, where it opened in April 1990 and ran until March 1991, with Ann back in the role of Rose.

How was she able to transfer? You tell me. One hundred per cent guts and courage and hard work was what got her back into shape, and she was able to do the run on Broadway. She performed in orthopaedic shoes especially designed for her, and whereas in the West End our stage floor had been cobbled – a typical Maria touch – on Broadway it was painted so that Ann would be more stable.

All of which brings me on to the story of *Aspects* on Broadway.

Chapter 39

When you're doing a show, all the talk is about what happens next. If you're out on tour, is it going to the West End? If so, what theatre will it be going into? If you're in a new show in the West End, is it transferring to Broadway? Is it going on tour? Is it closing? How is it doing at the box office? Are we over? Are we getting our notice?

Of course, when we began our West End run there was only really the vague hope rather than the expectation that we might transfer to Broadway. The slightly muted critical reaction notwithstanding, *Aspects* was a hit in London and therefore a money-spinner and so, at some point in the run they pushed the button.

'Who's going with it?'

'As far as we were concerned, well, Ann and Kathy would go, they're American.'

But then it's, 'Is Kevin going to go?' 'Is Michael going?'

When transferring, it's very much in the producers' interests to make it the best show it can be on Broadway. Not necessarily because Broadway has more prestige than the West End. That's a debate for another day. Just because you want a hit. The West End? For us that was sold out. Things were taking care of themselves as far as that was concerned. Broadway, then, is the next step. But the thing is that on Broadway it's way more expensive to put on a show, therefore way more risky, so you need to give it absolutely the best chance you can. And the most effective way of doing that is to use the same cast that had attracted the big numbers in London. I was in.

Oh, but then there was a bit of a news angle. Will Michael Ball's visa be sorted out in time? Will Equity insist on having an American in the role? Until, finally, after a good few column inches and maybe the odd sweaty palm or two, it was announced that I was definitely going. Then come the negotiations, of course, but quite frankly I would have done it for free. Get the Visa sorted, get me on Broadway – my first time – boom.

Of course there was some trepidation. Those reviews that had appeared in US newspapers hadn't been especially positive. Frank Rich – remember him? 'The Butcher of Broadway' – had written something rather disparaging as part of a West End round-up, so it wasn't like the transfer was a no-brainer. Heads were scratched and beards stroked in the making of that particular decision.

Something else that didn't help was the fact that we'd effectively been snubbed by the Olivier Awards in the UK. The big winners that year were *Miss Saigon*, *The Baker's Wife* and *Return to the Forbidden Planet*, which won Best Musical. Even *Metropolis*, which was more like *Flop-opolis*, got a nod. But nothing for

Aspects. Not even a nomination. Trevor got a nomination for *Othello*, but there wasn't so much as a mention for Andrew.

That, of course, created a bit of a siege mentality. Certainly we felt like the maverick outsiders of the West End crew. We were like, 'Hey, forget you, we're selling out here.' Which was all very good for morale, but privately, it takes the wind out of your sails a bit.

Anyway. Meh. We were off to Broadway while the show would continue in the West End with Susannah staying on as Rose; my understudy, David Greer, taking over from me, and Barry Ingham coming in as George.

Leaving the show in London was – to quote Vinnie Jones in *Lock, Stock and Two Smoking Barrels* – emotional. There's a video of my final performance, and it was incredible. Not the performance, which I'm sure was incredible but you know what I mean, I mean the feeling of goodwill in the auditorium.

And then afterwards. I mean honestly, Beatlemania had nothing on Michael Ball's *Aspects* swansong. You think I'm joking? We literally stopped the traffic outside the theatre with all the fans who had gathered outside, me waving out of the window, *Evita* eat your heart out. The thing was, this was big news, me going to Broadway. There'd been this story around me from the moment things kicked off with *Aspects*; it had all gone into another gear with the hit single, then a sense of stepping even further into the limelight when Roger left. It was like, 'local boy makes good', even though I was born in Worcestershire. People were really behind me and I was enjoying my moment in the sun, loving the fairy-tale journey that I had the good sense to appreciate at the time.

All the negotiations had gone well. I wouldn't have to work

for free, while included in the contract was the fact that I would be put up in a hotel, after which they'd help me find and pay for an apartment.

Me being fairly clueless, and again, don't forget, this was before the internet, it wasn't as though I could Google, 'Where's nice to live in New York?' and so I just said Greenwich Village. I'd heard of that. It sounded cool. After that, I disappeared off on my first-ever exotic holiday, to Speightstown, Barbados, staying in a place called Cobblers Cove. I was by myself, which I think we can all agree was fairly brave of me, but on the other hand a decision partly born of having no other choice. Cathy was busy and I had this brief window in which to take a break between West End and Broadway. It was either solo holiday or no holiday.

And you'll never guess who I met while I was there.

Left: Last night of *Aspects* in London, celebrating my transfer to Broadway.

Right and below left: The opening night party at the Rainbow Rooms in The Rockefeller Center with Ann Crumb (*right*) and Sarah Brightman (*below*). (Before the reviews had been published!)

Below: Winning MVP in the Broadway Show Softball League, sadly the only accolade I won during my time in America.

Right: What a night. It was my first-ever tour, and I celebrated my 30th birthday with a sold-out Hammersmith Apollo show, during which Cameron presented me with a gold disc for a number one album.

Left: Eurovision 'glory'. Being number two seems to come naturally to me.

Right: Nipples to the stars. Celebrating Gillian Lynne's birthday with friends Wayne Sleep and Elaine Paige.

© Alastair Muir/Shutterstock

A few of the roles that stand out for me. *Passion* (*above left*) with Maria Friedman, *Chitty* (*middle*) with Emma Williams as Truly, and (*bottom*) *Mack and Mabel* with Rebecca LaChance and the company.

© Nils Jorgensen / Shutterstock

© Alastair Muir / Shutterstock

Backstage at *Sweeney* with Imelda, and in the wings of *Hairspray* at the Coliseum with Les Dennis, Rita Simons, Marisha Wallace and members of the company.

© Johan Persson / ArenaPAL

© Johan Persson / ArenaPAL

Rehearsal and backstage at *Aspects* with Jamie Bogyo, Anna Unwin and Laura Pitt-Pulford

© Danny Kaan

© Danny Kaan

Great production shots and backstage moments from *Aspects*.

© Johan Persson / ArenaPAL

© Johan Persson / ArenaPAL

© Johan Persson / ArenaPAL

© Danny Kaan

Left: With the long-suffering Andrew, making sure I'm smelling nice for the ladies and gentlemen.

Above and right: Gill and Maureen who run my fan club, then and now. They've been with me every step of the way.

Left: Seat J17 at the Wales Millennium Centre, dedicated to my Gran.

Above: The company surprising me on my last matinee. What a load of Balls.

Below: With the love of my life, my darling Cathy.

Chapter 40

I didn't know this when I booked Cobblers Cove, but next door to it was a grand house called Bellerive, the island's only plantation house facing the beach.

Owner of said house? Claudette Colbert. As in, Claudette Colbert the legendary film star, whose career went way, way back. Her first-ever film was silent, directed by Frank Capra, but unlike many of that generation, who when the talkies came along found that their services were no longer required because they didn't have the dialogue chops, Claudette's career had gone from strength to strength.

Her next movie was a gangster flick in which she co-starred with Edward G Robinson, and throughout her career she worked with people like Fredric March and Ginger Rogers, and of course with Clark Gable in *It Happened One Night*, the film for which she won an Oscar, although she was nominated plenty of other times. I mean, there's legend, there's legend – and there's Claudette Colbert.

The manager of the hotel knew Claudette. He'd told her about me. 'One of our guests is a dashing and really rather charming young man who's about to go and wow them on Broadway,' he'd said, or words to that effect. Claudette was like, 'Wonderful, darling, I'll invite him for lunch,' and before you know it, I'm getting a note, the good kind, the kind that goes, 'Love you to pop in for lunch, love, Claudette.'

I was round there like a shot. I mean, this is the wonderful thing about my job. As soon as you get a certain amount of success, doors start to open, people want to meet you. Such-and-such knows such-and-such, would you like to meet them? Yes – yes, I bloody would. Now bring me the tea and the Battenberg.

Bellerive was absolutely incredible. I climbed the steps to an ornate front door, rang the bell and was shown in by a butler, an actual liveried butler, who took me through a reception area and into a lounge.

There in the lounge was a grand piano, and on and around it were framed pictures of just about every movie star you can imagine, all of them signed to her. 'Darling Claudette, love you, Clark,' that kind of thing. Plus, oh my God, the Oscar that she won for *It Happened One Night.*

And she was lovely. I mean, you're probably wondering if I've ever met a legend who *didn't* meet my expectations, and the answer is that of course I have. But perhaps it's a measure of their longevity that the biggies – the likes of Joan and Claudette – are, if not *nice*, necessarily, just *exactly as you want them to be.*

So it was that Claudette spent the afternoon regaling me with stories, instinctively knowing that I'd be a willing audience, which I was. And although she was in her eighties, she looked fabulous and was still vibrant and full of plans, telling me that she intended a Broadway return soon (although she would eventually leave us in 1996 after a series of strokes), and generally being a grand old Hollywood movie star holding court in her Barbados mansion. Pinch me.

So that was great. Brilliant.

And then I got a call. They'd brought *Aspects* rehearsals forward by a week. There was no time to go home and pack. I was going to have to travel straight from Cobblers Cove to New York.

Don't forget, this was January, and although the weather in Barbados was gorgeous, it was bitter in New York, and I wasn't exactly prepared, to put it mildly. The 'crazy limey' wandering around a freezing January New York in wildly unsuitable clothing? That was me.

Not that I did much wandering, if any. Arriving in the city, it had belatedly occurred to me that in all the excitement of reaching Broadway, it had slipped my mind that New York had something of a reputation – as in, a bad reputation. Certainly in 1990. This, after all, was the city of *Death Wish*, the place where muggings were commonplace; you didn't dare go out at night, and merely to look at Central Park, even to glance in its general direction, was to take your life in your hands. To go in there – especially after dark – was tantamount to suicide.

Well, I thought, *as long as I steer clear of Central Park, then I should be okay*. The taxi driver – no, wait, I mean *cab* driver – who picked me up from the airport cast an eye over my inappropriate clothing but said nothing. 'The Ritz-Carlton,' I told him, and settled back to take in the scenery which, and I know that this is a huge cliché but it's true, made me feel as though I were stepping on to a film set.

I mean, really. How many films have you seen beginning with a cab drive from the airport? Roger Moore made the exact same journey in *Live and Let Die*. As we approached Manhattan, I could see Central Park in the middle. *Stay away from there*, I told myself. *As long as I stay away from . . .*

'Here y'go,' the cab driver said, and sure enough, we had indeed drawn up to the pavement – sorry, sidewalk – outside the Ritz-Carlton. I looked across the street. Opposite was Central Park.

'You don't want to go into Central Park, man, it's dangerous in there.' The words were ringing in my head to the extent that I imagined it having some kind of Death Star tractor beam, so that if I so much as stepped on to the sidewalk outside the hotel then I would be pulled into it, never to return. My response, in the three days I had prior to the beginning of rehearsals – two or three days during which I could easily have spent exploring this wonderful city – was to stay in my room. I mean, honestly, this is true. I practically barricaded myself in. That was where I stayed, in my room, ordering room service, listening to the sirens at night and imagining all sorts of terrible atrocities taking place in the park opposite.

The thing was that I was going to be in New York for a long time. My Barbados holiday had been cut short with the aim of making sure that the show was as good as it could possibly be, for reasons I've already mentioned. We planned to build a lot; we wanted to work on it. Could be that I'd be cooped up in my hotel room for a long, long time. I mean, it was the Ritz-Carlton. First-world problems and all that. But even so.

I spent my time in solitary trying to get my head around the business of relocating to New York. I'm somebody who travels light. I don't really sweat the details. My younger sister, Kat, eight years my junior, moved into my flat in London to take care of things there, while my dresser and assistant, Tina, sorted out clothes to bring with her when she arrived in New York. Not gonna lie, it's a lifesaver having an assistant. Having an assistant allows you to airily say things like, 'I don't sweat the details,' primarily because there's somebody else sweating the details on your behalf.

Mind you, even if you took Tina and my sister out of the equation, my attitude to the move would have been the same. I didn't care about anything else apart from starring in a show on Broadway. I'm in New York, loves. Everything else can take care of itself. And anyway, once the clothes are sorted out, what else do you really need? Wash bag. That's kind of it, isn't it? For me it was.

Chapter 41

It came to our first rehearsals, in other words 'the first day of school', and Biddy Hayward of the Really Useful Group, the show's producer, turned up at the Ritz-Carlton.

'I'm going to take you down to the first day of school,' she told me, as though she were my bodyguard, which in this case, she probably was. 'We'll walk down,' she added.

Walk? *Walk*? I'd been expecting an armoured car, but okay, we'd walk. It wasn't that far, apparently. Four blocks away, or whatever it is they say. Should be fine.

And literally the first thing that happened was that somebody tried to mug her. We were on the sidewalk right outside the hotel, when from nowhere came this guy who tried to snatch her handbag.

Now, Biddy Hayward was invented in order that the word 'formidable' should find a suitable home. You don't mess with Biddy. Even New York muggers don't mess with Biddy, as this guy found out to his cost when, instead of relinquishing her handbag and cringing away in abject fear, as she was supposed to do, Biddy instead elbowed him and told him to fuck off.

Seeing that he was beaten, he scarpered, and then – and this is the really cool bit – Biddy shouldered her handbag and continued her journey, just as if nothing had happened.

I promise I'm not making this up. It was one of the coolest things I've ever seen. And when you consider that I live with Cathy McGowan, who practically invented the 1960s, the bar is fairly high when it comes to cool.

'Just be aware, darling, that's all you need to do. You'll be absolutely fine.'

I had no doubt that Biddy would be fine. As far as Biddy was concerned, it was the muggers I worried about. Me, though? I was a lot less certain. The strangest things were going through my head. I literally wondered whether the whole thing had been staged for my benefit, some kind of initiation-cum-education thing. If so, it had failed, because there and then I resolved not to leave my hotel room again. Clearly *Death Wish I*, *II* and *III* had been underplaying the reality. New York was a crime hellhole, promising death on every street.

I did eventually leave my room, of course. Not least because I needed more permanent digs. Between me, Tina, the guys from Really Useful and a local realtor we found a two-bedroom apartment in Greenwich Village, on West Ninth and Eighth Avenue, which was very dark, very green, and looked as though it hadn't been decorated since the 1970s. It overlooked the dirty well in the middle of the building where all the pigeon shit accumulates – a real, proper, tenement view, like something out of *A Streetcar Named Desire* or *Rear Window*.

By the time I moved in there, we were deep into rehearsals,

which were in rooms on 51st Street just off Times Square. There I made the unconscious decision that playing up the idiot Englishman would be the best way to gain a good introduction to New York life. Being such a scaredy cat (with good reason, I think you'll agree) I'd been getting cabs everywhere, but thanks to information provided by the other guys in the company I was able to pluck up the courage to use the subway. Their advice boiled down to, basically, 'The subway is fine, just be careful what you're wearing and what you're carrying. Make sure you get the right train and, whatever you do, don't go to 125th Street.'

These days, 125th Street is lovely. Like everywhere else in New York, it's been fully gentrified, and Bill Clinton has an office there. Back then, it represented the centre of Harlem and was known as being really very dodgy indeed. When Lou Reed scores smack in The Velvet Underground's 'I'm Waiting for the Man', guess where he goes to get it? I mean, this was New York in a nutshell: it was all down to being on the right block, sometimes the right street in the right block. You could literally be on a safe block, cross the road and find yourself in a dangerous area. It was why the native New Yorkers seemed to have it all going on. They came across so wise and world-weary. It was like they had The Knowledge.

Anyway, so there I was, slowly getting acclimatised. The show was open and I'd even been allocated a personal trainer – very New York – because they wanted me in good shape for the show. (And yes, he sighs, that's the life of a performer. 'We want you in good shape,' they say, the implication being that you're carrying more timber than they'd like. And you? You just take it on the chin.)

So anyway, one day in the early summer, I set off for my training session, which was near Carnegie Hall. I'm cringing thinking about it now, but I was wearing a vest and shorts, proper freshly bought training gear, and was listening to one of the new Sony Walkmans. Honestly, I must have looked like one of the kids from *Fame*, like a walking advertisement for the 1980s (already a throwback, then, when you consider that this was the summer of 1990).

What's more, I was wearing a very particular sort of trainers. If trainers are your bag, then you may well remember them. Released at the tail end of the previous year, the Reebok Pumps were so called because of the 'revolutionary internal inflation mechanism', which basically meant that you pressed the little pump button and the trainers would embrace your feet.

Anyway, the other thing about these trainers was that being so very new, revolutionary and on-trend, they were also eminently stealable. Kids would think nothing of making you remove your shoes at knifepoint and making off with them. It was win-win as far as they were concerned. They got the shoes, and you couldn't give chase.

So there I was, getting the subway, might as well have been wearing a T-shirt saying, 'Mug me for my Reeboks and Walkman,' and fully aware of the fact (I wasn't that stupid), but feeling enough like a native New Yorker and, anyway, knowing that my stop for my trainer's studio wasn't far away.

Perhaps distracted by how 'fly' I looked, I must have got on the wrong train. As I sat on the subway, I gradually became aware that all the stations we normally stopped at were flashing past. My train was the C-train, and I was supposed to alight at 64th Street, but it dawned on me that in fact I was on the

A-train, and the A-train didn't stop at 64th Street, it didn't stop at all – until it reached 125th Street.

Which, you will remember, was the place I had been told to avoid at all costs.

This was one of those trains from a New York revenge movie: graffiti inside and out. I looked around myself and having emerged from a Walkman-induced trance into the horrible reality of my situation, realised that nobody else on the train looks like me. They were not . . . *prosperous* people. Looking down at myself, in my athletic gear, Walkman and bleeding-edge trainers, it looked as though I was taking the piss.

It's Robocop. It's Sylvester Stallone in *Cobra*. It's the Warriors. It's *Assault on Precinct 13*.

Now, I realise that I'm currently regurgitating this story as an amusing anecdote for my book, but the fact is that while it might be funny now, possibly because it's self-evident that I've lived to tell the tale, at the time it really wasn't at all bloody funny. Darlings, I was absolutely, genuinely terrified. I felt as though I had made a terrible, possibly life-threatening mistake. I felt like a magnet for every mugger in the near vicinity, and knowing that I was travelling towards a higher concentration of muggers only intensified the feeling.

Okay, so think, Ball, think. My new pals in the company had given me a piece of advice should I ever find myself in a threatening situation. Act mad. That was it. Act like you're mad, because it'll freak people out. They'll think you're more dangerous than they are.

So that's what I did. I started twitching, moving my hands about in sudden gestures, barking out random words like 'fishwife' and 'lager top'.

And do you know what? It worked. Whereas before I had been receiving various glances varying from pity to outright hostility, now they were looking away, all of them studiously ignoring the weird disco athlete talking to himself in the carriage.

All of which meant that I made it to 125th Street alive. There was that to be thankful for, at least.

And now I had a choice. Did I get out at 125th Street, presumably taking my life in my hands, cross over to the other side and return downtown? Or did I stay on the subway, continue my twitching and end up God knows where – probably Coney Island, somewhere that sounded good but was nowhere I wanted to be.

I chose the former. Continuing to act weird, and still with my Walkman clamped to my ears – although switched off now, so I could hear properly – I got off the train and made my way over to the other side. Even that wasn't as easy as it sounds. Cue some sweaty-palmed moments as I tried to get my bearings, still behaving like I was hearing voices, 'acting mad' in the very non-PC parlance of the times.

I found my way to the platform. There were guys there. Guys who looked at me, not with curiosity in their eyes, but like I was prey, and I considered bailing on the plan there and then. But then do what? Go up to street level? No thanks. Go back to the other platform? Just as risky.

And then I saw her. Standing on the station was a little old lady who held shopping bags. It wasn't the same little old lady with shopping bags who had saved my bacon when I froze during 'Love Changes Everything', because for a start this one was American and what's more, she was black. But there's no denying that it was a little old lady with shopping bags, and as little old ladies with shopping bags are liable to do, she was about to save my life.

She saved it by doing nothing. Simply being there, as I moved along the platform and went to stand right next to her.

Not a word was said. I mean, I was in her personal space, and she could have sold me out. She could have given me a disgusted look, perhaps even shouted something rude at me and moved away, in which case I was toast. But she didn't. She looked at me, up and down, and she knew exactly my predicament, and I knew that she knew, and she allowed herself to be used, even as the train pulled into the station. She got on to an almost empty carriage, and I took a seat next to her, and still not a word was said, until we went our separate ways – by which time the train was in much safer territory.

As for me, I breathed a huge sigh of relief and thought that if I ever write this up into a memoir, I'm going to thank that lady from the bottom of my heart.

Chapter 42

It was partly because of that scaredy cat introduction, and indeed, experiences like the one I had at 125th Street, that my love for New York was sealed. It's the kind of city that can make you feel at once as though you're in the centre of the world, yet also as though you're a trench warfare survivor. No, you couldn't go into Central Park after dark, but you could go into Sheep Meadow in the evening, and as I went fully native, I responded to a notice on the theatre noticeboard and joined the Broadway Show Softball League. In one particular game, I was MVP, which sounds like a distressing condition, but is in fact 'most valuable player'.

At the same time, there was a show to do and we were all taking it very seriously indeed, right from day one. That 'first day of school' when I went from Biddy versus mugger straight into the thick of rehearsals – everybody was there. Andrew, Trevor, Don and Charles. Maria, Gillian and our principals, Kevin and Kathy, and – not fully recovered but fit enough – Ann.

Everybody else was local, of course. We're talking lighting, stage management, wigs, make-up . . . all the on-the-ground technical staff were American. Equity is very strong in New York, and the pay and conditions of workers more tightly controlled. This meant that, for example, there was no going over time. You didn't do anything that should have been a job for a union member. Move a prop, for example, and you'd be told, 'That's a job for stage management, not performance.' Fair enough, you soon learned. It was a situation that had its plus points as well as its negative ones. Those late nights we'd had in London were practically a thing of the past, and Kathy delighted in showing me and Kevin around the city after hours, adding to my growing sense of belonging.

Another thing that struck me was that the community on Broadway was – and no doubt still is – very close, much more so than in the West End. Of course, there's a sense of community in London, no doubt, but geographically the Broadway theatres are closer to one another, which tends to foster more interaction between cast and crew. The Broadway Show League being a good example. They also have this thing called the Gypsy Robe, which is, as it sounds, an actual robe that was first made in the 1950s.

What happens is that the robe – since subject to a name change to the Legacy Robe, for PC reasons – is handed to the newest Broadway musical to open, where it will be left in the care of the ensemble member with the most number of Broadway credits. That person has to add a little bit of stitching or appliqué to the robe and keeps it until a new musical is due to open. Before curtain-up on opening night, the company will gather on stage, an Equity member will explain the history of the robe, and it is then passed on to a new trustee. The new recipient will wear the robe and then walk around the company so that everyone can touch it for good luck. They then go through the rest of the theatre, anointing the stage and auditorium with good luck from the robe.

There are all kinds of rules about doing it counter-clockwise three times and wearing the robe while visiting each of the principals in their dressing rooms. When the robe is full with mementos (and there are quite strict rules about what sort of mementos can be applied), it is retired and kept at the Smithsonian, and a new one introduced.

Now, I don't know about you, but that, to me, is what it's all about. Just absolute class. And just to see that taking place, to share in the magic, was really wonderful. Not saying that it was 'better' than the West End, not at all. Just different, and especially for a young lad from England. I really dug how that midtown area of New York just lives and breathes the theatre. How it gives the community such a strong bond. Often, having finished the show, we'd go to a place called Don't Tell Mama, a sort of dive piano bar where you'd pay a dollar then get up and do a number. We were among the first to start going to this place, after which different shows would turn up. You probably know the name Billy Porter. He's a huge star now. Way before he was big, he was practically a resident at Don't Tell Mama, often singing into the early hours. I remember getting up with him, he and I singing 'Pity the Child' and 'Anthem' from *Chess*, and me thinking he was one of the most gifted singers I'd ever heard.

Not long later, Billy Porter was in *Miss Saigon*, and now of course is a huge star thanks to *Pose*, *Dreamgirls* and *Kinky Boots*.

But that was his start, a penniless guy who came to New York to try to make a wage, getting up, having talent, being noticed, getting on. It's a lovely story, a somehow quintessentially Broadway story.

I remember taking Sarah Brightman there. This was towards the end of my run. Sarah was taking over as Rose, replacing Ann, and I was helping her to integrate with a new cast. By then, of course, we were practically part of the furniture at our favourite dive piano bar.

'Right, we're all going out. We're going to take Sarah to Don't Tell Mama,' I announced. She was lovely. This was a difficult time in her life: her divorce from Andrew had been followed by a bit of a break from performing, and she was feeling the pressure coming back, especially with such a big show. But she was so relaxed, and it was one of those legendary nights.

So all was good, then. No dark spots on the horizon, you might think.

Well, there was one. Just a small one. Once again, the press were less than kind . . .

Chapter 43

We had arrived on Broadway as the creative team behind hits such as *Les Misérables* and *The Phantom of the Opera* – Andrew Lloyd Webber's profile had never been higher, and the same for Trevor. We came knowing that in London we had generated revenues of around £10 million and on Broadway already had an advance of around £8 million.

When you have that kind of success, you can't expect any quarter from the critics. So for example, a struggling composer might hope for a little slack. Not Andrew. A production lacking our advance could expect the critics to focus more on the positives than they do the negatives. Not us. A home-grown show might assume a little patriotic loyalty. We weren't that. A show with excellent notices in the West End might wonder if a critical consensus would form. We didn't have that luxury.

What's more, *Aspects* isn't an easy show. It has a somewhat downbeat feel at times, and its characters behave in ways that are occasionally unpalatable. As somebody who has lived within the story for so long, I find it endlessly fascinating. I love its ambiguities, the way that it isn't necessarily laid out for you in 'by the numbers', easy to understand terms. I love its semi-operatic, melodramatic feel. Don't get me wrong, I'm not for a moment saying that anybody who doesn't like the show simply doesn't understand it. Just that of those who didn't like the show there must have been a significant proportion for whom that was the case.

Factor in that Andrew Lloyd Webber was at that point worth in the hundreds of millions, and that his shows were basically assumed to be critic-proof, and what you have are the ingredients for a perfect storm of critical tsunami.

So firstly let's thank God for Clive Barnes of the *New York Post* who called *Aspects* 'easily the best musical currently on Broadway', and added that it was a 'delicious and deliciously sensual piece of musical theatre'. Yet at the same time we have to admit that Clive was very much in the minority. Others, while noting that Andrew had a seemingly review-proof production on his hands, went for the jugular anyway, criticising his music (repetitive, trite) before going on to rope virtually everybody else into the drubbing, including Maria, Gillian and Trevor. Ann came in for particular criticism, which was especially wounding given what she'd been through. Kathy, according to critics, seemed to lack the bohemian spirit her character required. Kevin largely escaped any mauling.

Me? Mixed, you'd have to say. The *Entertainment Weekly* review noted that I have a 'big, beautiful voice' while also calling my performance 'banal'.

Hmm. As a performer, something kicks in when you read

that. Did I read that my voice was 'big and beautiful' and think that I'd somehow pulled the wool over the reviewer's eyes? And when I read that my performance was 'banal' did I think, 'Oh my gosh, found out at last'?

The thing is that it's a complicated business getting your work out there into the public sphere and then having people you don't know pass judgement. We've glanced at the issue of imposter syndrome, where you assume that everything positive written about you is bollocks and every negative thing the truth. We all get it. At least we all say we do. And let's not forget that there was still that tall poppy syndrome going on. It's supposed to be a typically British thing. 'You don't get it in America,' you hear. Not true. Our apparently 'critic-proof' show came with an advert directed by Joel Schumacher (a good friend of Andrew's who later directed a movie version of *Phantom*), and there were plenty of critics happy to try and prove that wasn't the case.

Of all the reviews, by far the most damaging, and the one we still talk about now, was Frank Rich's in the *New York Times*.

'If you get a thumbs down from Frank Rich, you don't stand much of a chance,' sighed Trevor all these years later. 'And, I mean, it *was* quite difficult material for Broadway.'

Frank Rich is the critic we've heard of before, called 'the Butcher of Broadway' during his 13-year run between 1980 and 1993. They called him that simply because as the chief theatre critic of the *New York Times* he had the power to significantly impact a Broadway show's success and did not necessarily abide by the Spider-Man rule that with great power comes great responsibility. If Frank Rich didn't like your show, he said so and said it in the bluntest possible terms. And he didn't like *Aspects of Love*.

Rich's review of *Aspects* pretty much tore into every single feature of the production. 'Though *Aspects of Love* purports to deal with romance in many naughty guises – from rampant promiscuity to cradle-snatching, lesbianism and incest – it generates about as much heated passion as a visit to the bank,' he said.

Yes, well. He didn't like the music, of course, saying, 'The composer's usual Puccini-isms have been supplanted by a naked Sondheim envy,' and for good measure added that 'Seeing is Believing' echoes 'Tonight' in *West Side Story*, while 'She'd Be Far Better Off with You' was reminiscent of *A Little Night Music*.

We all got it in the neck. Ann was 'unconvincing'. Kathy was 'a brassy belter' (which I think is supposed to be a bad thing). And as Alex, not only did I 'cut a preposterous figure as a libertine', but I came across as 'a beefy juvenile who would fit right in with the Von Trapp family singers'.

Yes, well. If you've got this far you'll know what I took from that. Unless you're Ian Botham or a burger from the Tesco Finest range, you don't want to be described as 'beefy'. What was the point of having a personal trainer, for God's sake? And as we're on the subject, what on earth does he mean that Alex is a libertine? Is he? Really? Answer: no, he's not.

Of course, Rich picked up on the Jenny situation ('When men thank heaven for little girls in *Aspects of Love,* chances are the girls will turn out to be jailbait.') But also found space to attack what he saw as Andrew's 'misogyny'. According to him the general rule in Lloyd Webber musicals was to present female characters as either prostitutes, as in the case of *Evita*, *Cats* and *Starlight Express* (him saying this, not me), or sainted virgins, as in *Jesus Christ Superstar* and *Phantom*. The women of

Aspects frequently 'behave like bitches and whores, to use the epithets of the male characters. Their men, meanwhile, are overgrown English schoolboys.'

In fact, 'overgrown English schoolboy' is much more accurate than libertine. Alex is immature and petulant. He begins the show hoping to somehow control or at least understand the fluctuations of the heart only to realise that it's just not possible. That's his journey, his arc.

Rose, meanwhile, has a different journey. She sees herself as a free-spirited yet poverty-stricken actress, only to end the show knowing that just one of these things is true. Her signature song, 'Anything But Lonely', is her acknowledgement that she needs love in her life. That she would rather be anything but alone.

Meanwhile, and although Frank Rich seemed to quite like Kevin as George – damning him with the faintest of praise – pretty much everybody else was defenestrated. Maria's 'unflattering' costumes; Gillian's 'scant' choreography; Trevor's 'sexless casting' which, he said, 'only adds to the musical's icy emotional infantilism'; Andrew Bridge's lighting. No, wait, he liked the lighting, even when it served only to highlight the flaws in Maria's scenery.

Still, Rich saved some of his most vicious barbs for Andrew himself. He didn't like any of Andrew's music and there, to some extent, you have the crux of it. If you don't enjoy Andrew Lloyd Webber, and more specifically if you don't like Andrew's score for *Aspects of Love*, there's literally no way you're going to love the show. *Aspects of Love* is through-sung, for God's sake; there's no respite from the Andrew Lloyd Webber-isms throughout. If the repeated snatches of 'Seeing is Believing' aren't your bag, and if the interstitial, between-scene snatches of music are not so much an earworm as a bug, then you're probably not going to enjoy the show.

I don't know. Again you're straying into the territory of claiming that anybody who doesn't like the show doesn't get it, and I really don't think that's the case. What I do think is that Frank Rich, for whatever reason, didn't like Andrew, or didn't like the Brits. He'd been fairly savage about *Phantom*, and particularly unpleasant regarding Sarah, whom he'd called bug-eyed and chipmunk-cheeked. He was very tight with Stephen Sondheim, so maybe there was some competition there. Perhaps it rankled with him that his review wouldn't have the effect it normally would. Or maybe he felt that because the show had opened with such a huge advance we were cushioned from the effects of anything he might say, so he could be as savage as he liked, inflicting as much damage as possible, knowing that it was still going to run for a while. Personally I don't think he would have cared about whether or not he affected people's livelihoods. That, after all, is not the concern of a critic.

What I do know is that the review strayed beyond what I considered to be fair criticism and into something much more personal. The way he had ripped into every department of the show in forensic detail. His blank refusal to try and understand what we were trying to achieve. Sweeney Todd had nothing on the Butcher of Broadway.

Could we survive such a drubbing? That was the question.

Chapter 44

Any other show would have been given its notice in two weeks after a review like that. For us, it was different. Our huge advance cushioned us from any immediate fallout.

Which is not to say that his review had no effect. I've used the word 'critic-proof' several times, but while you can always point to the advance you still have to acknowledge that reviews have their place and if you're going to accept that the good ones will drive traffic towards your show, then you also have to acknowledge the other side of the coin. Broadway is expensive. It's expensive to put on a show and for the public it's expensive to go and see one. When folks go on a trip to New York and decide to 'take in a show', they're not going to see something that hasn't got good reviews. They don't want to spend all those dollars and take a punt on something Frank Rich thought was crap. They want to see the big, buzzy hit that's wowed critics and audiences alike, whatever it is.

The frustrating thing was that those who came loved it.

Whether the critics got it or not, it certainly felt to us as though the audiences did. We were getting lots of repeat business and word of mouth was good. It's just that the critical reaction may have prevented the show reaching that next level. The bookings were not consistent with the advance. We were looking around us. *Phantom*, sold out. *Les Misérables*, sold out. Us? Not so much. Empty chairs.

Then that other measure of success rolls around: the awards. Actually, looking down the list, we were less snubbed at the Tony Awards of 1990 than we had been at the Olivier Awards in London the previous year. Both Kathy and Kevin were nominated. Trevor got a nomination in Best Direction and we were nominated in the Best Musical and Best Book of a Musical categories.

No wins, though. *City of Angels* was doing well that year. A revival of *Gypsy* with Tyne Daly from *Cagney & Lacey* was also making the critics purr.

All these years later, and it's not the Frank Rich bitch that Andrew remembers, or even the fact that *Aspects* on Broadway was, by most measures, a birrova bomb.

It was those Tonys. He's always felt that, particularly on Broadway, *Aspects* was not done quite right. 'It comes back to the thing I was saying of how every element must be together. People are often saying to me how they'd like to revive it or do it in different ways. Perhaps visually it wasn't quite right.'

He also recalled something that had happened years and years ago when the legendary Hal Prince had gone to see 'my disastrous *Jeeves* musical in London, the one I did with Alan Ayckbourn'.

By Jeeves! In 1975, this was. A notable flop. After seeing it,

Hal had written Andrew a note on Savoy notepaper, advising him to 'bank the score of *Jeeves*', and two things had come of that note. Firstly, Andrew took his advice and withdrew the commercially released recording of *Jeeves.* And thus was able to reuse much of the material in subsequent shows, some of it turning up in *Evita*, and some in *Sunset Boulevard.* Added to which, over two decades later, Andrew was able to revive *By Jeeves,* as it was then called, and it did rather well. Altogether an incredible act of recycling.

The second thing to come out of that note was that Andrew and Hal Prince met.

'What are you doing now?' Prince had said.

'I don't know at the moment,' Andrew had replied, 'but Tim Rice is very keen on doing the story of Eva Perón.'

'Well, if you ever do finish the score, give me a call. I'd love to hear it.'

The rest is of course history. Andrew and Tim wrote an album of *Evita* and sent it to Hal Prince, who ended up directing the show in the West End. A show that, if you recall, made the list of Andrew's near-perfect productions, the elusive ones where all of those elements came together successfully.

I think what he's saying is that when one door closes another one opens, and you never know quite what is going to be inside.

It's saying something when a composer with the clout of Andrew Lloyd Webber feels that the staging of one of his shows had got out of control. I wondered then whether he'd approve of our 2023 version. Time would tell.

Back in 1990, ours was a nine-month contract for Equity reasons, after which there would be a cast change. It wasn't as though the show was such a flop that it closed early, only for the cast to be sent home with their tails between their legs. At least I would have the full New York experience, the entire Broadway run under my belt. But at the same time, it was obvious that *Aspects* in America was not going to do the same for me in the US as it had done in the UK. Michael Crawford had gone with *Phantom* to the US and become a huge star, but that wasn't going to happen here. I wouldn't be whisked off to another Broadway show and then find myself making movies in Los Angeles. I was going to do my time in New York and trot off home, which is just what I did. I went straight back.

Looking back now, it almost feels as though it was a sad end to that phase of my *Aspect*s story. Actually, nothing could be further from the truth. I mean, don't get me wrong, it could have been better. It could have been Michael Crawford. But the fact was I still came back as Michael Ball. I had a future in showbiz ahead of me, a life with Cathy to plan. All was better than good, it was brilliant.

And so, for the next 30 or so years, that's what I did. I lived my brilliant life, knowing that so much of what I loved about it was as a direct result of *Aspects*. Until one day I had the idea to do it all again.

PART FOUR

Rocking the Blocking, Wrecking the Tech

Chapter 45

And now let me take you by the hand and spirit you forward in time to early 2022, when having had the idea for *Aspects II*, secured the blessing of Nica Burns and then, at my famous Rules lunch, Andrew, the next step was to attend a meeting at Andrew's office.

Present were me, Nica Burns, Andrew, Don and Charles and members of Andrew's musical team – basically the creative backbone of the show plus the money (oh and me) in order to talk through the show and get a few of the major points decided – major points being what changes we were going to make.

Jenny. The whole Jenny thing. That was going to have to change for reasons already briefly discussed and shortly to be discussed in greater detail. For now, that was all anybody needed to know: when it came to Jenny we were all on the same page, and it was a different page to the page we'd been on before.

Another issue was the placing of 'Love Changes Everything', which ended up being a relatively simple decision. After all,

I'd already decided that, firstly, I was going to play George and, secondly, I wanted to sing 'Love Changes Everything'. Now – and I do hope this isn't a spoiler – George dies shortly before the end of the show, so he's definitely not going to sing it at the end.

Should he sing it at the beginning? He could, but if he did, then it would mean employing the same framing device we'd used the first time around, and nobody was especially taken with that solution. *Aspects of Love* has several time shifts as it is. The idea of adding another one, a 'backwards in time' shift at that, had only ever been a means to end. We didn't really want to introduce it again.

Much better, we decided, was to have George sing it part way through Act I, when, as Andrew said, it becomes a statement of his creed. I would still have to do a big money note, of course, but slightly lower, and it wouldn't come at the end of the show.

We also talked about the length of the show. *Aspects* is a through-sung musical, don't forget, and our original had a lot of recitative, and a fair bit of music in between scene changes. It also had quite a bit of spoken dialogue, and if you speak in a through-sung musical then those words have got to be important, otherwise why are you breaking the moment and speaking? And some of those moments weren't that important.

In the event, we shaved off about 10 to 15 minutes and were quite happy with that. As Don says, 'You don't write a musical, you rewrite it.' Shows are always evolving. Famously, *Chess* has gone through a million different permutations and they still never got the book right. Same with *Mack & Mabel*. *Sweeney Todd* was changed, as was *Passion*. Sometimes it's for timing reasons, as with *Les Misérables*. Sometimes it's just because the show isn't quite right and needs a tweak. The instant smashes tend to stay the same, even during revivals. It's the ones that maybe didn't reach their full potential – and, yes, I'd include *Aspects* in that – that tend to get rewritten the most. You have to be open to that; you have to be on the lookout for ways in which the show can improve, and with a show like *Aspects*, which is built around many different scenes in quite a filmic way, the challenge is to keep the action moving so the audience doesn't get bored. Changing technology makes the transition between stages faster and smoother; audience expectations have changed in the intervening 34 years. Things need to happen with a bit more snap, crackle and pop.

A harmonious meeting, then. I tell you what, though. The best thing about it was just looking around the room and thinking how bloody great it was to be back in a room with these guys. Honestly, I'm getting all misty-eyed just thinking about it now. Of the creatives I'd worked with on the original *Aspects*, each had in their own way contributed to a show that had become part of my DNA, not only a chapter in my life story, but in many ways the key to it. And although *Aspects* possibly didn't figure quite as prominently in the lives of Don, Charles and Andrew, I knew they had a soft spot for it and were just as pleased to be revisiting what had been a strong bond between us.

Besides which, the first time around I was just a turn. My focus was on 'my bit', and as we've already established, my bit was pretty manic in 1989. My situation now felt like being offered a seat at the table. Or like going back in time and being able to see things from a different perspective.

*

Now, you may be wondering why no Trevor on board this time. It wasn't a snub, promise. Nobody decided that they didn't want to be Trev'd. Just that it was thought, mainly by me, although there was general agreement, that having Trevor on board would make it too much in terms of revisiting the material. By assembling the same band we risked playing the same songs the same way, which was not quite what we wanted to do. We needed a fresh set of eyes. At the same time we needed a director who would command the respect of Andrew, Don and Charles, someone from whom they would willingly take suggestion. In other words, he had to be a veritable giant in our field.

I proposed Jonathan Kent. He'd been artistic director of the Almeida Theatre for all of the nineties, working with Ian McDiarmid to stage some of the greatest productions of that era: *When We Dead Awaken, All for Love, Medea, The Showman, The School for Wives, The Rules of the Game* and so on. He's worked extensively elsewhere and has also directed opera, and in 2016 was made a CBE for services to theatre and music. Far more important than all of this, of course, was the fact that he had directed me in *Sweeney Todd,* a production that, thanks to his direction and some truly wonderful chemistry between me and Imelda Staunton, was one of the most perfect I've ever been involved with.

Other names were proposed, of course. Such-and-such could bring this to the table. Such-and-such could bring that to the table. All discussions were absolutely valid and of course an essential part of the process. As with the casting later on down the line we looked into every name put forward. But in my head, the director I wanted was Jonathan, added to which

I was hoping to get Nick Skilbeck as musical supervisor on board, and they often came as a package. Nick had worked on dozens and dozens of shows including the Tina Turner musical, *Sister Act, Chitty Chitty Bang Bang*, and the Kate Bush Concerts at the Hammersmith Apollo. He and I had worked together on *Hairspray* and *Sweeney*, and I thought he'd be amazing, and that he'd bring a totally different sensibility to it, especially as he had not previously worked with Andrew and didn't know the show.

That to me was the essence of getting something new: it was presenting seasoned talent with material that was fresh to them.

After that, more meetings. I know that Jonathan met with Andrew. I also had a one-to-one with Jonathan on the south coast. He came down for the day and we just sat around with the script, the two of us going through it, saying, 'Well, that needs to change, that doesn't work, nothing wrong with that,' just to get the brain cells working so that he was informed enough to then sit with Andrew, Don and Charles and put forward his vision in order that they could then go away and make the necessary changes. Nothing major. It's not like we decided that Jenny should attack Alex with a chainsaw. Just a series of what were virtually invisible amends in order to bring the production more in line with, firstly, 2023 sensibility, and secondly Jonathan's creative needs.

*

It was at this stage that I took my leave. It's a bit like teaching a kid to ride a bike without stabilisers. You get them to a stage where they no longer need your help then step away and watch them go. Once you engage the creative team, get them going so they're just as excited as you are, it's over to them. You can discuss things with them, but they're the ones who'll have to sit down and actually make it work.

Besides which, it wasn't for me to insist on how I envisaged the show and stamp my feet until my monstrous and outrageous demands were met. One of the reasons I love this job so much is the excitement of getting the right people for the right jobs, then standing back and, like a proud parent, watching them do their amazing work. Even though I'd originated the idea, and going forward would be the public face of the 2023 *Aspects of Love* revival, it wasn't as though I was the sole pilot. From then on, my job would be to act as a figurehead for the show. Be the mouthpiece, the front man, get people's juices flowing.

Chapter 46

Which does of course raise the question as to who has the final word in a production like *Aspects*?

As we've already discussed, if Andrew ever came good on one of his threats not to let the orchestra play his music, then no doubt that would be the final word in final words. You might say that he has the final veto, certainly where the music is concerned. Then again, the director will say that they're the most important, because it's their vision. The writers will say they are, because they've created the whole damn thing. The turns will say they're the most important because it's us the public want to see, darling.

But the buck stopping? I mean, really to a halt? Well, I guess you'd have to say that it stops at the money. And the money is the producer, Nica in our case, whose job is to finesse and negotiate terms, and in short order to tread a fine line between the creative vision of the composer, director, writers and designers. If anyone falls out with anyone else, it's up to the producer to calm things down. And when it comes to getting paid, it's the producer who signs the cheques.

As for me, I'm the one who'd have to go on telly to talk about it. But at no point was I ever making those big, controlling decisions. I mean, I could probably throw my weight around and demand a Jacuzzi in my dressing room. But I was never going to do that, partly because I have my 'nicest guy in showbiz' reputation to uphold, and mainly because the last thing I wanted to do was sully my memories of 1989 with a fraught and unpleasant production in 2023. *Aspects II* would be a diva-free zone. What I wanted was hard work, a challenge. What I didn't want was needless pain and stress.

Another of Nica's many jobs – and perhaps the most important reason that the buck stops at the producer – is that producers do what they do to raise the money. Firstly, they put their own investment into it; secondly they raise funds from outside investors. Was I investing cash? No. Never invest money in your own production. You have to have a producer on the case.

Now, the original *Aspects* came on the back of *Phantom*, when everybody wanted to see the brand-new Lloyd Webber musical, and so they'd filled the seats and made £10 million before it even opened. Not a note was sung and the show was recouped.

That was never going to happen with *Aspects II.* It's a very different world now – that sort of thing doesn't happen. But the West End of now is slightly different, dominated by jukebox musicals and big special effects-led productions.

Back then: *Aspects of Love* was *boof*, the new Lloyd Webber. Where do I sign?

Now? Well, now, it has a slightly chequered history. It's

Andrew Lloyd Webber's strange oddity of a show that failed to replicate the success of his previous work and outright flopped on Broadway.

So not necessarily an easy sell for Nica, then. But perhaps made easier with certain names attached (cough). Her task was to juggle that potential appetite for a revival with the cost of production, ticket revenue, the fact that it's a limited run, all the kind of stuff that I could never in a million years do. What's useful in our case, of course, is that she also owns the theatre, so she could do a deal with herself for the rent.

Aspects was never going to be a huge money-spinner. Truthfully, you don't do theatre to make money. It's not where the fortune lies – me, I'd make far more doing a concert tour. We did it because we loved the thought of it, because it was exciting to revisit one of Andrew's shows, a challenging but beautiful piece. We did it because we love the art form and because it's something that felt new, not just another *Joseph*, another *Sunset Boulevard*.

It's also a show that still has relevance now. When do affairs of the human heart ever lose relevance? It was always one of the things that made it a fascinating outlier in Andrew's back catalogue. It's not based on a biblical story. Not about South American leaders, chandeliers or trains. It's a show about people. A smaller, much more intimate piece based on a fairly obscure novel that nobody saw coming from him and all these years later it still looks like a slightly atypical entry in his catalogue. For all these reasons, I thought it could find its place in 2023.

Or at least I really, really hoped so.

Of course there was lots being done behind the scenes. I've explained the process with the casting director. That was taking place around then. Meanwhile the producers were working out all the other bits and bobs. Who to employ for PR, who was going to be stage manager, who was going to be company manager? – actually the last one was a no-brainer; I first met Jo Miles when she was assistant stage manager on *Les Misérables* and have worked with her ever since. She takes no shit from flaky snowflakes but somehow does it in a kind way, which is quite a talent. Also what about the costume department, the wig maker?

This is a Nimax production so you're not working with people fresh out of college, you're working with the best, experts in their field, and for that reason, they usually have a pretty full dance card and can't just drop everything and move over to *Aspects* on a whim. There's an incredible amount of diary juggling that goes on.

Regarding a designer, Jonathan had approached a few people, and a number said no for varying reasons – busy, didn't know what they could do with it, didn't get their juices flowing – and that was disappointing but par for the course. After all, we are all masters of our own destiny, and I've said no to loads of things simply because I couldn't do it at the time or it wasn't something I felt was right for me.

In the end, Jonathan hit on the idea of John Macfarlane, who had not done musical theatre before but was very experienced in opera design. He had been under Jonathan's nose the whole time. Fortuitous, perhaps, that other designers had turned him down.

The benefits? John Macfarlane certainly fulfilled the brief of coming to the show with a fresh pair of eyes. What's more, he is an incredible artist and painter.

The drawbacks? 'I've never done something this quickly,' he told us, having come up with a bunch of designs we were to look over. They were brilliant, but the timescale remained an issue. In opera you have two years or so to get a thing up and running, we . . . well, we didn't have that.

The other thing John had to do was fit in with our stated desire to have the scenes moving quickly, establishing a flow that takes the audience along with them. We couldn't have clunky scene changes. The recitative was being streamlined in order to facilitate that, so the designs needed to fall into place as well.

Lots to do, then. What's more, we would soon be passing the point of no return. We'd be announcing to the world that *Aspects of Love* was back, back, back.

Chapter 47

As we moved into the last few months of 2022, I was busy with the business of being me. There was a Las Vegas special with Alfie Boe, various things in the run-up to our new album, *Together in Vegas*, and my first novel, *The Empire*, was published, which meant promotional duties, recording the audiobook, going on *Loose Women*, *Saturday Kitchen*, various bits and pieces. It's a full-time job, you know.

Regarding *Aspects*, I started dropping little hints on social media. Something new coming up. Can you guess what it is? Most were wrong, but some of them right. You know who you are, you clever clogs.

I'd mention things in interviews, too. Obviously you go into these gigs supposed to talk about one thing – the novel, the album – and your PR people for that project will be saying, 'No, you can't talk about the novel / the album, you have to talk about the album / the novel,' and then the next set of PR people for the other project would say the same, but I'm pretty wily in interviews. I've got good at letting the interviewer ask a question and then being able to shoehorn everything I want to say into my answer. And so as well as keeping my novel and record people happy, I was also dropping in hints for my big announcement to come.

And then, at the beginning of October, the announcement was made when they ran an advert. It was 'Michael Ball' (big letters) 'in Andrew Lloyd Webber's' (smaller letters. I mean, quite a lot smaller) '*Aspects of Love*' (okay, really, really big letters. Cameron is right. The show's the star.)

And that's when the buzz really began. Then as I toured the country doing book signings, appearing on *Lorraine* and Zoe Ball's breakfast show, *This Morning*, I'm talking about the book. I'm talking about the album with Alfie. And I'm talking about *Aspects of Love.*

The reaction was really great, both from the media and the general public. The forums of theatre websites were alight. You had some people saying, 'Oh my god, I can't wait! This is where I fell in love with Michael Ball.'

And you got others going, 'I'll go, but only on the understudy day.'

And this one I loved: 'It's just a vanity project.'

Now look, love. If it was a vanity project I wouldn't be playing an old man for starters. If it was just a vanity project, I'd do a one-man show. Boom. It may be many things. A trip down memory lane. But it ain't a vanity project.

And then, as the month wore on, there came an article in the *Daily Telegraph*. The headline was: 'Incest, skinned rabbits and 007 – why Andrew Lloyd Webber's worst musical should be buried forever.'

Uh oh.

Now this was quite a hatchet job. The article, by Marianka Swain, began by pointing out that *Aspects of Love*, with its tales of bed-hopping and partner swapping, is a bizarre concept and then quickly swooped in on the whole Jenny issue, specifically her age, as well as some of the more, erm, 'challenging dialogue' associated with her growing affection for Alex.

Marianka, whom I later met, called it a 'truly outlandish, and often queasy melodrama', and is not necessarily wrong about that. It is indeed intended to ask questions of its characters and its audience; secondly, it's worth repeating that the show was never meant to be an upbeat and joyous celebration of love, rather an examination of it. When Alex meets Rose at the beginning, he is an impressionable and immature young man who falls in love with a woman who doesn't even know her own mind, let alone her own heart; by the show's end, a much older and more jaded Alex has caught the eye of an impressionable young girl. Nobody is saying that any of these characters are role models whose actions are to be admired and copied. We watch them with a mixture of horror and amusement.

The *Telegraph* piece pointed out that while *Aspects* had enjoyed a respectable run in London, it had flopped on Broadway, losing its entire $10 million investment in the process. She pointed out that the 'bombastic staging' had undermined Andrew's stated intention of staging a 'chamber musical' only to add that lower-key revivals (Trevor's 2010 production at the Menier Chocolate Factory, a 2018 staging at the Hope Mill Theatre in Manchester that transferred to the Southwark Playhouse) only 'seemed to magnify the show's flaws'.

She came close by saying that 'the planned 2023 revival at

the Lyric Theatre in the West End . . . is reportedly making changes for this new production. But what exactly can they do to make it palatable for a post-MeToo world? We're now on high alert for power imbalance in relationships, or for older men taking advantage of young girls.'

And just for good measure, the piece ended with, '[The show] makes *Lolita* look positively wholesome. Maybe love does change everything, but so does time – and I can't imagine that it's been good to this curate's egg of a show.'

As Tony the Tiger might say, 'Grrrreat.'

Chapter 48

Once the announcement was made and I began promoting the show in earnest, my thoughts turned to the past, and I found myself reflecting on what *Aspects* had brought to my life. It had cemented a great relationship with the fans who have, I'm pleased to say, stayed with me (although what they don't realise is that I exert a sinister form of mind control via my albums and performances. I'm doing it now); it had brought me incredible experiences in London and in New York; and it had brought me love.

At the same time, I thought in a bittersweet way about the passing of the years, memories prompted by feedback from people who were there in 1989, and were involved in the original, or even just came along to see it. We'd trace a line all the way back, thinking about what's happened to us over the intervening years, how we're still here, some of us – I never forget that we've lost quite a few along the way – only now we're playing the older role.

I know it was that metaphor for life that had proved a decisive factor for Jonathan in signing on. He found it profoundly moving that as a young man, I'd played snotty-nosed Alex ('libertine'! I ask you!) and now was returning to play George. For him, the idea of the boy now being the older man was a compelling one.

That's why the idea of doing *Aspects II* was never simply about wallowing in nostalgia. For me, doing the show, and indeed writing this book, was all about showing who I was then and who I am now; showing how we've all changed and mellowed; how the show has changed, and how love has changed.

Which is not to say there's no nostalgia involved. I'm not completely daft. Of course there are going to be those who will have seen the 1989 version and then go to see the new one expecting that warm rush of nostalgia.

My instinct, though, was that even if they went in feeling that way, they wouldn't come out thinking the same. Right from the start it was my intention to bring something new to the production. Did I feel it needed saving from the dustbin of history? No, not really. It was never in the dustbin of history. Yes, it didn't do so well on Broadway, but by any normal standards it had a decent run in the West End, just that it wasn't the big Andrew Lloyd Webber blockbuster that people had been expecting. *Cats*, 21 years, *Starlight*, 17 years, *Phantom*, still playing at the time of writing. These were shows that never really lost their allure or glamour, whereas *Aspects* probably *did* lose its shine, was overshadowed by other, bigger, sexier things and so when it closed, it closed not in a blaze of triumph and glory, but with a whimper.

But maybe that was because of the show it is. It doesn't have a satisfying pay-off. Its characters are selfish and hedonistic. Even the 'nice' characters like George often behave in quite unpleasant, self-serving ways. Their saving grace is gifted to them by Andrew, i.e. his beautiful score, and if it's always been a source of amazement to me that the score doesn't get as much love as it should, then perhaps that's because of the story leaving people scratching their heads. If you don't get the fact that 'Anything But Lonely' is Rose finally baring her soul after what may be years of hiding her true self, then maybe 'Anything But Lonely' won't land quite the way it should. Perhaps you don't appreciate that the song is in fact one of Andrew's greatest 11th-hour female torch songs, up there with 'Memory' from *Cats* or 'One Look' from *Sunset*. That was always the challenge we had. How to make these occasionally selfish characters appealing. How to get the audience to care what happens to them, to engage with them, and maybe see something of themselves in them. Most theatre transports you, it takes you away from yourself. *Aspects* doesn't do that, certainly not for any sustained amount of time. And as Alex falls in love with Rose, you might think, 'Ah, a sweet love story,' only for the show to pull the rug from under your feet when Rose goes off with his Uncle George. Truly, this is a production in which love is yucky and messy. It doesn't lead you towards a life-affirming climax where two characters we've been hoping will get together eventually end up with each other. It's not 'sail off into the sunset, everything is great'. It's hand me the wine and the dice. What happens in the future? Who knows? It's not written.

I didn't mention much of this during my promo duties. That's not what they want to hear on the sofa at *This Morning*. I didn't tell them about the ambiguous ending or the fact that this one is Andrew's 'difficult' show. I focused on the personal changes it brought me, and I namechecked 'Love Changes Everything'.

And maybe at times I asked myself, *Am I doing the right thing here?* I mean, if I'm reluctant to talk about the subject matter of *Aspects of Love* during interviews in which I'm supposed to talk about the subject matter of *Aspects of Love*, then is it possible I was backing the wrong horse?

Chapter 49

After various costume meetings came the photo shoot at which the principals for *Aspects* would be together for the very first time. I'd had lunch with Laura and, as I said before, I'd invited Jamie on to my Radio 2 Piano Room appearance, but at no stage had we all been under the same roof. Here was where we'd try our character costumes (not necessarily the finished versions), shoot little promotional films, and get our pictures taken for the poster and promotional material.

Nica Burns was there, too. She had something she wanted to talk to me about. And what she wanted to talk to me about was 'the Jenny situation'.

*

Okay, so here's the bit where we go into that particular issue in some depth. And the reason we're dealing with it in detail is that it evolved into a fascinating talking point that somehow encompassed so much that was relevant to us. It became about the era in which the show is set, and the society when the play was first performed compared to society now; it became about character, how Jamie and Anna approached their roles and interpreted certain lines. And a little bit. Just a little bit. It became about where the buck stops.

So, okay, quick recap. Act I of *Aspects* is all about boy meets girl. Then girl goes off with his uncle and marries the uncle.

In other words, it revolves around Alex, Rose, George and, to a lesser extent, Giulietta, who gets her same-sex kiss right at the end of the act.

By Act II, Rose and George have had a daughter, Jenny. Alex is George's nephew, which makes him and Jenny cousins. Over the years Jenny develops feelings for Alex and subsequently makes them obvious. He, for his part, struggles with his own growing affections, thus his conscience and the disapproval of those around him, especially his aunt (and former lover) Rose, and his Uncle George.

George is especially affected. In fact, when he realises the extent of Alex and Jenny's relationship, the shock of it is so great that he keels over, dies (and then, after a short rest in his dressing room, reappears to lead the cast in a bow).

So all of this was a little bit tricky in 1989 when we did it. A bit of an issue.

In 2023? A really big issue.

Which is not to say that we were in any way cavalier in 1989. Oh no. Far from it. We went into great detail and were crystal clear that Alex was never at any stage secretly lusting after Jenny. He liked her, for sure. He found her charming company. But only as his young cousin. There was never any sense that he was 'grooming' her. For him it was just a huge irony that when he was young he went crazy for an older woman, who then goes off with an older man, together they have a child and the child becomes fixated on him. He, no stranger to the heart's strange ways, understands the impulsivity, but he doesn't encourage it, quite the reverse.

For Jenny's part, there's no coercion involved; her love for Alex is just the way she feels, and she's been brought up not to be ashamed of her feelings nor be shy in expressing them. Her agency is actually empowering her as a character and as a person.

'I was a bit uncomfortable because I find that sort of thing creepy,' said Charles when I raised the issue. 'Especially all that business in the bedroom – but I'm not sure the audiences were particularly worried.'

He was right. There was far more attention given to our lesbian kiss. But here we are, 34 years on, and the whole idea of grooming and relationships of vastly differing ages is just too much of a hot potato. (And bear in mind as you read on that while there was much effort involved in downplaying and rejigging the relationship between Alex and Jenny, we increased the prominence of the same-sex kiss to general approval. That's the changing times for you.)

So anyway, it was a given that the Jenny situation needed to be addressed. That day that I spoke to firstly Nica and then Andrew at Rules, I had agreed that something needed to be done, I just wasn't sure what, exactly, or to what extent. Just that we needed to acknowledge how sensibilities have changed over the intervening years. I should mention here, by the way, that broadly speaking, I don't mind making an audience feel uncomfortable, as long as there isn't a happy ending for the people who behave badly. See *Sweeney Todd* for details.

When we subsequently met with the creatives and the issue came up, it was decided that Jenny's age should be increased by a year. In 1989 she had first appeared at 12 (though nothing of any romantic nature occurs in that section), and then later at 14 prior to her 15th birthday, after which she made her feelings for Alex clear.

Now she would be 16, thus the age of consent, while certain other moments in the script would be tweaked. The bit Charles referred to. 'All the business in the bedroom' (and also the source of my Favourite-Ever Corpse, if you recall), would have to go.

But that's not quite enough, because in 2023, we're much more aware of different power dynamics. We know that it's not as black and white as saying, 'If it's legal, it's okay'. Even we ageing ladies and gentlemen in that meeting knew to ask ourselves, 'It may be legal, but is it moral?' And if so, does it matter? My point was always that Alex never grooms Jenny, doesn't act on his emotions, and ultimately rejects her invitation, so no harm was ever done.

'It'll still have the same impact if she's 16,' I was told.

Maybe. Maybe not.

To be clear, my mind was not yet made up on the issue. I didn't want this to be distasteful, but at the same time, I was aware that the piece relies on high-stakes emotions. This, after all, is a situation that doesn't just anger and outrage George, it actually *kills* him. You as the audience need to share his shock somehow, otherwise he just looks like he's overreacting.

So anyway, I agreed. I didn't think it had quite the same punch, but fine: she'd be 16. Don and Charles made their tweaks, and when the first libretto was submitted, Jenny's birthday was removed; in fact, all reference to Jenny's age was taken out.

Chapter 50

That libretto came out before the piece in the *Telegraph*, and the piece in the *Telegraph* came out before the photo shoot, where Nica wanted to speak to me. Having been moved by the piece, Nica had reached out to Marianka Swain. She didn't go into great detail on what was said, just that she and various other people, by which I took to mean investors, had got cold feet about the issue. 'We don't want the only conversation about *Aspects* to be about underage sex and grooming,' she told me. She was proposing that Jenny be 18.

For me that changed things a lot, and performance-wise made it a slightly tougher proposition, particularly for Jamie, playing Alex, and Anna, who plays Jenny. With less that was overtly 'wrong' about their relationship, they would need to explore the less obviously uncomfortable facets of them being together, basically that they were cousins and had known each other since she was 12.

Still a bit icky. No doubt. Just lacking that dramatic heft.

I spoke to Anna about it. Bearing in mind that Anna is 19, and therefore quite capable of playing Jenny at 18 or going down to play her at 16. How old did she think Jenny should be?

Sixteen, she said. Absolutely. The lines are written for a girl of sixteen. They're how a 16-year-old would speak.

I talked about it with Laura, too. 'You know, the first boy I kissed, I was 15, he was 25, and it was fabulous. I just wanted to snog all my teachers. That's how you feel at 15. That's the reality. No one's thinking, "Am I old enough to do this?" And I was never coerced into it. I was just a normal 15-year-old girl who had pashes.'

This was it. Sixteen to 18 was just a matter of two years, but it seemed to make all the difference. It recast the attraction from that of a teenage 'pash' to a grown woman – who can vote, marry, fight in a war – forming an attachment to a man who's much older. What's more, there were still lines that painted her as being very young. George, at one point, calls Alex a 'selfish little cradle snatcher'. We had Jenny saying lines such as, 'Grown-ups are so funny, they're not grown-up at all,' which an 18-year-old would never say.

'It doesn't really make sense,' I contended. 'Why would an 18-year-old say that?'

'Well, maybe she's led a very sheltered life,' they told me.

'She bloody hasn't,' I retorted. 'Her mum is Rose, for God's sake. Rose has a husband and one, maybe two lovers.'

For me as George, the question is, am I playing a guy with a 16-year-old daughter who's becoming a woman and feeling the feels. Or am I playing a guy with a slightly backward 18-year-old daughter who talks like a child and probably should get out more.

So these are things that were in the mix, issues up for discussion. It's surprising how big it can get, not knowing the age of one of your central characters, how it can throw things into disarray.

However, whereas we in the cast were finding it difficult to deal with, as far as Nica was concerned, it was very much a hill she was prepared to die on, and with her enjoying buck-stopping status, as well as having a firmer opinion on the matter, it was at some point decided once and for all that Jenny should be 18. The birthday party stayed scrapped but so was the idea that her age should never be mentioned. Again to ward off any accusations of whatever it was we were worried about, Don and Charles inserted little lines that specifically referred to her as being 18. Other references – the line about grown-ups, the line about being a selfish cradle snatcher – remained, and I'll leave you to make your own mind up about whether in context they work or not. Do they make her appear a little backward for an 18-year-old girl? Are they simply appropriate to the era? You can read them different ways. Jenny's line could be interpreted as being a protest at what she perceives as being infantilised. George, the overreaction of a protective father.

I went back to the issue with Charles shortly before the run started, when he visited me in my dressing room. 'You think we've done the right thing?' he asked me.

'Now I do,' I said. 'At first I thought that just because people are uncomfortable doesn't mean we shouldn't show it. And after all, the bottom line is that Alex behaves morally correctly. But now I think it's right, and I think that Jamie and Anna have found a way to make it work.'

'Also,' he said, 'I think there's a difference between making an audience uncomfortable and making them uncomfortable as they enjoy the show. I mean, if you watch a horror film, the audience are uncomfortable watching somebody's head get chopped off, but they're not horrified that somebody would even make a film where a person's head is chopped off. There's a distinction.'

So, had we put it to bed? Had we successfully headed off all criticism at the pass? Spoiler alert. No. Possibly we had merely mitigated it. Watch this space.

Meanwhile, the last word goes to Charles: 'However people leave the theatre, we don't want them to go out with an unambiguous message that our lives are much better for love. This show isn't entirely pink. It's got shadow in it.'

Couldn't agree more.

Chapter 51

There's nothing like heading the cast of an upcoming West End show to focus the mind when it comes to looking good and feeling fit. I'm not a huge drinker, honest, but even so, as 2023 made its presence felt, I gave up the grog.

I have to say, the results were instantaneous. I'd already had one costume fitting, but by the time of a second I'd lost an inch on my waist. Combined with a healthier food intake, I ended up losing well over a stone. Expect my *Aspects of Love*-Plan diet book any time soon.

And so it came to pass that feeling a little trimmer, I trotted off to this photo shoot, the one I've already mentioned, where Nica collared me about Jenny's age.

That particular discussion was just one facet of what was by any measure a brilliant day with jam on top. Not just a photo shoot, it was also a chance for everybody to get together, try on costumes for the first time, do a bit of promo work and generally behave like excited parents wrapping presents for a family Christmas. The world knew we were doing *Aspects* and that I was to head the cast. But that was it. After today we would be able to announce more names and faces and start to really shout about what we had to offer.

The first thing to note was that everything fitted. God knows how many times I've stood there like Coco Chanel's muse, having my measurements taken, only to turn up to a fitting and have nothing actually fit. Out come the safety pins and gaffer tape. Look at a studio shot of a performer, and you can bet your bottom dollar that out of sight are pins and tape, the full *Blue Peter* keeping their clothes snug – or, in some cases, actually *on*.

But not this time. Everything fit! Diet and everything.

Now, I'd told them from the very beginning: don't give me a linen suit. Honestly, you put me in a linen suit and I'll look like a dishcloth in 20 minutes.

That was all I had to say regarding my costume. Literally my one bloody stipulation. At the first fitting they'd been wheeling out various fabrics. 'We've got this beautiful . . .'

'Yes, beautiful *linen*.'

In shops, Cathy has a fabric test. She gets the arm of a garment, scrunches it, lets it go and if it stays wrinkled then that's what it's going to look like after two seconds sitting down.

So that's what I did to prove my point. I did my professional crinkle test. 'You see? This is what's going to happen to me. If I wear this suit for two minutes, I'll look like I've been on a six-month bender.'

'Yes, but this is the South of France . . .'

'Yes, but in that suit I won't look like I'm in the South of France. I'll look like I'm in Luton town centre at closing time on Saturday. Okay, look. For the second half, fine. He's an old man doddering around his house, so he can look like that. At the beginning, I want more David Niven than Boris Johnson.'

Mainly, and this is testament to our designer John Macfarlane, the whole business of creating character through wigs and costumes is a collaborative process. John had ideas about the colour palette for the show and would definitely have dug his heels in on that score, but otherwise he was completely open to how we wanted to play the character, and thus how the character would dress themselves.

I'd be like, 'I love the idea of this, but a double-breasted suit doesn't work on me; go for a single, go for a waistcoat.' (We went for the waistcoat.)

'Do you want a tie? Or a cravat?'

'George is a cravat kind of guy, so go for that.' (We went for the cravat.)

And then: linengate. I arrived at the photocall only to discover that they were *still* trying to sneak me into linen. Cue the crinkle test and a little bit of toy / pram action (Me? Never!) and we were all good.

Hair. That's another thing. On the day of the shoot we went for a side parting, like my dad, knowing it wasn't the look I would necessarily end up with, just as long as it looked George-*ish* – a hairstyle that George might have worn at some point in his colourful and hedonistic life.

All these decisions are all very well, but what really excited me was the fact that the day marked what I hoped would be the beginning of a brilliant bond between us all. I knew Jamie and Laura, although I'd yet to see how they looked together and wanted to watch that chemistry form, but I'd only briefly met Dani, who because she knows Alfie had come backstage at one of our concerts. And I hadn't met Anna Unwin, our Jenny, at all.

And I loved them, of course. I loved how Jamie used the opportunity to get a free haircut; I loved how they all instantly seemed to get on with one another. You worry, you do; you go through the casting process thinking, firstly, *Is this the best person for the role?* And secondly, *Are they going to integrate with others in the company?* Here's where you get your first clues as to whether your instincts have been correct. You step into this atmosphere in Holborn Studios, which isn't actually in Holborn, it's in Hoxton, but never mind, with S Club 7's 'Reach' blasting out – my go-to deep, deep joy song – and you're immediately confronted by loads of other performers in various states of dress and undress, technicians setting up lighting and cameras, people filming, people filming the people filming; you've got producers Nica and Laurence buzzing around, so you say hello to them, and then somebody's offering you a coffee ('Yes, lovely, thank you so much.'), and a biscuit ('No, darling, thank you, how do you think I maintain this svelte physique?'). Somebody else is handing you a jacket they want you to try, and you hand it back. ('Linen, darling, linen.') Then you go into make-up where they're creating your look, giving you a bit of powder, deciding what to do with your hair. 'Are you keeping the beard for George? Maybe change it . . .'

And throughout all this, we principals are like planets moving around each other, occasionally colliding: 'Hello, my name is Michael, we'll be snogging later,' until it gets to what you might call 'our bit' when we assemble in groups for photos. And because they were asking us to go straight into poses that represented our relationships, we were embracing, we were snogging, we were entwined and there was no wall up, no awkwardness or hesitation. I don't think I'm speaking just for myself when I say that we felt an instant fraternity form.

After that – or maybe before, or maybe even during, it's all a bit of a blur – we were doing a bit of social media in the form of little videos, soundbites and behind-the-scenes action.

'Describe *Aspects of Love* in three words.'

So Laura's going, 'Passionate. Sweeping. Romantic.'

Somebody else is going, 'Intensity. Beauty. Love.'

And I'm going, 'Starring. Michael. Ball.'

That's me. Never knowingly undersold.

There were more chats with Nica and Laurence, who seemed pleased with our progress and thrilled with a dynamic that they could see beginning to develop. The one thing that hadn't been sorted was an alternate for me. Because I do my radio show on a Sunday morning, and knowing that after a week of shows, two on Saturday and then the show on Sunday I'd be dead on my feet, I had elected to take Monday off. Thus, we needed walking cover for me.

Hands up who remembers what 'walking cover' is? That's everybody. Good. It means you were paying attention during the Roger Moore chapters when Kevin Colson was Roger's walking cover. From that you will also recall that the walking cover, or alternate, was required to shadow the person they were covering, thus, as you can probably appreciate, it was important to get the alternate sorted as soon as possible.

I had thrown a few names into the hat, but nothing had so far progressed. It was a difficult role to cast. We needed someone who was established which, because of George's age, was practically a given. On the other hand, that person, who would have to have some miles on the clock, would also have to be content to accept just one show a week, plus any shows that I might miss due to ill health or otherwise. (It would take a while, and it went down to the wire but you'll remember that we eventually managed to tempt my old *Phantom* pal Dave Willetts on board, which was quite a coup, and my original suggestion.)

So that was a worry but also not my concern. Later, we were shown the various pictures taken during the day, and they talked me through a mock-up of what the poster would look like. The idea was that this poster should be used for an initial phase of marketing prior to production photos that would go front of house, in the programme and, eventually, on the proper posters. They had this idea of the letters LOVE, with four of us appearing around the letters.

There's all sorts of trickery and dark arts that go on, especially regarding the particular image that we used. My arm was separate to my body, and they had to flow it in so that it went around the L of 'love'. Half joking, I said to them, 'So you'll make it look nice, will you? You'll Photoshop it to make it right, yes?'

Possibly they took me a little too seriously, because the next day new versions arrived and I don't know who was playing George, but he was very thin, very handsome and very young.

I showed the new images to Cathy. 'Oh, they're lovely,' she said.

'Yeah, they're lovely,' I said, 'but they're not *me*.'

It's possibly the first time in the history of entertainment that the turn has gone back and said, 'Actually, can you make me look a bit older and fatter?' I am not by any stretch of the imagination hench, and they've got me looking as hench as a hench thing.

So anyway, after that frankly stupendous day came the second phase of the announcement, during which the full cast was revealed. Jamie had already been revealed, but to him we added Laura, whose casting gained universal approval within the theatre community, as well as Anna – and it was very exciting that she should be making her West End debut – and Dani, who briefly made the headlines by pulling out of that production at Glyndebourne in order to do *Aspects* – something made even more eyebrow-raising by the fact that she's married to Gus Christie, aka Mr Glyndebourne.

All very exciting. And I couldn't have been happier with the way things had progressed so far. Next? Only bloomin' first day of school.

Chapter 52

Rehearsal rule number one (and this was the memo Roger missed): you wear comfortable clothes that you don't mind getting knackered, because rehearsals are usually long days during which you might find yourself grovelling around on a dirty floor.

Me, I go in T-shirts, jeans and so on, although I did buy myself a pair of Jordan 1 trainers, just to make an impression on the first day. I told myself I may be the old fart in the company, but I'm still down with the kids. Not in denial. Oh no.

Our rehearsal rooms were to be on the fourth floor of Holborn library which is, I'm happy to say, a proper, working library and genuinely located in Holborn. I'm even happier to say that literally the first thing I saw as I walked into the library on that first day of school was a copy of my novel, *The Empire.*

A-ha, I thought. *This is going to be a good day*.

I swear that the book wasn't put there deliberately, just

because they knew I was coming in. I was very much incognito, darlings. But if they did, then, well, I thank them – it gave me a real lift. And if they didn't, then I still thank them.

On the fourth floor, I was met by our company manager, Jo Miles. I mentioned knowing Jo from years back, but what I didn't say was that her grandfather was *the* Lord Bernard Miles who had opened the legendary Mermaid Theatre in London and was a renowned actor in his own right. He was a friend of my dad's and I remember, just before I started drama school, how he'd stayed with my parents, and together we did a scene from *Henry IV, Part 2*.

Anyway, Jo was his granddaughter who'd worked on *Les Mis*. And because I'd known her for so long, we were instantly catching up on life: 'How are you, darling? Can you believe what we're doing? We must be mad.' Straight away going into full-on luvvie mode.

Our new base was made up of one main rehearsal space with smaller rooms coming off it that we could use either as green rooms, as extra rehearsal or for stage management to work their magic. There was also a great balcony, in case anybody needed to vape (ahem).

As rehearsals proceeded, we also made use of another large space which was located beside the offices of Nimax in Maiden Lane. If, for example, the principals were using the main area at Holborn, the rest of the ensemble could make use of the second space.

Arriving that morning, most of the company were already there. Jonathan was there, of course; John Macfarlane; Don and Charles in a corner with laptops.

Dani was flying in from Boston, having played a concert the

night before, but she's an opera diva, so she's allowed to be late – it's practically in her contract. There were teas and coffees, and lots of introductions.

'Darling, aren't we all marvellous? How exciting. I've no idea if it'll work, but let's just see!'

That kind of banter going on.

'When was the last time I saw you? Oh my God, you were fabulous.'

All of that. Very lovely and positive and upbeat.

We trooped through to the main rehearsal room and took seats, oohing and aahing at a model of the set that had been created by John and his team and laid out in front of us.

Andrew wasn't there, of course, the death of his son, Nick, being so terribly recent. The day before, a Sunday, I'd paid tribute to Nick on my show, sending out love to Andrew and playing 'Pie Jesu', which had got an enormous response from listeners. Now, ahead of any *Aspects* business, Nica stood and gave a lovely speech about Nick, and we took a moment to think about the family, which was very moving.

Next to speak was Jonathan. Oh, Jonathan. He's like your favourite don at university. Very clever, smart and funny. He was, as ever, hilarious, talking us through his love of the show, his ideas for it, and then introducing us to John Macfarlane, who went into more detail on the stage model. We were using lots of backcloth and painting in order to reflect the artistic world in which the show is set, and so there was a screen set up in addition to the model. John's a brilliant artist himself and had designed beautiful drapes and paintings.

Also noteworthy was the fact that we would be using a triple revolve. I had first used a revolve in *Les Misérables,* of course, so I was more than familiar with that particular bit of kit, but never a triple: a revolve within a revolve within a revolve.

John had clearly worked incredibly hard to fulfil the brief, which was that we wanted to get real fluidity and flow into the scene changes. To incorporate so many scene changes, we were using back-projection, front-projection, screens that would slide across the stage – I remembered those well from the 1989 incarnation – as well as various other bits and pieces. The girl operating the model was having difficulty keeping up, and this was just a demo. 'To warn you now,' John told us, 'this is going to be the worst technical in the history of your lives.'

Yeah, yeah, I thought, not daring to look at Don and Charles who were no doubt thinking the same as me: no way could any technical rehearsals be as bad as they were for the original *Aspects* in 1989.

The most important thing, though, was that it looked great. George's house at Pau in the South of France should look warm, open and romantic, and indeed it did. Paris on the other hand, as the base for the dodgy theatre where Rose is first seen performing *The Master Builder*, was rainy and cold. Later, the city is shown in a much more glamorous light, as Rose's career catches fire, and for this, Jonathan visited the city in order to capture our own footage (during the recent riots, no less).

Around the rehearsal room we had paintings and pictures to create a feel for the various settings, as well as bare-bones props. If you've seen the show and bought a programme (you *have* seen the show? You *did* buy a programme?) then you'll know what I mean from the rehearsal pictures: we marked out areas of the stage using tape on the floor, pretending it's the real thing until we moved to the Lyric five weeks later, at which point we went to the next level, working out how the space fit, how it would be lit, how it would sound, what working with the orchestra would be like – the dreaded tech rehearsals.

But that was all to come. For now, we were luxuriating in our first day of school, where with the pep talks having run their course, and the process of bringing the *Aspects* world alive had begun, we broke for lunch.

Two things about me and lunch. Firstly, I tend to use it for a bit of alone time. ('But Michael, you told us that you used to spend every lunchtime with Roger Moore!' 'Yes, reader, I did, but that's because HE WAS ROGER MOORE.') Secondly, I'm a creature of habit so I tend to eat the same thing every day.

On that first day, I found a lovely little poke bowl place and began a daily diet of raw tuna or raw salmon on brown rice, and with the odd exception, that's pretty much what I did every day of rehearsals in Holborn.

Dani had turned up by then, so during the afternoon she and I spent about 40 minutes going through our first scene together. After which, the rest of the day was spent note-bashing.

What's that? Okay, 'note-bashing' is a process where singers will lock themselves in a room somewhere and go through the songs with a fine-tooth comb. The way I do it is that I put it down on tape, then sing it through and find where the difficult bits are, looking at tempo and rhythm, and then, once the technical elements of the song are in place, thinking about adding touches, little bits of flair, colour and interpretation.

The beginning of the process is always about that exercise of note-bashing and learning the music; there's no point trying to incorporate movement until the music's in your head – for a start we won't have learned it, we'll still be on script – so you're just concentrating on the major architecture, the big moments, which in a musical is always the music, and in our case – or at least for me – was 'Love Changes Everything'. For example, I wanted to look at how we transitioned into it halfway through the first act. I had an early, exploratory idea for an interpretation and wanted to try a few things out, first with myself and then with others as sounding boards. It was early days, but what we eventually came up with was pretty special, even if I do say so myself . . .

And as we were doing all of that, Don and Charles were tinkering and Jonathan was flitting from department to department. It's up to him and the cast to identify those moments where tweaks are needed in the script, then for Don and Charles to make them, and then for those changes to be presented to Andrew, who tends to have the last word and can often be reluctant to approve changes to his work.

(And I could tell you that I have my ways and means for getting changes past Andrew, but that would be revealing too big a trade secret . . .)

Chapter 53

And that, essentially, is how the rehearsals progressed. The schedule would be assembled by Jo and Jonathan. At the end of each day, they'd ask us, 'Right, what do you need to work on tomorrow?'

After which they'd work out who was doing what, where. So say if the principals were due to work with Nick Skilbeck, then the ensemble could go away with the rehearsal pianist to learn their harmonies – and Jo would draw up call sheets, which were given out before we went home for the night.

It's the same with every show. As a performer, all you know is that you have to be available between 10am and 6pm every day, but as for what you'll be doing, at what time and in what rehearsal space, you need to refer to the call sheet. God knows how they do it. Must be like herding cats, which is exactly what actors are. Feral, really.

Travelling to and from Holborn Library, I'd get a car in the morning and then often a Tube home, which is my regular ride.

Occasionally another passenger will look at me and think, 'Is that him?' and then think, 'Nah, he's not gonna take the Tube,' but I'm not recognised that much. I'm pretty good at being invisible when I want to be: glasses on, headphones on, buried in my work. Besides which, it's not as though I'm a contentious and controversial public figure. Nobody's going to hassle me for releasing the *Coming Home to You* album. Not yet. Those who recognise me tend to be pretty nice and respectful about it.

When rehearsals are good, they're hard work but bloody fulfilling. Some days I'd find myself singing almost non-stop from 10am until 6pm. You're having to retain harmonies and sing with other performers, who are also trying to retain harmonies; you're trying to assimilate a mass of information constantly coming your way from the various departments, wigs, costumes, music.

At the same time, there's other behind-the-scenes work going on. Stage management are building rehearsal props. Mostly these are for use in the rehearsal room and will eventually be replaced by proper props, also being built. It's all happening in rooms off the main rehearsal space. You'll be trying to do your bit in the main room to a background of hammering and drilling.

*

I'd thought it would be an advantage knowing the show as well as I did. But it turned out that, no, that's not the case. If you're learning something from scratch, then you're learning it right. If you think you remember something accurately from 34 years ago, you're probably wrong. Not to mention the fact that it was a different part.

I found that I'd misremembered notes and timings, and what I soon worked out was that to do a good job I needed to *unremember* stuff, a bit like that mind-zap thing in *Men in Black*, except I didn't have a mind-zap thing, I just had the same old slightly faulty grey matter I've been relying on for the past 60 years, and it turns out that it's easy to unremember where I put the car keys, less easy to unremember things I did 34 years ago. Who knew?

As I said right in the beginning, I don't read music. I do everything by ear and instinct, and that can sometimes hinder my progress, too. What I also discovered as the five weeks of rehearsal wore on was that I was pleased with my voice now. I loved where the music sits in it, and I loved the other voices – my God, they're fabulous, it's a really terrific sound.

There's a particular song, 'Falling', which comes in Act II, which during Roger's tenure on the show was always his downfall. Easy to see why, because it's a complex piece of music with a lot of it a cappella – or 'Acapulco' as I always call it. One afternoon was spent just on this song, and by the time we were able to sing it through it sounded glorious, absolutely wonderful, one of those moments – and I'm glad to say I have them often – when you just skip out of the rehearsal room knowing that something has really come together, that you've created a real moment.

I was also enjoying using my seniority to enjoy a bit of creative input, and not just on my own character, either. It had always been my intention to use *Aspects* as a way of bringing on performers like Jamie and Laura, guys who deserved a big leading West End part. Because I was singing 'Love Changes Everything' earlier in the show, it had been decided not to end

Act I with Alex singing the reprise, as we had done in the first incarnation. Indeed, the original libretto has Alex ending Act I with a reprise of 'Seeing is Believing'.

For me, that didn't quite work. I really wanted Jamie to have that big 'Love Changes' finish for Act I, and so it proved. Jamie was thrilled that he got the big money note at the climax of Act I.

*

The other thing is that you really start to get to know these people. Prior to rehearsals, you know that you'll be spending every day with this rabble and you stress about a personality clash, or that you'll simply decide you don't like working with somebody, or that they'll turn out to have terrible habits you hate. Not flushing the loo, for example. Or maybe they will be the dreaded Company Seafront!

My favourite one like that was in *Hairspray* with Mel Smith. Mel, God rest his soul, smoked cigars, drank and didn't have the best oral hygiene I've ever encountered. Let's not beat about the bush: he didn't have the best hygiene, full stop. I know that possibly better than anyone because I had to snog him every night.

Now, the way it worked backstage in *Hairspray* was that my dressing room was two rooms knocked into one on the first floor. In the corridor outside was a toilet, which was supposed to be solely for my use because, turns out, I'm a bit funny about that – I don't like public loos and sharing it with the rest of the company fell squarely under the definition of 'public' as far as I was concerned.

However, that rule was roundly ignored, with everybody and

his uncle using the toilet, and it was doing my head in, so I asked stage management, 'Could we not make it so it's *my* toilet?' I'm sure they said rude things about me behind my back, but they complied and built what they called 'Ball's Barrier', a ply wall so that the toilet was incorporated into my dressing room.

And look, if this sounds terribly diva to you, then firstly, allow me my foibles, I really don't have many; and secondly, I'm about to get my comeuppance anyway.

So, one afternoon I was in my dressing room, doing my make-up, when in strolled Mel, a newspaper under his arm.

'Just using your lav,' he announced, gurning, and let himself in. There I sat, thinking, *I can't bloody believe this. What is the point? I mean, what is the bloody point?*

He was in there about five minutes.

And then ten.

Until, after about 15 minutes, we heard a flush, and out came Mel, gurning.

And the smell? My God, it was unspeakable. My hair and make-up girl, Sue, was cringing. My assistant, Andrew, the same. Smells from the pit of hell followed Mel as he emerged, with his newspaper under his arm. Approaching Andrew and Sue, he said, 'See you later,' taking care to touch them both at the same time and knowing that they knew what he knew: there was no sink in that toilet. As he left the room, wipes were immediately dispensed, the place was hosed down.

Me, I thought it was funny. He was welcome to use my loo any time. (Which, of course, is easy to say now.)

But that's a story from when the show was up and running. Rehearsals is when you get a flavour of people. But when you really, *really* get to know them is during the run. I never forget, either, that there's so much going on with the cast that I'm not party to. Sometimes you want to know everything that's going on. Sometimes you don't. Sometimes you don't have much choice. Was it *Hairspray* where they set up a WhatsApp group chat and didn't invite me?

To a certain extent, the group may splinter a little. Although you'll see the entire company at warm-up, there may be some characters you never meet on stage. As a result your paths never cross; they naturally gravitate towards the performers they're working closely with; ditto you. You don't really *want* that, necessarily, but sometimes it's just a natural part of the process. Little groups form. People go out on the town together.

On *Hairspray*, there was a real age divide. There were loads of youngsters who weren't interested in hanging out with me, Les Dennis and Rita Simons, and so we formed a threesome who would meet in my dressing room to bitch about everybody else, with the wonderful Marisha Wallace flitting between the two groups.

('Perhaps that's why you were never invited to the WhatsApp group, Michael?' Good point.)

Sometimes, performers will come in a little worse for wear, but I never have a problem with that, just as long as they bring their A-game to the stage and to the rehearsal room. In fact, I'd encourage them to go out. It's what it's all about, forging friendships and relationships. The closer the performers are in real life, the better the performance. They develop a kind of psychic link.

For *Aspects II*, I was the old hand. But that never made me an island. At least once a week I made sure to visit everybody's dressing room, usually before the Saturday matinee, taking them a different something, often with a theme (strawberries and cream at Wimbledon, Sherbet Dip Dabs for Pride), just checking in on everybody.

Part of my job is to set the tone – that drip-down effect, discussed before – and make sure the tone is one of camaraderie, fun, support, hard work and mutual respect. I think by doing that it goes some way to mitigating those little cliques and exclusivities I'm talking about.

I could be talking out of my backside, of course. For all I know, the rest of the company were having nightly meetings and bitching about me.

Thing is, I really don't think so. And the reason I don't think so, is because *Aspects of Love* was one of the – if not *the* – best companies I've ever worked with. Oh my God, I was having *the best* time.

Chapter 54

As the first week became the first fortnight, we moved on from note-bashing and learning our respective parts to working as a group, running scenes together and working more interpretation into the musical numbers.

This bit can be make or break for a group of performers. It's where you start to see the chemistry – or the lack of it – become apparent, but for us, it was make, not break. And although I talked about how you only really get to know your fellow performers when the run begins, I'm now going to contradict myself, because what was truly wonderful about the squad we assembled for *Aspects* was that we bedded in almost immediately, going straight from zero to bad behaviour in 60 seconds. From day one the place was alive with piss-take, stories and back-and-forth banter.

And it wasn't as though the novelty wore off. As the fort-night turned into three weeks, we only became even more harmonious and happy. The standing joke was that things were so good we simply must be heading for a full-scale disaster. It was like one of those films where one character turns to the other and says, 'It's quiet.'

And the other character says, 'Yeah. Too quiet.'

And then all hell breaks loose.

After all, we'd all been in situations where a fractious rehearsal had been followed by a brilliant show; we'd all been in situations where a seemingly smooth-running rehearsal process had been followed by a production beset with problems.

But this – this was great. This was a really happy working environment.

Oh, but then I caught a cold. I was pretty sure I got it off Nick Skilbeck, the musical director, who came in on the first day, going, 'Oh, don't come near me, I've got a cold, or it might be asthma.'

I'd given him the old 'oh it doesn't worry me' hug but can tell you now, it wasn't bloody asthma – and it turned me into a snot factory.

I did the best I could but had to have a Friday rehearsal off (I hated it. Hated not going in. Terrible FOMO) and duly passed it to Jamie, and then Laura, who completely lost her voice.

If somebody gets a cold in a show, everybody gets it. We're luvvies. We're constantly hugging each other and anyway, *Aspects* is that kind of show. There's a lot of physical contact.

*

As surely as day follows night, week three followed week two, and we moved on to the blocking stage.

Blocking is working out where you stand, how the changes

work, how you move from scene to scene and what you do within a scene. Basically, it's about where each performer puts themselves in the show at any given time. A decent company – and ours was better than decent – will make this stage as much character work as it is the technical business of who goes where, when, using the opportunity to develop character by understanding where you are in relation to other characters; how, physically, you'll respond to the space. You're working out your playground.

Once you've blocked it and have the shape of the show and how the scenes interlock, you literally go back to the beginning and start running sections to see how everything ties in together. At the same time we're doing more in-depth work on character, what we're trying to achieve, what positions are going to work and how those positions work in relation to other characters, and how that dynamic develops.

What was especially great about this phase – and actually the entire process from day one – was the incredibly collaborative and collegiate feel we had fostered within the company. I'm not going to blow my own trumpet and say that insisting on hiring Jonathan Kent was the best decision I've ever made, and that a combination of his vision and my leadership of the company achieved a situation in which we managed to catch lightning in a bottle, because that would be very gauche, not to mention big-headed of me. Nevertheless, between us we did indeed manage to evolve a situation in which everybody was able to have their say, and personally, I was brimming with ideas. I used to wonder if the rest of them were thinking, 'Bloody hell, Ball, give it a rest, why don't you?' As an old lag, I might find myself having to resist the opportunity to show younger members of the cast what to do. Sometimes it's the case that you already knew the shorthand, how to make something work, but you have to let people find their own way. It has to be their process, and so I bit my tongue, sat back, watched people find their own ways and, actually, loved that process.

As all this is happening, we had one eye on the upcoming sitzprobe, and then the technical rehearsals after that, because when you're blocking in the rehearsal room somebody says, 'And at this point, the doors will sweep us on to the next scene,' and that's it, you maintain your own tension and fluidity and stay in character in order to move on to the next scene, but knowing that in tech rehearsal the 'doors coming in' will take ages to get right; that moving on to the next scene could take 20 minutes as stage management rush around trying to finesse the scenery. The bed will be here. The chairs will be here. The lighting will be this.

Right now, in our little rehearsal room bubble, we were able to concentrate on character and performance, which at that stage of the game was like driving on the open road. Feeling free and as though nothing was going to stop you reaching your destination. Except then Orna Merchant comes on the radio to warn you of severe traffic delays up ahead (and that's the upcoming technical rehearsal).

Nick Skilbeck was like that. Full of ideas and ready to incorporate mine. You go in thinking, *Right, this is how it's going to be. This is what the tempo will be like.*

And he goes, 'No, let's try this instead. Don't take a breath here, make this bit much quicker, make this an entire line. Have a different thought here,' and what he's doing is opening up the song for you, reinventing it.

Obviously, the most eye-catching example of this policy was 'Love Changes Everything'. That interpretation I was talking about exploring on the first day had grown into something quite special. If you've seen the show (and you *have* seen the show, right?) you'll know what I mean. You'll know that the song opens in a different manner to the one you expect. It becomes a character moment, as opposed to 'here's the bit where the bloke off the radio sings his famous song'; it has a thoughtful, reflective feel, as though George is ruminating upon, and then finally accepting, the central message of the song.

This was something that came up during those rehearsals. Firstly, it became obvious that we had made the correct decision in giving the song to George and placing it where we had; secondly, the changes we made were not changes simply for the sake of it, because we felt we wanted to shake it up or wrong-foot the audience. Nothing in the show was coming from that place. It all came from situation and character.

And in the case of 'Love Changes Everything', because it's a different character singing the song at a different place in the show, the meaning of it slightly changed. What we did was to reinvent the song without – I hope – disappointing the audience. And just as it starts in an unexpected manner, it finishes as you expect, because we're not in the business of denying the audience what they want.

In other words, we don't miss out on the money note. Not on my watch.

Chapter 55

In the fourth week Andrew paid a visit.

Prior to that it had been almost what you might call a closed set. We'd reached that point where we were so close that we were starting to pick nits out of each other's hair and eat them.

Well, not quite, but we were certainly at the stage where everyone is massaging each other constantly. All walking around with personal nebulisers in order to keep the voice going, and me thinking, *Oh my God, I bloody love the theatre, I really do.*

Dramas there were none – apart from when poor old Laura had a call from her dog walker to tell her that her dog had slipped its leash and run off. Oh my God, she was frantic, the poor thing.

'He doesn't know about roads. He's frightened of everything.'

I'm happy to say it all ended well. We prayed to St Anthony, the patron saint of lost things, and Laura's dog was discovered hiding under her car, having somehow made its way back home.

That aside, it really was the most drama-free experience you can imagine. I wasn't sleeping. I was waking up at 4am or 5am with the brain whirring, having these wonderful, creative flashes of inspiration, thinking, *I know! Let's do this . . .* some brilliant idea so genius that by the time I awoke properly at 7am, it had completely slipped my mind. It was also the beginning of that common malady: the showbiz anxiety dream. (Usually a wrong-character scenario. Or wrong song, wrong costume, no costume at all – naked on stage.)

The Wednesday of that week we did our first run-through of Act I and Act II together, having been concentrating on Act II prior to that. In *Aspects*, they're a very different kettle of fish. Act I goes from scene to scene very quickly. It's pacey, hardly stops. Act II is much stiller, being based mostly around the house in Pau. Compared to Act I it's practically Ibsen, and in many ways feels like a different kind of musical.

For this reason Act II requires a little bit more of the audience; they have to be really captured and involved, and if they are, then there's a huge pay-off with 'Anything But Lonely', which is gut-wrenching. I had been hearing Laura do it in rehearsals and she was breaking my heart each time. There's not much levity in Act II. Everybody seems to get their heart broken (apart from Giulietta, who's practically bulletproof in that regard) and if you're going to offer up that much heartbreak, you'd better make it good, otherwise you'll lose the audience.

So anyway, back to Act II and we had been spending a lot of time working through that. For me, the advantage was that George dies just before the end, so I could sit in and watch almost as an audience member, appreciating, not just the performances – destroyed by 'Anything But Lonely'. Every. Single. Time. – but the way the stage management people wander around with sofas and chairs, pretending they're on a revolve doing strange things with planks of wood. Honestly, a play watching people improvise a play would be amazing. (But then how would you improvise that play in rehearsals?)

So. Andrew's visit.

The morning he was due to arrive, there was a definite frisson in the air. Don and Charles had been in earlier that week and although they hadn't seen a great deal of what we'd achieved were very encouraging.

But Don and Charles, bless them, weren't Andrew Lloyd Webber. They didn't have quite the same effect on the rest of the company.

Aside from Nica and Rosie Ashe (who plays Elizabeth), I was the only one who'd worked with Andrew closely before, certainly the only one who knew him well, so I gave them a little pep talk. He'll want to keep it low-key, I told them, doesn't want to make a fuss. But for all my talk, I was feeling pretty nervous myself – hyped and nervous and weird, and certainly not heeding my own words about this being a no-fuss, low-key visit.

Andrew arrived, and we assembled ready for a run-through. Watching was what can only be described as the Politburo in front of us: Andrew next to Jonathan, and the heads of the various departments, sound, lighting, stage, who just sat there completely stony-faced as we launched into Act I.

We performed Act I.

The songs become so familiar to you, you forget how good they are. In Act I of *Aspects of Love* you get 'Seeing is Believing', 'Love Changes Everything', 'Everybody Loves a Hero' and –

in our new, far less sexist version – 'She'd Be Far Better Off with You'.

Classics all. And don't forget it was just us, the cast, with a lone pianist accompaniment.

Andrew was beaming, absolutely beaming. As the first act came to its conclusion, I said, 'Now, at this point in proceedings, I'll come out and sell merchandise in the interval.'

'Fabulous,' he grinned, 'I've got a lot of Phantom masks hanging around if we could flog those. And I'm now working on a megamix for the end of the show.'

For 'George being deceased' reasons, I was able to watch him a little more closely in Act II. I noticed that most of his time was spent looking at the score, following that rather than the action in front of him, because at this point, it's all about his ears – aurally what's working.

Act II was the one in which the most changes had been made. Andrew had been making lots of notes. As it ended, he said, 'Why does she have to be 18?'

'Welcome to my world,' I told him, at which point Nica said, 'Look, she has to be, okay? She just has to be.' And that was it. No more was said.

'Okay,' said Andrew, accepting that particular point, 'it's a wonderful cast. I'm very, very excited. There are things I'm thinking . . .'

And indeed he was. You could see the cogs whirring. It was almost as though he was picturing himself at the piano stool. 'I need to look at . . .'

What?

Need to look at what?

We weren't sure, so left them to it – by which I mean Andrew,

Nica, Jonathan and Nick – and ducked into a side room in order to speak to the troops. Although it felt like we were awaiting the results of 'who's going to judges' houses?' on *The X-Factor,* there were plenty of compliments and hugs.

Followed by the news that Andrew wanted to change the ending.

If you'll remember, in the very first incarnation of *Aspects of Love,* back in 1989, the show had ended with a reprise of 'Hand Me the Wine and the Dice' which, with its message of living life to the full and letting the chips fall where they may, neatly summed up the show's two main themes.

We'd rehearsed the play with that ending, but then, fearing that the audience weren't getting sufficient release, it was changed in order that I (as Alex) could sing a reprise of 'Love Changes Everything', my big exhausting ending complete with money note.

In Don and Charles's new 2023 libretto, the show still ended on 'Love Changes Everything' except with George being dead they'd given the final lines to Alex and Giulietta who were to sing them together. But now Andrew was proposing a return to that very first ending. The original ending, with just Giulietta singing 'Hand Me the Wine and the Dice'.

It was a really interesting thing to do, almost as though he wanted to take the show back to his initial vision: a small chamber piece devoid of the usual Andrew Lloyd Webber bells and whistles. Personally, and while I could see the benefit of being a little braver in our approach, I was also mindful of the need to send the audience out on a high. It wasn't my call, but in retrospect, I wish that we had explored the ending more.

Either way, that was the finale we went for. Rewritten and

re-orchestrated, we had exhumed the original, intended ending for *Aspects of Love*.

Week four became week five, and our time at the Holborn Library, with its superb selection of fine fiction on the ground floor, had to draw to a close, and it was with some sadness that we waved goodbye to that space. It had been quite the best rehearsal period I had ever enjoyed: convivial, creative and collaborative. All the Cs, in fact, except one. The company 'seafront'? There wasn't one.

Oh, wait a minute . . .

Chapter 56

Ahead of the sitzprobe, we finished at the library and took ourselves to a rehearsal studio in Waterloo that I knew well, having been there with Shirley Bassey – *Clang! Name drop! Shirley bloody Bassey* – to sing with Alfie Boe for our Christmas show in 2019.

So there I was, making my return to the room, which is a really nice room, and who should be there but the entire orchestra for *Aspects of Love,* complete with our conductor, or 'carver' Cat Beveridge. (Carving – it's what we call the waving about of the orchestra wand.)

Before that, we as the company had been in one place doing our thing and the orchestra had been in another place doing their thing. Our musical accompaniment at Holborn Library – even for Andrew's visit – had been a single pianist. But now, like Rocky and Apollo Creed, we met, and together ran through the show, the first time that the orchestra and performers were all singing and playing together, and . . .

It was glorious. I was literally welling up with pride.

Come the day of the sitzprobe, and as a company we agreed to sing without mics in order to get the 'live room' feel. Andrew arrived, came up to me, gave me a great big hug and said, 'So sorry we're having to cut your big number.'

'Not a problem,' I said to him. 'No one likes the song anyway, and I think that replacing it with a tap routine and a dream ballet is really going to work.'

Bit of banter. Good start.

Andrew took a seat close to the harp. Now we had the Politburo; we had the company and the orchestra; we had the performers and orchestra doing the show, without blocking and scene changes; just the music and the words.

You can see why it's my favourite bit. If you were my psychiatrist, you might even trace my love of the sitzprobe back to my start in musical theatre, listening to all those cast recordings in my mum and dad's house. It's literally musical theatre stripped back to its bare bones. Music, narrative, performer. Bosh.

We began the run-through. It sounded glorious. There were moments that were over-embellished, but that didn't matter. This is why you have a sitzprobe. It's about listening to what's going on, deciding what you like, what you don't like.

But . . .

I could see Andrew becoming agitated. Points to remember: he was sitting close to the harp and that we were doing it without amplification and therefore had no sound mixing. A mistake, in retrospect.

He continued looking agitated. Until, just after Laura and Jamie sang 'Seeing is Believing' he stopped everything.

Which isn't quite as catastrophic as it might sound. It

happens. He just wanted to offer direction to our conductor, Cat Beveridge, in charge of the carving.

Cat was nervous. Come on, everybody was nervous.

So we continued, moving on to the section which leads into 'Love Changes Everything' and the way it now started, which was a cappella (Acapulco), almost spoken. I did the song. Did my big note. The orchestra swelled.

I looked at Andrew.

He wasn't happy. A marked contrast to his genuine pleasure during that previous run-through. In fact, I think it's fair to say that things were going downhill, and continued to go downhill from there. Without going into details, Andrew . . .

Well, he 'left the session'.

I'd been here before. I knew that this was . . . Andrew. I had warned people that Andrew had a tendency to go nuclear. I had also reminded them that with everything going on in his life he was under an awful lot of pressure, and therefore any negatives might be amplified.

I had, in other words, warned them that the shit might hit the fan.

But it's one thing being told something might happen and another thing actually having it happen. And although nobody was going to blame him for leaving, least of all me, you have to recognise that it has an effect on everybody in the room. This guy is a hero to most of us. If he literally storms out during something that you're trying to show him, an adaptation of his work, then there's no point in pretending otherwise.

Andrew, before leaving, didn't fully articulate exactly what it was that had disturbed him, other than saying that the harp was too loud. In a talk afterwards, I assured the group that it sounded extraordinary and beautiful. Which it did. Over-embellished, as I say. A lush score perhaps being rendered a little over-lush. But otherwise, amazing. We waited to see what would happen next.

Overnight, there were toys hurled out of prams. People were threatened with the sack. There was a bit of 'if he goes, I go' action.

Then, as if by magic, it was sorted. And this is why I don't want to go into too much detail about it; I don't want this to be the headlines, because it was just one of those little things that happen during a show. In short order, Andrew clarified what it was that he didn't like about the music (and sure enough it was the fact that it was over-embellished) and at the same time took pains to tell the performers that he absolutely loved what they were doing, which, after a couple of days of upset, was much-needed encouragement. Andrew is actually quite open and 'heart on sleeve'. If he doesn't like something, you'll know about it, but on the other hand, if he's pleased then he'll say that, too, and he's especially encouraging to the younger members of the cast.

What can I say? If you have a mercurial genius as your composer then you have to expect him to behave like a mercurial genius every now and then. And hey, we'd laughed about things going suspiciously well. ('It's quiet.' 'Too quiet.') This, then, was our bump in the road.

Chapter 57

So that was our sitzprobe. After that, we decamped to the Lyric, which would be our home until the end of the run.

We arrived to find the sets were still in the process of being built. The production of *2:22*, starring Cheryl Cole, had moved next door (though not with Cheryl, with a new actor in that role) and our stage management had been given a day in which to transform that set from *2:22* into *Aspects of Love.*

So I walked in to find the place looking like an explosion in a carpenter's workroom. These guys were doing an incredible job taking apart *2:22* and replacing it with *Aspects of Love.* We had the stage guys still building stuff; we had the lighting guys tearing their hair out. And we still had technical rehearsals yet to do.

All that bonding we'd done at Holborn Library. Those great times. That incredible dynamic we'd built. This was when it all came into its own; this was when we needed to lean on each other and on the relationships we'd formed in order to try and retain that magic and bring it into the show, when we had to combine all that stuff that we'd achieved in the rehearsal room with the practicalities of putting on the show – the 'who does what, when', the 'how does this scene become this scene'. Lights, sound, staging – so many things you have to take into account.

The problem is that it's so slow. For example, on one particular day of technical rehearsals we spent 24 hours getting ten minutes of the show right. You end up forgetting what you've achieved as you stand still, and wait for lighting / sound / stage to get it right, while at the same time trying to maintain your performance.

The revolves don't work. The big French windows are in the wrong place. The table's in the wrong place. It all takes time to fix.

The slightly frustrating thing in this situation is that if, for example, we'd been asked to record a cast album, we'd have been brilliant. The cast was ready. *So* ready. It was just that pesky technical thing of needing the show to actually work on stage. Tsk.

At last, things sped up. But then it's as though they're going too fast, and as a performer you're transformed from someone watching paint dry to a swan who looks serene above the water while its feet frantically paddle. I'm carrying a typewriter. I'm doing quick changes on Laura and Dani behind the scenes. I've got a donkey in my hand. Not a real donkey. A cuddly toy donkey. What am I doing with this donkey? I don't know. And now I'm on stage, but then again, so is one of stage management, standing with headphones on, looking at me like, 'What are you doing on stage?' And I'm like, 'What are *you* doing on stage?' And then I'm trying to act while people in black T-shirts are trying to move bits of stage around me.

'Jamie's forgotten to put the chair in the right place for the revolve.' Panic-stricken faces.

'Don't worry. I'll sort it.' And so I'm going on, picking up the chair, moving it into place, making it part of my performance. 'Leave it to me! Super Ball.'

(It's one of the first lessons I was taught: never leave anything on a stage. If somebody drops something it's your job to pick it up.)

Another time, I almost got my head chopped off at the end of 'Love Changes Everything' and had to do a swift limbo in order to avoid decapitation.

And you know what? You know what I'm going to say, don't you? I love it all. I absolutely love it. Tech rehearsals are hard, there's no doubt about it. The days are long and they're either frantic or mind-numbingly boring, no in between. But at the same time they're also incredibly rewarding and funny and creative and, really, everything you want from the theatre experience.

Even when you're nearly getting your head chopped off.

*

One day I was in early and didn't get on to stage until 9.45pm, which you might imagine was annoying, but (*whisper*, don't tell anyone) was actually quite handy because I had the opportunity to put my dressing room together.

You spend an awful lot of time in your dressing room when you're doing a show, so I like to have a nice one. I'm at that stage where I can ask for certain things. I like a pull-out bed.

A fridge. Certainly a loo, as you know, hopefully a shower. They'll usually decorate it for you as well, and you can put up your own art, get the lighting just how you like it.

I like to have an open-door policy (unless I'm naked, nobody wants to see that) so that anybody can come in if they want to have a chat or ask me anything.

That day, I also had the opportunity to do various bits of business. I had my hair cut and went through all my costumes. I decided that I was going to steal the dressing gown they'd got me for my entrance – a big, gorgeous silk thing from Harrods. I had another fitting for a suit and also attended to the business of working out what George is going to smell like.

And yes, that really is a thing. Every character I play has to have their own smell, a practice I first instigated on *The Woman in White*, so part of the process for me is working out what the scent will be.

For Edna in *Hairspray*, I wore Madame Rochas, which both my mum and gran used to wear and which to me represented a warm, motherly, matronly figure – perfect for Edna. For *Sweeney* I learned how to do a wet shave using a cut-throat razor at Geo F Trumper, and Sweeney's scent was Bay Rum. For Mack (in *Mack & Mabel*) it was Eau Sauvage.

I found George's scent at a beautiful Italian perfumer in Piccadilly Arcade called Santa Maria Novella. These are scents that have been made by monks since the middle of the 13th century, and George's smell, I decided, was Russa, a Russian cologne that had been popular in the 1800s.

Whatever happened in the tech and then the previews and then the press night, one thing was for sure: George was going to smell like a dream.

Chapter 58

Tech rehearsals looked set to go over time, so we had to announce a postponement of the first preview, early enough to warn those who had purchased tickets.

It's never something you want to do. It doesn't inspire a huge amount of confidence. But then again, it's not especially unusual, and it's almost always a decision made for good, practical reasons. If you recall, we had to cancel an *Aspects I* preview. Why? It's the age-old story. Despite knowing that we had a really hard technical rehearsal ahead of us, we didn't schedule enough time for the technical rehearsal. As Forrest Gump might say, shit happens.

So the second preview became the first preview, and it went really well. The response from audiences and those who posted on social media was fantastic, while Andrew Lloyd Webber, who came and sat in the third row, not far along from Cathy, was ecstatic. Gathering the company on stage afterwards, he gave a properly inspirational speech about how much he'd liked it.

Poor old Laura had been sick at the beginning of previews. I still don't know how she managed to get through it, but she did. Complete trouper. I think that basically we all fed off what was a very positive energy in the building. You could tell there was so much goodwill when everybody started applauding my final big note of 'Love Changes Everything' before I'd even finished it.

And so, we went into the run. Using previews to work out applause points, smooth out bits of the show, change the odd line here and there, as we headed towards opening night, the press night.

And for me, getting into the old way of life was like slipping into a warm bath. All of my familiar pre-show routines and rituals returned. I am one of those who is incredibly superstitious. Oh my God, I nearly punched Charles Hart on the opening night of *Aspects* in London. The two of us were standing on a stage looking out, and he said, 'Well, bloody hell, we've made it,' and then quoted the Scottish play, saying, 'I would applaud thee to the very echo,' which if you know anything about theatre you'll know is absolutely verboten.

I looked at him. 'Have you gone mad?' I said.

Instantly he realised what he'd done. Hand to mouth.

'So anything bad that happens is your fault,' I told him.

And don't think for a second that I was joking, doing any of it with irony; it's absolutely deadly serious.

'Right,' I told him, 'you know what you have to do, don't you? Go outside to the street, turn around three times, spit, swear, knock, ask to be let back in, and pray that the gods of theatre smile kindly on us.'

I know that it all seems completely mad, but it's absolutely baked into me at a cellular level. Charles quoting the Scottish play gave me an actual physical reaction.

Whistling. That's another one. Whistling in the dressing room is one thing. I don't like it and I make people go outside. Whistling on stage – that's the real problem. If I hear anybody whistling in the theatre my heart stops, and I have to tell them again to go out of the stage door, turn around three times, spit, swear, knock, and ask to be let back in.

Of course they think I'm crazy. And of course they think they're just going to disappear for a minute or two and then come back claiming they've performed the ritual.

But I'm not crazy, and what's more, I watch them do the ritual.

The funny thing is that, as with many superstitions, both of these have quite rational roots. The first-ever performance of the Scottish play was apparently beset by disaster, with at least two of the principal actors dying. An 1849 riot in New York, during which loads of people died, was started because of the rivalry between an American and an English actor, who were playing in competing versions of the play. There have been plenty of instances of accidents, mysterious deaths and so on. Laurence Olivier almost got brained by a falling stage weight in 1937.

We're not in the theatre so I could say the name of the play if I wanted to. The one that begins with M and rhymes with 'black death'. It's just that I get a bit of a *brrr* feeling, like a shiver when I say it, wherever I am, and no way would I have said it in the confines of the theatre or even hear it be said, even a line from it.

And the line quoted by Charles was from Act V Scene III: 'I would applaud thee to the very echo.'

As for whistling, this dates back to when stage managers would whistle as a cue to let in scenery. So if anybody whistled at the wrong time, something could come flying down from above and even kill an actor. These days, of course, it's all done with lights and radio, but back then it was whistling and so whistling was banned in the theatre unless the stage manager was doing it.

The interesting thing is that when I tell people about this, they respect the rule. I'll say, 'Go on then, whistle.'

'No, you're all right.'

Or they take me up on it and whistle.

'You know what you need to do now, don't you?'

'And what'll happen if I don't?'

'I don't know, but something will. Do you want to take that risk?'

The one I'm not too fussed about is the whole 'good luck' and 'break a leg' thing. But that's a bit of an outlier. In every other respect I'm pretty superstitious. For example, everything I do on the opening night I have to repeat for the entire run. The order in which I get dressed, for example – left shoe, then right shoe – how everything occurs in the wings when I get a prop. You'll also find me doing a tapping exercise, EFT, or Emotional Freedom Technique, a trick taught me by Stephen Gately of Boyzone. (And I can tell you exactly when. It was Wednesday 6th May, 2006, when we were doing *The Rocky Horror Picture Show* together.) I'm not sure if all this is a ritual or out-of-control OCD, but that's the way it goes.

Over the years, I've also worked out that it's better for my performance if I can sleep for an hour or so beforehand. Before I came to that conclusion, I'd get so worked up before a show, so hyper, that I'd end up exhausting myself, and then get to the show and find it difficult to concentrate through the fatigue.

What I discovered was that giving myself an hour to rest would really help. I put on an audiobook or a play, concentrate on that and allow myself to drift off. When my next conscious thought is, *What are they talking about in this audiobook?*, I'll know I've had a rest. I'm forever wondering who killed Lord Edgware.

I also make sure to join the company warm-up. A lot of the leading turns won't join in the 15-minute physical and vocal warm-up where the whole company assembles on stage before they open the house, but personally I think it's really important to do, and very much a part of the process. It's that moment of being together, talking and finding out how everyone is doing, a few parish notices, points of order, who's on, who's off, covering arrangements, that kind of thing. I mentioned how you can have members of the company with whom you don't really interact during the show itself, so this is a moment to just touch base with those guys.

So say if the show begins at 7.30pm, I'll probably want to be at the theatre by 4.30pm, have my sleep, eat something, get myself prepared before the warm-up which will be at around 6pm or 6.30pm before the house opens at 7pm.

Normally, I then have about 20 minutes before the half-hour call, and in that time either I'll go to somebody's dressing room to chew the fat, or somebody will come to mine, just having a cup of tea, checking in.

Then comes the half-hour call which means it's time to start getting prepared. I usually do my own make-up, and certainly do for George. The make-up itself will have been designed by a make-up artist and the chances are they'll be with you in the dressing room, but I find that doing it myself is really useful for getting into character.

After that, it's wigs and costume. George in the first half doesn't use a wig; in the second, when he's nearing 80 and has greying hair, I have one. Wigs are a terrible faff. I'm allergic to the glue, so it's a real drag. Saying that, I love getting them on. Wigs, make-up and costumes. I love that idea of being slightly unrecognisable. During *Sweeney Todd*, people used to go to the box office saying, 'When's Michael Ball coming on?' They didn't even recognise me. It's great to let yourself sink into the character.

Then I go for a wee. You always feel like you need a wee before you make your entrance. There's nothing worse than hopping around desperate for a wee on stage.

And then – very important this – the last thing that we do in the dressing room is that my assistant Andrew will say to me, 'Are your flies done up?' which is another superstition with very grounded roots, because I used to be notorious for flying low and going on stage. And secondly, he will say to me, 'Are we smelling nice for the ladies and gentlemen?'

And so I check my flies, dab on the scent, and that's it, I'm George.

By the time of the interval, I'm back in my dressing room where I have a nice cup of tea, and then, especially for this one, get the complete make-up transformation, ageing me by 12 years. It's actually quite a major transformation, but George doesn't appear until a little way into Act II, so I have enough time. As you get into the run – any run – you're acutely aware of exactly how much time you have to do everything. Is it worth going back to the dressing room, for example? Or do you wait in the wings for your next entrance? After months of doing it, you have everything down to a fine art.

Afterwards, I like to be really quick. I don't sit in my dressing room, gazing into a mirror with light bulbs around it, a glass of neat gin and prescription medication not far away. No way. In *Hairspray*, I'd do the bows and then, as the play-off music started, be back in my dressing room, out of the clothes, the fat suit, the wig and down to my pants before the music had finished. Andrew would be going, 'For God's sake, it doesn't have to be like this,' but it was part of the game. You've just finished the show, you're buzzing with adrenaline – you want to *do* something.

So Andrew's wrong there: it does have to be like that. But mainly he's right. He's super-organised. Totally military about it. He'll tell me off if it looks like I'm in danger of being too much of a prima donna. 'Do we really need to behave like that, Michael? I don't think we do, do you?' I have no inhibitions around him, and you really need that in a dressing room.

Sometimes you get people to see you after the show, and in that case you have to do your second show, maybe open a bottle of wine if you're entertaining them. I try to have drinks ready on the off chance that someone is coming back, but nine times out of ten it's just a case of getting out of my show clothes, getting into my civvies and going home.

At the stage door I stop and greet fans and sign autographs. I'll do selfies, but truthfully, I hate them. Nobody looks good after a show, having just scrubbed off all the make-up.

During the first few nights of the show, you're buzzing. It can be really difficult to get to sleep. But as the run goes on, well, it's just work, isn't it? The key to making it through the run is making sure you get plenty of rest, preserving your energy.

And that was pretty much how it progressed with *Aspects of Love*. Did I miss anything out? Oh God, yes, opening night. Press night. The reviews.

Chapter 59

Just prior to press night, I was interviewed by Marianka Swain, the *Telegraph* writer who put the cat among the pigeons with her piece following the announcement.

Perhaps because she had since spoken to Nica and also came to my dressing room to interview me, she was a little more, shall we say, even-handed or open-minded in her approach to the follow-up. Quoted in the piece, Nica pointed out that following the rewrite 'all the relationships are consensual and transparent'. Jonathan was also quoted as saying, 'The complexity of the relationships is very engrossing and in no way offensive. It's a very sophisticated evening.'

Meanwhile, we in the cast were able to make the case that while *Aspects* is not necessarily an easy proposition – I repeat, it's not supposed to be – it's a story that reflects the messiness of human relationships. We were also able to make the point that we had looked very carefully at the Jenny issue. That not only had her age been changed, but the relationship slightly recalibrated in order to make it absolutely certain (and I think it always was, but just to really hammer the point home) that Jenny has her own agency. Marianka ended by admitting scepticism, but looking forward to seeing the new, redrafted show.

Well, we never got to find out, certainly not officially, what she thought of it, because it was the paper's chief theatre critic, Dominic Cavendish, who wrote the official review. And, at the risk of equating 'liking it' with 'getting it', Dominic did both.

He acknowledged that it's a complicated, occasionally challenging proposition. He called it a 'fleet and classy revival', and picked up on the poignancy of me having played Alex as a younger man and now stepping into George's shoes.

Four stars. Not bad.

The Sunday Times was great, too. Quentin Letts, this was, who gave us four stars and called it 'dreamy, judiciously done and, with Michael Ball and Laura Pitt-Pulford leading the cast, well sung . . . this production is an easy, old-fashioned pleasure.'

Adam Bloodworth of *City AM* started by saying, 'I think I must be mad, but I really enjoyed this absolutely morally bankrupt musical . . .'

Well, yes. 'Utterly gorgeous', he also called it, and 'staggeringly beautiful' as well as saying some very complimentary things about me and the rest of the cast. Another four stars.

Time Out had some nice things to say. True, *Aspects* was according to them 'wildly problematic', while the writer, Andrzej Lukowski, found the plot a bit difficult to swallow. This was something that would become a recurring theme among the reviews. Unlike many others, however, Andrzej loved the music, calling the score 'up there with Webber's best'.

The *Daily Mail* went for mixed, giving us three stars and picking up on perceived problems with the plot, but being extraordinarily kind about our performances and rightly pointing out that 'much love has been poured into this *Aspects* by all involved, and thankfully the sweetest moments make it worth the effort.'

The *Daily Express* again was mixed, praising the performances and the music, but ending by saying, 'inconclusive, bittersweet and decidedly out of tune with the current climate, it is an unsettling experience garnished with great songs.'

Kate Kellaway in the *Observer* sort of summed up the mood. 'This is a spectacular production,' she wrote. 'Everything I assumed it would not, could not be. So much talent has been lobbed at it that it overrides the musical's many and varied faults.'

The *i News* was great, too, again a bit of a link between the whole 'getting it and liking it' thing. 'This is not your typical overblown West End musical – and is all the better for it,' said their writer Fiona Mountford, who also declared herself moved by the 'haunting lyricism and romantic longing'. She picked out Laura as being a particular standout, and asked readers to ignore the detractors.

Ah, yes. The detractors.

The *Evening Standard* was not kind. In a two-star review, the show was called 'creepy and downright silly', and although he was nice about the music, he called Don and Charles's lyrics 'unintentionally cringeworthy', ending by saying, 'But really, the score and the daft narrative aren't substantial enough to make us care about these smug, silly people and their lazy, messy, pervy liaisons.'

As for the *Guardian*, they called it a 'well-oiled show, easy on the eye and ear', but also laid into the 'preposterousness' of it. Again, their reviewer felt that there were issues with the story.

The Times called it 'a shallow work'. 'The anthemic "Love Changes Everything" still casts a spell in this Jonathan Kent production, yet the rest of the through-sung score remains anodyne.'

Fair to say that those who didn't like it really sharpened their knives on it, which was especially the case with Sam Marlowe in *The Stage*, who took a real dislike to it. 'Thin, sugary musical', it was called. The show had 'offensive sexual politics' and was 'mawkish and meandering'.

And then, 'What's most howlingly problematic is the plot: a textureless glob of sexist cliché that surely must have seemed faintly nauseating even three decades ago, and now looks creepy and, at its most flagrant, startlingly offensive.'

Come on, tell us what you really think.

Chapter 60

In 2012, when we opened *Sweeney*, the first review I read was in the *Daily Telegraph*, a four-star review which was nice about the show, but not very nice about me.

I immediately felt as though I was going into a complete decline. I believed every negative pixel of that review – until I saw the next one, and the next one. And every brilliant one after that. Complete triumph. The *Daily Telegraph* guy ended up re-reviewing *Sweeney* and apologising for his initial review.

The point is that he had his initial reaction to the show, just as I had an initial reaction to his review.

The other point is that sometimes critics are right, sometimes they're wrong.

And the other point is that you have to take the rough with the smooth, and that if you're going to accept it when critics say nice things about you, you have to do the same when they have negative points to make.

For *Sweeney Todd* and *Hairspray* I was lucky, because the critics were very kind about me, and they loved the production. I always knew that *Aspects* was going to be a difficult show and that there would be varying responses to it. How did I know? Because of the reviews we got last time, and because as I've said, time and time again, *Aspects of Love* is not an easy prospect. If, as a critic or audience member you don't connect with the music then I dare say you're not going to find it redeemed by the plot. On the other hand, if you're slightly baffled by the plot but enjoy the music, then that's half the battle won.

The negative reviews hated it. You can't do much about that. The mixed reviews tended to like most elements of the production but took against the whole David Garnett-ness of it all.

Again, it would be great if critics enjoyed all elements of the production. But you can't have everything. And plot is one of those things that's very much down to personal taste. After all, if you analyse the plot of say, *The Marriage of Figaro*, or *Rigoletto,* or indeed any opera, you're probably going to be coming out of it going *WTF*.

The thing, though, was that even though we had some great reviews – two that were proper raves, and more than enough quotes and top-star ratings that we were able to pull them out for the poster – the negative reviews still hit home. It's just a fact of life that if you have three good reviews and one bad one, it's the bad one that you fixate on. Anybody who works in entertainment will tell you the same. It's just human nature.

In short, they do have an effect. They have an effect on the public who when they're booking a show might prefer to book one with great reviews as opposed to the one described as problematic. And they have an effect on the cast.

That first one is out of my hands. In which case, my job

became about acknowledging that, yes, some of the press could have been kinder, because there was no point in ignoring that particular elephant in the room, while at the same time trying to keep enthusiasm and confidence in the company high.

How do you manage that? By making sure that we never lost sight of that rehearsal-room vibe, how we felt as we came together. And by making sure that we rejoiced in what we had and in the knowledge that we were doing good work and doing it well.

I think for me one of the greatest things was watching Andrew's reaction to our work and knowing that it had given him a bit of solace, and provided him with some help at what was an almost unimaginably difficult period in his life. For us to see his work revisited on a huge West End stage with all the production values and the talent, and the fact that he came to that preview and absolutely loved it, was brilliant.

A couple of nights later I spoke with Madeleine, his wife. I said to her, 'This is where all our stories began. *Aspects of Love* was the beginning of your journey with Andrew, the beginning of my journey with Cathy.' For that reason alone it's been worth the journey. For if not a career maker for either Andrew or me, it's a memory of a happy moment, and the chance to create even more memories from that time in the rehearsal room was very, very special indeed. Of course I wished that that happy time, followed by the challenging tech and then well-received previews, had been followed by a universally positive press reaction, but that's showbiz.

The reviews made us glad that we'd erred on the side of caution and opted to age Jenny. Thank goodness Nica stuck to her guns.

Talking of which, the one review that made our producer really cross was the one in *The Stage*. That one was vitriolic. I mean, you don't give a production like this one star. One star suggests that it's objectively bad, amateurish, even. And you cannot deny the artistry and professionalism of what we're doing. How can you go from four stars in the *Telegraph* to one star in *The Stage*? Nica responded by taking out an advert on *The Stage* website drawing attention to what was an obvious act of deliberate critical sabotage.

The night after reviews appeared we gathered for the warm-up. Nica came in that night and we both gave little speeches about not losing faith in what we were doing, pointing out that most sides of the production had come in for praise. The one person to really get it in the neck was poor old David Garnett.

*

Meanwhile, with the press night over and the show locked, the creatives left us. We were on our own now. Jonathan would come back and various writers, producers and composers would pop in sporadically, but now it was just us, and that's where my work really started in keeping the company buoyed, tight and still enjoying our work.

There was a moment in late June during Act I when George sees Rose wearing his deceased wife's red dress. A warm Saturday matinee, it was. In the scene, I sang, '*Do forgive me, so unlike me*,' and there was supposed to be a pause, a moment of electric silence as something passed between me and Rose and the seeds of one of the show's many relationships were sown.

Except on this occasion not complete silence. From the audience came the *loudest* snore.

I should say that we were really lucky during *Aspects*. None of this rowdy and boisterous crowd behaviour you read about. Audiences were respectful of the performers and of the work. And this was an old chap who was very swiftly woken by his no-doubt irate wife.

Laura and I looked at each other and of course we both knew that the moment had gone and that we'd broken character, and the great corpse began.

But we hid it, of course. And if you were there, you didn't know.

You also didn't know that during that performance they gave us neat cranberry squash instead of the diluted stuff we use for red wine and we almost gagged to death. You didn't see Jamie pour the self-same wine all over my hand.

Oh, but you might have seen poor old Anna fall over during 'The First Man You Remember', although of course she recovered like a true pro.

I had some visitors after the show. They had no idea it was strewn with catastrophe. They could feel the emotion, they said.

It's moments like that I live for – that I dare say we all live for.

Critics schmitics. That's what being in the theatre is all about.

Chapter 61

I'm often asked what roles I would like – or have liked – to play.

People say I should play Henry Higgins, but I'm not especially interested. They say I should do *The Rocky Horror Picture Show*, but actually, I've already done it, sort of – I played Frank N Furter in the second half of the anniversary concerts at the Royal Exchange. To be honest, I looked like a cross between Pauline Prescott and Imelda Marcos, but it was great fun. And – exorcising that particular demon – I even got to play Joe Gillis in *Sunset Boulevard*, in a stage concert for the BBC opposite Petula Clark (great kisser, by the way).

Playing in *The Woman in White*, complete with fat suit, wasn't an altogether happy experience on Broadway, but you can't win them all. I loved doing *Sweeney Todd*, Edna in *Hairspray* and Mack in *Mack & Mabel*. I adored being in *Chitty*, where through the super-clever use of mechanicals and lighting, it really did look as though the car was flying. I'd look out into the audience, see grown men weeping and think, *Yup, just like me. Obsessed with the movie as a kid.*

But all of these experiences, good and bad, stand in the shadow of my *Aspects* journey, on which I was first a passenger, then the conductor and then the driver. Opening it in London in 1989 changed my life in the most profound ways, bringing me success and fame and even love. Revisiting it in 2023 was a joyous experience, bringing the story full circle.

It would have been nice if . . .

Well, okay, before we get into that, let's talk about the twist ending, shall we?

*

We had an issue with the poster. The one that accompanied the first roll-out was never supposed to be a permanent piece of marketing, just a placeholder, and the more time passed the less I liked it. In the view of my assistant Andrew, it looked like it was advertising *The Play That Goes Wrong* does *Cluedo*, and I campaigned to get it updated, something I wanted done sooner rather than later, because we knew that we were experiencing that same downturn affecting the whole of the West End and were hoping the summer holidays would bring in the visitors. Looking out into the audience, we could see that the auditoriums weren't full. In particular, we were having trouble getting decent audiences for Mondays, and there was talk of axing that night altogether.

In other words, there were rumblings. In no way was the future of the show assured.

But of course we carried on. It was disappointing to see

empty seats out there but those who came loved it, and we were really enjoying performing it.

And then it got to my birthday, which was 27 June, a Tuesday, when Nica sent me a note wishing me a happy birthday and also requesting a meeting the following day, Wednesday, our matinee day.

And I knew. I mean, I'm not just saying this to look like Mystic Meg, I really did. As I say, we knew that it wasn't selling as well as we'd hoped; matinees we were always full, but the evening performances not so great. No doubt that had something to do with the demographic. We'd never quite attracted the younger theatregoing public that we hoped might come. Inevitably, the cost-of-living crisis had its say in this regard.

The thing was that when I'd dreamed it all up, I'd always intended it to run for three or four months. I knew that was a safe timescale. But Nimax were investing a lot. They wanted six months which I had agreed to in the hope that it would make money and everybody would walk away with a smile on their face. No, it wasn't what my gut was telling me, but hey, fortune favours the brave, and the fact is that as William Goldman always said, nobody knows anything in this business. If we knew what makes a hit we'd all be billionaires. With *Aspects*, I was aware that it wasn't *Cats*. It certainly wasn't a slam-dunk in any way shape or form. I'd always been unsure of it finding an audience in 2023.

*

So, anyway. My birthday was just lovely. We had a full house and at the curtain call, Laura surprised me by making a speech and leading the audience in a rendition of 'Happy Birthday', which was lovely, until the very end when I turned to Laura, she jumped on me, and I put my back out. (They sent me to see the West End's go-to physio, a guy called Fabi in King's Cross who worked his magic and clicked me back into place.)

The next day was the Wednesday. Matinee day. Nica day. She arrived at midday, took a seat in my dressing room and brought out the spreadsheets. This is the amount we need to make in order to wash our faces. This is what the receipts have been so far, and this is what we have coming up. And as you can see, it's not working now and it's not going to work in the future.

We talked it through. We touched on the marketing strategy (i.e. the issue of the posters), but I think the horse had bolted as far as that was concerned. We talked about ways of trying to shore things up via royalty cuts, wage cuts, slashing the budget. We talked about closing early.

And in the end, that was what we decided to do. We had a natural break coming up on 19 August, and so I suggested taking it up to there and closing, lopping almost two months off the intended run.

Nica was in tears as we made the decision, and my own reaction was in sorrow, not in anger. One thing we both knew was that everyone – and I mean everyone – involved in this production had worked their arses off.

Nica is amazing. I'm telling you, there are so many shows – especially on Broadway – where closure would be announced with a notice on the board and performers given next to no warning. Nica volunteered to come in the following day and break the news to the company, in order to let everyone know they had eight weeks of the show left and give them time to start auditioning for the new season. She promised to send complimentary tickets to every casting director and producer in order that they could come and see the company.

She was lovely about it.

I told Cathy when I got home. I also told my assistant, Andrew. Other than them, nobody else knew, which was hard. Two shows, knowing full well that we were going to close. Three if you count the Tuesday show, when I knew the game was up.

The next day, Thursday, when Nica was due to break the news to the entire company, I decided Laura should know. It wasn't like I could tell everybody individually – it was painful enough as it was – but as the leading lady, I thought she should be aware. Besides which, I knew she'd be great with the news. Sure enough, she was. Devastated, of course, just as I was, but taking it on the chin.

For Saturday matinee warm-up we often dressed up according to a theme decided beforehand. This was Thursday, but that night, Katie Mitton, one of the three actresses who played the young Jenny, was missing her school prom so we decided to break with tradition and come to warm-up dressed for prom.

So we did the warm-up, and I presented a little tiara that I'd been wearing to Katie, after which we moved on to parish notices, which is when we attend to any company business.

Nica stepped up. She'd been hanging around unobtrusively prior to that, but still attracting the odd cautious glance. What was Nica doing here, again?

In a short but beautiful speech, she delivered the news,

ending by saying that after the show she'd be opening the bar and ordering pizza, so please everybody stick around.

The effect on the company was devastating. The full gamut of emotions. Some resigned, some shocked, some upset. Perhaps the best reaction was young Katie, who said, 'Well, that's showbiz, isn't it?' Out of the mouths of babes . . .

After the warm-up we had 25 minutes to do our hugging and chatting, go into little groups, bitch, moan, cry or say, 'Fabulous, I can book a holiday,' whatever. And then we did what we do, which was put on the best show we could. Which we did. And it was phenomenal.

It's only happened to me once before: *The Woman in White* on Broadway, which was a different situation, a lot more ruthless, a lot more like, 'The reviews are bad, you're out.' Nica was different. She does her job because she loves the theatre, and she loved the show. She was genuinely emotional, and in some small way that really helped. It's appreciated by everyone in the company that she cared, that it hurt her at the same time as it hurt us, and that she was doing her utmost to soften the financial blow.

Meanwhile, those ticketholders who had booked past August were contacted and given the option of a refund or rebooking. We had about £400,000 worth of sales, but it wasn't enough. As word leaked out, we found that houses improved. We weren't sold out but still, we saw a little uptick, and matiness were doing very well indeed. I never wanted to limp to the finish line – at least there was no question of doing that.

Chapter 62

And of course, I ask myself why – why were we unable to attract sufficient crowds to sustain the run?

Firstly, as I've said all along, *Aspects of Love* is not a traditional musical. We knew that from the beginning. It's a complicated, dark piece that demands a lot of an audience. It was just a question of whether that fact was a bug or a feature. (We thought a feature. The world at large? Hmm, maybe not so much.) Nor was it what's in vogue. It wasn't an adaptation or a jukebox musical; it was a show very much of its time, two times, actually – the period in which it's set and the late 1980s – and neither of them were now.

Added to that, there's a huge drop in footfall in the West End. Some shows are doing fine, but a lot are struggling to find an audience. You've got people who traditionally go to a West End show three or four times a year who are now only going once a year. They weigh up the costs and the weather, the train strikes and the traffic, and they think, *If I'm going to make that commitment I want to see something that I* know *I want to see,* and I guess people didn't feel that about *Aspects.*

Which brings us on to reviews. I think that if we'd had five-star raves across the board then that would have helped. Of course it would. But we had very few outright raves because it's not an outright-rave kind of show. It's a show that divides opinion, and if you're influenced by that then you'll take your money to something that everybody loves unreservedly. The fact was that we were going into the summer months – traditionally the busy time – and didn't have the bookings, so it was only going to get worse when the schools went back. You're into October and November then, which are the lean months. The nights draw in and people are starting to think about Christmas. My name had sold a lot of tickets, but that's not enough to sustain a thousand-seater house every night. Name recognition helps a show, and it'll give you a certain percentage, but it won't fill the theatre; you need all the other elements: great reviews, a show that people are fascinated and intrigued by, and a groundswell of support.

You also need good word of mouth, and part of that is down to the way you leave an audience at the end of the show, and perhaps, after all, we didn't get that quite right.

If you recall, the show in 1989 finished with me singing a reprise of 'Love Changes Everything', so the show had that big, money-note climax which sent the audience out into the street on a high. We had planned to have Jamie sing 'Love Changes Everything', but Andrew instead decided to reinstate the *original* ending, a reprise of 'Hand Me the Wine and the Dice', which ended the show on a more downbeat note. It may have suited the story and felt right for the creatives, but I wasn't so sure about it; I always maintain that we're performing for an audience and need to give them a big emotional pay-off, and in hindsight (it's a wonderful thing) I wish we had explored that issue more. We could have worked on giving the audience a better reason to applaud, but we didn't, and ultimately it was an artistic decision that may have lost us a little bit of that precious 'word of mouth' that every show needs.

Was it the only reason? No. It may not have been one of them at all. Likewise the marketing. Easy to say now, but I think we got that wrong, and I let it pass when I should have dug my heels in a bit. Was it *the* reason? No. Was it *a* reason. Maybe.

But look, you can pick it apart all you want. There's no right or wrong answer. Just that at the end of the day, Katie Mitton had it right. That's showbiz.

*

As for me personally, my initial reaction was sadness for everybody because I knew how hard they'd worked and how much they loved doing it; it was concern for where they go next and hoping they find work and are soon able to adjust; it was also huge pride that I got the show on in the first place and also of course a sense of resignation, because I get it: I work in commercial theatre, which only survives because people want to come and see you, and if they don't, they don't, and you have to accept that. You have to think, *What lesson can I learn?* and go do something else.

I'd feel worse if I thought that I'd been foolish, that I'd miscast myself and wasn't right for the role, if I'd done it for the sake of it, or for vanity reasons. But I'm confident enough in my own radar. I know if I'm crap, and I wasn't. I did what I set out to do, and if I could go back in time, I'd do it again, and maybe change a few things. But one thing I would not change is the people. Every single one of them.

Shortly after the announcement, my friend and songwriter Amy Wadge sent me a song she'd written in response to the show closing. 'On With the Show', it was called and although I didn't cry when I was told the news, nor later when I told Cathy, there were a few tears when I played that song. If all goes to plan, you'll hear it; we plan to put it on the next album.

So there's that album to make. There's work to be done on the TV adaptation of *The Empire*. There's my Radio 2 show. I mean, professionally, for me, things are fine. I didn't do *Aspects* as a career move; I did it for the love. And if Andrew Lloyd Webber was right when he said he doubted it would ever be performed again, then at least the show goes into the vault having had a fabulous outing that we're all thrilled about. Yes it was a risk. You take them, you need to keep taking them in order to keep moving forward. And for me, it was a risk worth taking. My only sadness being that we weren't able to deliver a great end run for what was a wonderful company.

What lessons have I learned from the experience? That nothing changes. You embark on every project full of optimism, commitment and bright ideas – and hopefully with a bit of talent at your disposal – and that's all you can do. You prize the moments you have on stage. You enjoy the company of those you're working with and appreciate the privilege of being in a position to do what we do. But at the end of the day, it's in the hands of the gods. A show will either catch fire with an audience or leave them cold. You just don't know. As I often say, if we knew the answers then we'd all be billionaires and shows would run forever.

And on those occasions when a production doesn't work, you have to find the resilience to pick yourself up, dust yourself off and start all over again. And you take the lessons you've learned in that job and apply them to the next one.

For me, no ending can spoil what we've achieved. I'll always remember the night of the opening when we all got together for drinks in the function room at Drury Lane Theatre. Assembled were the cast and creatives, the whole company, all the great and the good in their finery, and I looked around and thought, *I made this happen. I gathered these guys together and initiated this thing, and we've done it, we've opened. Wow.*

It was, to quote the show itself, a memory of a happy moment.

Acknowledgements

Much like a putting on a show, creating a book takes many people working away behind the scenes, without whom it could simply not happen. I am therefore extremely grateful to everyone who has contributed along the way and would like to extend heartfelt thanks to each and every one of you.

Firstly, a huge huzzah to Andrew Holmes for guiding, listening, cajoling, encouraging and making sense of it all . . . we laughed a lot.

To my literary agents, Gordon Wise, Alastair Lindsey-Renton, Helen Clarkson and Sheila Crowley at Curtis Brown who supported me right from the start of my publishing journey.

I'd like to thank my publishers at Bonnier Books UK, in particular my editor, Ciara Lloyd, who has been my cheerleader from the very beginning and has expertly steered this book through to publication. Additionally, credit to Emily Rough for her cover design; Ellie Carr for her editorial help; Natalia Cacciatore, Ellie Pilcher and Elinor Fewster for their wonderful work in marketing and PR; Stuart Finglass, Mark Williams, Kevin Hawkins, Andrea Tome, Vincent Kelleher, Kate Griffiths, Phoenix Curland, Stacey Hamilton, Kim Evans, Ruth Logan, Stella Giatrakou, Nick Ash, and Amy Smith for selling *Different Aspects* around the world; Laura Makela and Charlotte Brown for helping create the audiobook; and to Ella Holden for making it into an actual book. And thanks also to my copyeditor, Ian Greensill, proofreader, Chris Stone, and the wonderful Sophia Spring who took the cover photographs.

To all my friends and colleagues who were happy to let me pick their brains and rekindle our shared memories from the past and present.

I have been lucky enough to have my career supported from the very start by some wonderful individuals, far too many to name here, but I would especially like to thank my management team, Phil Bowdery and Sarah Donovan at Live Nation, and Andrew Ross for keeping me on track at all times.

Finally, to my wonderful partner, Cathy, who has been by my side every step of the way.